About Denise Linn

Denise Linn is an international lecturer, healer, and author at the forefront of the Feng Shui movement in the U.S., Europe, and Australia. She is the acknowledged pioneer of the Space Clearing movement that has gained so much popularity throughout the world. Her bestselling book, *Sacred Space,* has been translated into 12 languages. She is the originator of the groundbreaking Interior Alignment™ Feng Shui and Space Clearing system, and founder of the Interior Alignment™ Institute, which offers a professional certification course and weekend workshops.

***

Also by Denise Linn

Books
Pocketful of Dreams (1988)
Dream Lover (1990)
Past Lives, Present Dreams (1994)
Sacred Space (1995)
Signposts (1996)
Quest (1997)
Descendants (1998)—reissued as *Sacred Legacies* (1999)
Altars (1999)
Space Clearing A–Z (will be available in 2001)

Audio
Journeys into Past Lives (1999)

Video
Instinctive Feng Shui for Creating Sacred Space (2000)

Other Hay House Titles of Related Interest

Books

THE ESSENCE OF FENG SHUI:
Balancing Your Body, Home, and Life with Fragrance, by Jami Lin

THE HEALING HOUSE: How Living in the Right House Can Heal You
Spiritually, Emotionally, and Physically, by Barbara Bannon Harwood

HOME DESIGN WITH FENG SHUI A–Z, by Terah Kathryn Collins

THE WESTERN GUIDE TO FENG SHUI:
Creating Balance, Harmony, and Prosperity in Your Environment,
by Terah Kathryn Collins

THE WESTERN GUIDE TO FENG SHUI—
ROOM BY ROOM, by Terah Kathryn Collins

Audiocassettes

INTRODUCTION TO FENG SHUI, by Terah Kathryn Collins

THE WESTERN GUIDE TO FENG SHUI
(6-tape audio program and workbook), by Terah Kathryn Collins

***

All of the above titles are available at your local bookstore, or may be
ordered by contacting Hay House at:

(760) 431-7695 or **(800) 654-5126**
(760) 431-6948 (fax) or **(800) 650-5115 (fax)**

Please visit the Hay House Website at: **hayhouse.com**

FENG SHUI FOR THE SOUL

How to Create a Harmonious Environment
That Will Nurture and Sustain You

Denise Linn

Hay House, Inc.
Carlsbad, California • Sydney, Australia

I dedicate this book to
Interior Alignment™ Feng Shui practitioners
throughout the world

***

Originally published in 1999 by Rider, an imprint of Ebury Press Random House, London, England • ISBN: 0-7126-7081-5

Library of Congress Cataloging-in-Publication Data

Linn, Denise.
    Feng-shui for the soul / Denise Linn.
        p. cm.
    Includes bibliographical references and index.
    ISBN 1-56170-731-7
    1. Feng-shui. 2. Spiritual life—Miscellanea. I. Title.

BF1779.F4 L5755 2000
133.3'337—dc21   99-048222

ISBN 1-56170-731-7

03 02 01 00   5 4 3 2
1st Hay House printing, August 2000
2nd printing, August 2000

Contents

Acknowledgments

I am so grateful to have Claire Brown in my life. A remarkable human being, exemplary writer, and good friend, her suggestions added magic and soul to this book.

I want to thank my husband, David; our daughter, Meadow Linn; and Ellie Baker, Charlie Baker, and Antonia Chavasse for putting their love into my Interior Alignment™ Feng Shui courses.

I am also grateful to Louise Coe and Jerry Nowatzke for their assistance with research for this book. I especially want to thank Danny Sollene for his very generous support of Interior Alignment. Also, much thanks to my wondrous editor, Judith Kendra, and to Jill Kramer at Hay House.

In addition, I want to thank these friends for the depth of their love and support—and also for the contributions that they have each made to the field of Feng Shui: Jane Alexander, Maureen Bell, Tom Bender, Ron Chin, Terah Kathryn Collins, Dennis Fairchild, Lillian Garnier, Johndennis Govert, Roger Green, Andreas Hager, David Daniel Kennedy, Monica King, Karen Kingston, Bruno and Monica Koppel, Jes Lem, Pamela Laurence, Gina Lazenby, Robin Lennon, Jami Lin, Courtney Milne, Katherine Metz, James Moser, Helen and Micheal Oon, John Sandifer, Nancy SantoPietro, Stephen Skinner, William Spear, Sophia Stainton, Sarah Surety, Angel Thompson, Lillian Too, Carol Venolia, Derek Walters, Richard Webster, Rich and Christine Welt, Nancilee Wydra, Seann Xenja, and to Prof. Lin Yun for bringing heart into Feng Shui.

***

Note from the Hay House editor to American readers: This book was originally published in England, so some of the spellings and syntax reflect the British use of the English language. However, your appreciation of the content should not be affected. Thank you!

Introduction

As a child I moved house nine times. My roots would begin to take hold in a new place, only to be abruptly ripped up once again. None the less I grew like a weed, taking root wherever we lived. There didn't seem to be a common thread connecting the various places; each one was completely different.

My first home was a small wooden house atop a hill in Astoria, Oregon – a rainy fishing village by the Pacific Ocean. The house overlooked the sea, rolling mists and fog. A later move took us to the dry arid heat of King City, California, where we lived in abandoned army barracks. Whenever we needed more space my dad would knock down a wall, opening up another unit. Later we moved to Chicago and lived in a run-down tenement apartment. The fluorescent lights from the 'greasy spoon' coffee shop on the street below blinked endlessly into my bedroom window every night.

Better times in my father's career took us to a beautiful Tudor-style home in a middle-class neighbourhood near Chicago. After this we moved to a rural region of Ohio, where we lived in an old farmhouse surrounded by an overgrown apple orchard.

Later, I lived for two years with my grandparents near Los Angeles. Their home was a suburban bungalow in a transitional neighbourhood that was slowly being infiltrated by gangs. By my high-school years, we lived on a gracious tree-lined street in a mid-sized town in Ohio. Our three-storey, historical house had marble window seats, hand-carved woodwork, antique stained-glass windows, and an intricately patterned slate roof.

Disruptive as it was for a child to be uprooted so many times, I now know that every move we made prepared me for practising and teaching feng shui. The wide spectrum of environments that I called home when I was growing up gave me an intimate understanding of the spaces we occupy and how they influence us.

This understanding was accelerated by a near-death experience. When I was seventeen, a traumatic random meeting with a crazed gunman left me in critical condition, in an intensive-care unit of a hospital. I had been riding my motorbike on a country road, when I was run into and then shot by a man who had shot several other people. A farmer found me on the side of the road and took me to the nearby hospital. While the doctors were frantically trying to save my life, something remarkable happened: I floated out of my body and entered into a realm of golden radiant light. I was surrounded by a loving force that appeared to be infusing the entire universe with vitality and energy. It all felt so very familiar. I 'remembered' knowing that I was connected to all people and all life, animate and inanimate. I felt that this was something I had always known, but had forgotten. I was eventually pulled back into my physical body, but from that point onwards I saw the world through different eyes.

Human beings usually experience the world around them as comprising separate parts thrown together in a jumble of colour, sound and form. But this is an illusion. At death's gateway, I had an experience of not being separate from the world. In that exquisite moment I knew that we are all one with the sea, the mountains, and all creatures on this beautiful planet.

This awareness eventually propelled me towards the study of feng shui. I found this ancient tradition provided keys to access the rhythm of the ebb and flow of the natural world. By using feng shui principles to organise and clear living spaces, people could live more in oneness and balance with the environment.

In my book *Sacred Space*, I sought to unravel some of the mysteries of space clearing and feng shui and to demonstrate how anyone could create harmony at home. Since its publication I have had a deepening realisation of how important it is that our homes are not only retreats for our bodies but are also, in the profoundest sense, homes for our souls.

In *Feng Shui for the Soul*, you will find three approaches for transforming your dwelling into an environment for spiritual renewal and inner poise. Each approach is discussed in a separate section of the book. Taken together, the three parts provide a blueprint for creating environments of harmony and beauty.

The first section focuses on developing your aptitude for instinctive feng shui. Everyone has the ability intuitively to pinpoint exactly what is out of balance at home or at work, and then cure it. Because this ability has been blocked in most people, I have provided information and exercises for accessing this innate power. By unlocking your intuition and working through blockages surrounding home issues, you can understand the deeper meaning of your home. You will learn how to feng shui your home or workplace easily and in a way that brings remarkable results. The ensuing transformation will affect not only you, but everyone who lives with you and enters your environment.

The second section of this book presents little-known information on how to activate the forces of nature within your home. Living in an environment without the energetic signatures of nature separates us from our deepest heritage and reduces our life force, slowly but surely. Re-establishing our connection to nature in our living spaces is vital to our physical and spiritual health.

The third part of *Feng Shui for the Soul* is based on the ancient understanding of the importance of the Medicine Wheel, the four elements of nature and the four directions. Utilising the power of these traditions empowers the energy fields in your home and calls spirit into your life.

Writing this book has been an exciting process for me. My comprehension of feng shui and sacred alignment has become deeper and, at the same time, fresher for me. I have written this book because I want to help you create a place where your soul is nurtured, so that you can feel at home with yourself, wherever you are, and be at home in the universe.

Part One

A HOME FOR
THE SOUL

1

Creating a Home for the Soul

TWENTY YEARS AGO my husband and I, and our two-year-old daughter, squeezed together into our old Dodge pickup truck to move to Seattle. Every one of our possessions was piled on to that truck. Our mattress, roped on top of the load, flapped dangerously in the wind as we tottered down the highway. It seemed like a great adventure.

It was a rainy cold November day when we arrived at last in Seattle. We had very little money and nowhere to stay, so we immediately began looking for rented accommodation. We finally found a bungalow not far from Lake Washington. It was so tiny that what I mistook for a walk-in cupboard turned out to be the bedroom. We moved our household goods in, and we were home. David found work as a carpenter and I decided to stay home with Meadow. For a while everything was exciting and new, then slowly I became depressed. Every day was rainy, overcast and cold. I didn't have any friends in the area and David was away all day. I felt so alone and miserable. Not only were the skies grey, all the walls of our little home were grey. It seemed like my life was grey too. I doubted myself. I doubted my mothering skills. I doubted everything about my life.

Then one day I found some tall branches dumped in the alley. I dragged them home, propped them up in the living room so that they extended from floor to ceiling, and wove tiny Christmas-tree lights

through them. They looked great. The feeling of the room changed entirely. I loved the effect; it reminded me of a starry night in the forest. I noticed that I felt a lot better after I had done that.

Next I bought an inexpensive large round rice-paper lantern to hang in front of my 'forest'. I painted it a luminous colour so it would look like the full moon in the forest. When night fell, I turned off all the lights in the house and switched on my 'stars' and my 'moon'. It was magical. I felt so happy and uplifted. The little grey bungalow had turned into a sanctuary of beauty . . . it had become a home for my soul. This marked a turning point in our life together there. I continued to find odds and ends in thrift stores and began to assemble a home environment that was warm and inviting. Joy emerged in my life and my spirit blossomed.

Our homes have an enormous impact on our state of mind. They can make us feel as though we are plunging into the depths of despair, or they can be uplifting havens of beauty and rejuvenation. I believe the soul yearns for places of sanctuary and balance, ones that provide authentic reminders of what is truly important in life. It longs for dwellings that are in harmony with the cycles of nature; places where kindness, compassion and wisdom are cherished . . . and where these qualities can grow. It has been many years since we moved from our little home with the 'moon-lit forest', but I have always remembered how changing my environment made such a deep and lasting change in my life.

One of the ways we can create soulful places is through the use of feng shui. This ancient art shows us how to make our homes harmonious and balanced. The type of feng shui that most people are familiar with originated in China. However, every ancient culture has had rituals, myths and other traditions based on the fact that our living spaces profoundly affect our wellbeing. The intent of all these ancient systems has been to create environments which are in equilibrium with the forces of the universe.

Our yearning for places that nourish the soul, as well as the body, accounts for the rapid growth of feng shui in recent years. In my feng shui practice and in my classes, people invariably ask me how to create a feeling of sanctuary. They want to bring a sense of the sacred into their homes and workplaces. They want to know how to create a home for their soul.

The soul

 Soul is a word we use to describe the central or integral part of something; it is the vital core. In its most profound sense, it also describes the essence of every human being. It is that place within each of us that is infinite, eternal and universal. The soul is an enigma, a part of what Native Americans call the Great Mystery, which is the creative force underlying the universe. It is a source that gives rise to form, yet is unknowable. It is illusive by its very nature, yet it also must be nurtured and cared for. We can intuitively understand what its needs are, yet never fathom its depths. It is the substance within us that links our body and spirit to the greater forces of the cosmos.

The closest I have come to directly experiencing my soul was through the near-death incident that occurred when I was seventeen. It resulted in the realisation that I was more than just a physical body. I knew I had a soul.

Ever since that turning point, much of my life has been focused on recapturing the deep sense of belonging and connection that I experienced in those few moments on the other side of life. For many years I searched for ways to reconnect to that sacred place. I studied many traditions and travelled throughout the world, always yearning to find the pathway back to that place. At last I realised that it was in me all the time, and that by aligning the energy in my home I could create a spiritual template to help carry me to the centre of my soul. And any-one can do this. With a few very simple techniques, you can use your home as a template to reconnect to the sacred element in your life. You can create a home that will allow your potential to blossom and your heart to open.

What Your Soul Needs

I believe that there are four things that the soul requires in a home. First, it needs a sense of belonging, to feel truly connected to the land, to your roots, to your spirit. Second, a soul needs to feel safe, so that you can be yourself, be creative, and bring forth what you are without fear. Third, it yearns for harmony with the greater cycles of nature. And, finally, your soul needs sacred space. When you have these four things, your home will be filled with inner peace. It will become a gateway into deep, spiritual realms.

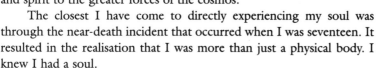

1 A sense of belonging

For your soul to feel balanced and happy it is essential to find a place on the planet where you feel truly at home. In my life, I have had the opportunity to spend time with native people in countries around the

15

world. In every location I have found that these people have a profound attachment to the land. Passion comes into their voices when they talk of their ancestral home sites. Their connection to their place on earth forms the very fabric of their soul. In some earth-based cultures, a new-born child is placed on the soil to instil a sense of symbolic connection between the child and the sacred earth. This way, even when life is hard, there is always a deep sense of belonging.

People in modern Western cultures move on average approximately once every five years. I believe that this results in a loss of a sense of belonging, which is felt as a subliminal malaise. In ancient times native people did not usually suffer from depression and the lack of self-esteem that modern people do. In part, this can be attributed to the fact that they had a sense of place.

Your home should give you a sense of belonging and provide a context for interpreting your life's experiences. It should be a reference place that you look forward to returning to, an anchoring point from which you venture into the world, and a place where you know that your heart resides. To gain a sense of belonging to a place, it is essential to 'ground' yourself. Even if you move often, in each location imagine sinking your roots into earth. If you live in a block of flats or housing estate, find a park or green near your home and take some time to connect to it. Locate yourself on the planet.

2 A feeling of security

When creating a home for your soul, it is vital to make it a place that feels truly safe. It should be a place where you not only feel physically safe, but also where you can truly be yourself. The soul needs a place where you can explore what you are and what you might become, a place where you can be creative and outrageous or quiet and still.

We feel most secure in an environment that truly reflects who we are. Just as an ill-fitting shoe cripples your ability to walk freely and comfortably, a home that does not express your true nature will restrict your ability to reach into the deepest corners of yourself to explore your potential. You can only do that when you feel safe.

A home that matches the contours of your soul subconsciously affirms that you are completely all right exactly the way you are. Knowing this encourages you to take the risks necessary to reach your dreams in life. A home that fits you provides a firm launching pad from which you can leap towards your aspirations, as well as a safety net you know you can always depend on when things don't turn out exactly the way you imagined.

3 *Harmony with nature*

Nature nourishes the soul. Our homes will either separate us from nature or connect us to it. A home for the soul will include tangible links to the world of nature – things you can see, hear, smell, taste and touch that remind you of the sky above and the earth below. Its four walls will form a kind of shrine where the spirit of nature resides as an honoured guest. In the natural home, the lives of the occupants will be in harmony with the cycles and rhythms of nature.

Ralph Waldo Emerson once said that 'the views of nature held by any people determine all their institutions'. The survival of early humans depended on their ability to live in balance with the natural world, and their homes reflected awareness of this fact. Modern homes are often separated from nature and the soul has suffered as a result. In the rush to create inexpensive, efficient housing, we have neglected the deeper yearnings of the spirit.

The natural world around us is composed of swirling vortices of energy which make up the four elements of the natural world – air, water, fire and earth. There are simple ways to call the spirits of these elements into your home. When you do, they can ignite the power of nature in your home; they can strengthen and heal you.

One easy way to welcome the spirits of nature into your home is by including natural objects there. Doing this subconsciously recreates feelings that you have when you spend time outdoors. Natural objects recall ancestral memories of early times when we lived close to the land. For example, although most modern bathrooms are miles from a river, lake or the sea, placing smooth river stones by your basin or bath can invoke memories of ancient times when people bathed in local streams and rivers. These objects serve as affirmations of your connection with nature. They honour the Spirit of Water and its powers of purification. When you bring things from nature into your home, they bring with them the feel of the breeze which once blew around them, the sun that warmed them, the rich scent of the earth which supported them.

Ancient homes were constructed from natural local materials. Adobe houses, for instance, were made from the red mud native to the region; wooden houses were made from felled trees from surrounding forests. Building homes from the gifts of the land instilled the energy of that land into the foundations, walls and roof of the home. By bringing objects native to your region into your home, you re-establish this intimate connection with the land. It is remarkable to see how even a few stones from your local river will expand and transform the energy in

your home. It will seem to come to life, to breathe and radiate joy when you activate the forces of nature there. A natural home nourishes the soul in a profound and powerful way. (Chapters 7 to 12 will show you many ways to call the energy of nature into your home.)

4 *Sacred space*

I believe that within the core of every human being dwells a yearning for the meaning that lies beyond the prosaic reality of everyday life. We reach out for evidence of something beyond the ordinary. This searching is a reflection of the soul's journey towards its destiny. Because no two souls are alike, no two people will follow exactly the same path in life. A soulful home is one which mirrors and supports the unique essence of the souls who live there. It is a home infused with a feeling of sacred space that allows you to tap into the hallowed places within you and discern the meaning of your life.

The renowned mythologist Joseph Campbell once said, 'To live in a sacred space is to live in a symbolic environment where spiritual life is possible, where everything around you speaks of the exaltation of the spirit. This is a place where you can simply experience and bring forth what you are and what you might be. This is the place of creative incubation. At first you might find that nothing happens there. But if you have a sacred place and use it, something will eventually happen. Your sacred space is where you find yourself again and again.'[1]

Our homes can be so much more than mere boxes in which to live. They can be places where, in the words of Joseph Campbell, 'the whole world is mythologized'.[2] In such a place the spirit expands; it feels set free. The soul connects deeply here, not only with other people, but also with dreams, the environment and the whole universe of reality beyond the home. The weaving of sacred space in your environment creates a web of context that will deepen your sense of relationship to all things.

A HOME FOR YOUR SOUL

In order to create a home for your soul, you must first establish a connection with it and get to know its needs. Just as every person is unique, so every soul has different needs. The following exercises can help you discover what your soul desires. Creating in your imagination a symbolic home for your soul, will help you instill some of that same feeling into your current home.

Envisioning a Home for Your Soul

Close your eyes and allow yourself to relax. Take a few deep full breaths, and with each exhalation allow yourself to enter into a serene state of mind.

- Now imagine that you are going on a journey deep inside yourself to reach your spiritual source point. Say to yourself, 'I am now connecting with my essence.' You might want to give a persona to this essence, such as a name or an image. By doing this you are connecting to the essence of your soul.

- Visualise your soul travelling to different locations in order to discover what kind of landscape makes it feel most at home: the top of a mountain, by the sea, in a cave, nestled in a valley, near a river, in a rainforest, surrounded by deep snow, overlooking a broad expanse of prairie, or somewhere else. The ideal landscape for your soul is important because it connects you to the energy of the earth.

- Imagine the perfect home for your soul. What kind of walls enclose your soul house? Are they brick, wood, stone, glass; thick, thin, open to nature? What are their colours and textures?

- Picture the roof of your soul house. Is it high or low, ornate or plain, open to the heavens, domed, flat, sloping, constructed with skylights? Are there beams? Is it rough or smooth?

- Now go through your soul home room by room. Imagine windows, doors, stairs, fabrics and lights; also sounds, smells, colours and textures. Move things around and keep going until your soul house is shining and bright, until it feels like a perfect match for you.

Once you have completed this exercise, take a moment to recall what you experienced and write it down. Make your description as detailed as possible. In the coming days you can continue to add to your list. This list will be useful in helping you to design your present home with some of the components of your soul home.

Doing this exercise will probably point out discrepancies between the home you actually live in and the home that your soul would find ideal. There may be aspects of your ideal soul home which it is not possible literally to reproduce in your present home. For example, your idea soul home may be by the sea, but you are committed to the life you are living inland right now. This is not an insurmountable problem. Because the soul dwells in the world of the spirit and is a part of your unconscious, it is powerfully affected by symbols. By adding to your

environment symbolic representations of what the soul needs, you can nourish it in a powerful, magical way. Find ways to recreate *symbolically* the *feeling* of your soul home within the context of the life and home that you have now.

When my client Sarah did this exercise, she found that her ideal soul home was an English country cottage surrounded by a lovely garden. She visualised the house filled with flowers – from sprigged curtains and cushions, to bowls of fresh blooms everywhere. Although Sarah lived in a third-floor flat in a large city, she was able to recreate the feeling of her soul home with pictures of flowers, flowery fabrics, and a lovely bouquet of fresh flowers every week.

An artist named John found that the ideal home for his soul was a cave. At the time, he was living in a loft in a modern industrial conversion with high ceilings and lots of windows. Although this environment was ideal for his studio work, John realised that it was not meeting his deeper need for a feeling of seclusion, so we set to work to add cavelike comforts. We hung beautifully textured terracotta-coloured curtains at the tall windows. When he was working during the day they could be pushed aside; but at night he could pull them shut to bring a warm, earthy feeling to the space. We also swagged across the ceiling above his bed several swathes of fabric in warm colours. This gave it a very enclosed cosy feeling, which made John feel more at peace at night. After living with these changes for a period of time, John noticed that he felt more at ease in all areas of his life.

When you have crystallised your thoughts about the perfect home for your soul, find a word that describes the *feeling* of this special place. One client said that the word for her soul home was 'celestial' and that her soul needed to feel a direct and living connection with the galaxies of the night sky. To bring this feeling into her current home, we decided to paint tiny phosphorescent stars on the ceiling of her bedroom and create curtains out of richly embroidered star-patterned fabric. She said that she felt such a deep peace as she fell asleep each night under the 'stars'.

Your home is like no other place on earth. It is special and unique just the way it is, and through your love, insight and care it can become the ideal place for your soul.

2

Home as Self

YOUR HOME can be your greatest ally in helping you to achieve your potential. This is true because your home is not only a reflection of you, but in its deepest sense, it also has the power to mould you and shape your future. When you implement changes in your home, you will notice that often your life is also transformed: instantly, dramatically and permanently.

Your home fulfils many functions in your life. On the physical plane, it provides shelter from the elements and offers you protection and privacy. Beyond this, it is also a place where you can relax and be yourself. It can serve as a canvas for your self-expression. Your dwelling is also an outward expression of your inner being, and on a very profound level it is also a place where you can grow spiritually.

In the deepest sense, your personal space is a sharply accurate mirror of your subconscious desires, hopes, fears and dreams. It reveals your beliefs and decisions about yourself and the world. It is a reflection of your identity.

A mirror of yourself

You cannot help but implant your identity on your home. Every object you place in it expresses some inner aspect of yourself. As you mature, your development is mirrored in the choices you make in your environment. The style of your home, your possessions and the colours you like all reflect your inner being. The Swiss psychoanalyst Carl Jung said that everything in the unconscious seeks an outward manifestation. This principle explains why we continually project our subconscious beliefs and feelings on to our home.

When you want to find out what someone is like, all you need to do is look around his or her home. The spindly teenage boy who plasters his bedroom walls with images of Arnold Schwarzenegger and Sylvester Stallone is subconsciously saying, 'I want to look like a body builder.' The data processor who decorates her home with photos of unspoilt wilderness, carvings from Africa and an animal-print duvet cover on her bed dreams of having some adventure in her life. A house with natural fabrics, hand-carved wooden toys strewn on the floor and biodegradable laundry soap on the shelf speaks of a belief in living naturally and organically. If you want to discover your subconscious dreams, fears and beliefs, just look around your own home. You will find them represented in every nook and cranny.

Our homes also chronicle our personal history. Our past experiences form a framework that gives structure and context to our lives. We use the past to define ourselves. Our history is carried into the present through the symbols with which we surround ourselves. Our past is displayed in the photos on our walls and in the objects we treasure. The teapot from your great aunt, the baby blanket from your childhood and the silver napkin rings from your mother are all physical relics embedded with memories. They all say something about the way you define yourself, based on your interpretation of the past.

An anchor to the earth

Your home can serve as an anchor to the earth and to your roots. Ken Colbung (Nundjan Djiridjaken) the senior male clan leader of the Australian Bibulmum Aboriginal tribe, spoke to me of how important this connection between people and their land can be. He said, 'Western man is connected materially to the land, but we are connected spiritually to land. It's important that we continue to secure our connection to the land because it is our spiritual embodiment.' Your home is the connecting point between heaven and earth. It is the place of your centre, your axis – it connects you to the land.

A template for spiritual growth

The soul is always yearning to expand and grow. This is the reason why we are subconsciously drawn to home environments that can give us what we need at a particular point in time. The homes we choose often provide what we most need to progress on our journey towards wholeness. Some of these environments may seem to lack harmony or even have unpleasant aspects, *but they always offer us an opportunity to grow.*

Just as we are drawn to individuals and experiences that contribute to our spiritual growth, so too we may seek environments that can help us to learn the lessons that we need in life. The Dalai Lama once remarked that you don't learn tolerance from your friends. What this means is that it is sometimes the people you find the most disagreeable who have the most to teach you. This is true with our homes as well.

Your soul is drawn to what it needs. In traditional feng shui, a home at the top of the mountain is usually considered bad feng shui because it is too exposed. The bottom of a valley is also inauspicious feng shui because it can be too cloistered and constricted. However, living on top of a mountain may suit your soul because the vast open expanses make you feel more expansive . . . *and this is what your soul needs.* And other people, living down in the valley, may find this environment perfectly meets their requirements for seclusion: its constrictions might help them to focus their otherwise somewhat frenetic energy.

There are no wrong homes. Each home offers you unique opportunities for spiritual growth. The so-called feng shui imperfections of your home may well be exactly what you need for polishing the rough edges of your soul. For example, a man I once knew lived in a rented home that had a very low entrance door. This is usually considered bad feng shui. Henry was a tall man, and every time he entered his house he had to incline his head. Sometimes he would be in a hurry and forget to do this. He would then hit his head on the door lintel which made him angry. Sometimes he yelled at the door. Occasionally he banged his fists on it. One day he came home, looked thoughtfully at the door lintel, humbly bent his head and walked in. It was a moment of truth, a moment that changed his life.

Henry was often in confrontational situations. Many people found him arrogant, because he was always trying to prove that his point of view was right. The instant he bent his head at his threshold, he was filled with an indescribable peace. In that moment, he realised that he could navigate around the obstacles in his life. Afterwards, whenever Henry walked through the front doorway, he bent his head in humility saying to himself, 'I accept my life with love and compassion,' and he found more harmony unfolding in his life.

Sometimes problems encountered in feng shui bring to mind the classic question about the chicken and the egg. Which came first? Do we subconsciously choose homes that contain metaphors for the issues that we need to work on? Or do we experience blockages in our life because of the bad feng shui of the home? Although the answer is probably some of each, I generally feel that we subconsciously choose homes because they have something to teach us. *On a soul level, there are no bad homes.* Every home is filled with lessons and opportunities for spiritual growth.

Sometimes the soul is drawn to a house because it has energy that will help activate hidden potential. Shortly after my husband and I were married we moved into a ramshackle little house by the sea. We did not have much money, so I decorated our home with things found in thrift stores and with treasures washed up by the sea. I framed paintings with driftwood, and placed on the windowsill pieces of glass from the shore that looked lovely in the afternoon sun. Our shabby little house began to glow, igniting an incredible creativity within me unlike anything I had ever experienced before. Without the limitations of our income and this tiny home, I might never have discovered this side of myself.

What is home to you?

To gain clarity about your home, you must first look at what 'home' means to you. The hidden symbols that you discover within your four walls can be decoded to reveal your overall beliefs about what a home is. This will be slightly different for each person.

For many people their home is the place where they sleep every night. Other people may think of home as the place where they were born and grew up, even if they have lived elsewhere for many years. For many native people, home is their ancestral village or the place where their ancestors are buried.

I have spent quite a bit of time in Scandinavia. Many people in these northern countries live in city apartments for most of the year, but for a month or more during the summer they go to a cottage by a lake. Often this will be the place they call home. Their definition of home is not determined by the amount of time they spend there, but the amount of happiness they feel in a place.

Some people's sense of home will be linked to a certain kind of geography, such as the moors of Scotland, the lakes of Sweden, the mountains of Switzerland, or the great plains in the middle of the United States. Whenever these individuals find themselves in this kind of terrain, they feel at home. It is useful to ask yourself, 'Where do I feel at home?' When you have discovered just what the word home means to you, then you can begin to create the kind of environment that has this sort of energy in it.

I once had a feng shui client, named John, who was a perfect example of how this process can work. When he considered what the idea of home meant to him, John realised that he felt most at home whenever he was in the mountains. I suggested that he place paintings and photos of mountains within his home and office to help create the feeling of mountains in his space. He reported that after doing this he felt much more at home with himself and his life.

For some people, ideas of home can be tied to the traditions, heritage or religion of a particular culture. (See Chapter 4.) They feel at home when they are surrounded by things that symbolise these associations for them. For example, one of my clients found that he felt at home in environments filled with things from the Japanese culture. He wasn't Asian and hadn't grown up in an Asian culture, but none the less he found that including Japanese objects in his home filled him with a great sense of peace and contentment. Another client found that she felt truly at home among relics and icons reflecting Spanish Catholicism. She said that she felt so serene after placing antique carved statues of Jesus and various saints around her home.

These yearnings to be surrounded by objects from a particular culture may be the product of early childhood experiences, ancestral memories, the collective unconscious, symbolic associations, or even former-life memories. Discovering the reason for the attraction is not always important. What does matter, however, is honouring the preferences of the soul. Something that may seem trivial, illogical or even somewhat silly to the conscious mind often fills a deep need on an unconscious level. Listen to the promptings of your soul. It will lead you home.

HOW THE OBJECTS IN YOUR HOME INFLUENCE YOU

The material items that surround you create a bridge between the realms of form and spirit. Because of this, objects in your environment have a profound effect on you in three different ways. First, the symbolism of the things in your home shapes and reinforces your identity, in either a positive or a negative way. Second, because these objects reveal aspects of your inner world, they can help you to move towards integration and unity. And third, the things in your home can be a vehicle for realising your potential.

1 Shaping your identity

Your home is filled with metaphors for your life. Your belongings not only reflect your values, they also are constantly shaping who you are. This is true even if you are unaware of their significance to you.

To illustrate how this works, let me tell you about a feng shui consultation I did for a single woman who wanted to be in a long-term relationship. As I walked through her home, I saw numerous paintings and sculptures of single women. In addition she had in her bedroom a beautiful doll collection that comprised single female dolls. The glass cabinet containing the dolls faced her bed. It was the last thing she saw before she went to sleep and the first thing she saw when she awoke in the morning. *All her prized possessions were a reflection of her identity as a single woman.* Although consciously she wanted to be in a love relationship, subconsciously she saw herself as single and had unconsciously imprinted this identity throughout her environment. Her home was a constant refection and *affirmation* of her identity as a single woman.

The things surrounding you in your home serve as subliminal reminders of who you are. They will continue to direct you towards old patterns of behaviour. Subconscious beliefs are generally so deep-seated that one is not aware of them. They affect our perception of reality in the same way that tinted glasses allow only certain colours to reach our eyes. In the example above, the woman who wanted a relationship was completely unaware of the clues her home provided about her resistance to this possibility in life.

Your environment doesn't lie. Go around looking at the objects in your home as if you had entered it for the first time. What do they say about you? Some things will not take you aback, but if you look with an open heart, you might uncover some surprising information about your inner beliefs which can be very helpful to you.

The exciting news is that you can use the items in your environment to release limiting beliefs about yourself and the world. Once you have identified negative inner beliefs, you can set about finding the ways you have represented them in your home. Then you will be free to make changes and your home can become a powerful affirmation of who you want to be. This method is a thousand times stronger than affirmations spoken or written, because it immerses you in a sea of metaphors that constantly support you in becoming the person you want to be.

Spending ten minutes a day writing an affirmation such as, 'I am prosperous and successful' has been shown to have a positive effect in reprogramming the subconscious mind. However, if you create an environment around you that constantly exudes the feeling of abundance, this idea will be embedded in your subconscious mind day and night.

Ruth had been trying to become more prosperous and never seemed to be able to get ahead. As I walked through her home I observed that although it was a very nice home it was also a very plain one, with few furnishings. Most of the walls were painted in monotone shades of grey and cream. The energy felt austere, almost impoverished. Even though Ruth religiously carried out her daily ritual of writing abundance affirmations, she was living in a home that felt drab and severe. It was a subliminal message affirming her diminished resources. Through our work together, Ruth discovered what abundance meant to her, and we found ways that to implement this *feeling* into her home.

Prosperity will not have the same associations for everyone, but for Ruth two things that symbolised this were big velvet cushions and the colour crimson red. To create the feeling of opulence in her home she painted her study a beautiful shade of crimson and made some sumptuous velvet covers for the divan pillows. She said those two small changes completely transformed the way that she felt in her home. She reported that she *felt* more prosperous. Then, no sooner did she feel more prosperous, her income was boosted: within two weeks she was given a rise at work.

2 Becoming more integrated

The objects we surround ourselves with are not random. Your soul is constantly, subconsciously, arranging and rearranging the world around you in remarkable patterns all aimed at intergration and wholeness.

It is the nature of human beings to invest objects with deeper meaning. The Panama hat on the peg isn't just a weaving of straw and ribbon. It is the shoreline that you walked along wearing it. It is your lover's arm linked in yours, and your laughter as you raced across the sand to recapture it when it flew off your head. You might not consciously remember all of these associations when you pass by this hat, but they linger. And they are affecting the way you feel about your life. Each thing in your home will either increase your energy or diminish it.

The great web of meaning that surrounds you in your home occurs because of a largely unconscious process of integration. Your mind is constantly rearranging pieces of reality in ways that have meaning for you. For example, when you place a piece of your grandmother's antique lace next to a silver comb that belonged to your mother, and then put these next to a photo of yourself on your dressing table, you might be trying, on an unconscious level, to understand and integrate the female relationships in your family history. Choosing a painting of a campfire for your living room, and hanging it next to a photo of a still mountain lake might indicate that you are trying to integrate your fiery impulsive nature with your desire for a quiet, reflective life.

When you understand the deeper meanings within your home and how they represent various aspects of yourself, you can begin to see how all the separate parts of yourself are linked together. You can consciously alter the symbols in your home to create wholeness and balance in your life.

3 *Expressing your individuality*

Even if you think you have no talent for decorating, your home is still a vehicle for expressing yourself. It is one of the ways of distinguishing yourself from others, of demonstrating who you are. When I was a child I had a tree house which I embellished with moss and twigs and pieces of cardboard and old bottles. I felt so alive, so creative and so uniquely myself when I was in this special place.

When teenagers throw their room into disarray, this might indicate that they are defining themselves as individuals separate from their family. The process of doing this can sometimes be difficult, and this turmoil will be reflected in the chaos of the teenager's environment. It is also very common for them to pick wild posters and very intense colours as they try out different identities. They often go through periods of choosing styles that are opposed to the dominant style of the home; it is a way of declaring their individuality.

Sometimes an environment can be used to diminish individuality, as is the case in the armed forces or in certain religious orders. I lived for several years in a Zen monastery, where our personal space was supposed to be simple and undecorated. This type of environment directed our attention away from our personal needs and towards a more universal awareness of self.

Your home can be a shining revelation of your truest self. Don't worry that you haven't got a classic sense of style. If you choose things that you love, objects that fully express the aspirations of your soul, you will create an environment that is perfect for you. The time, energy and care that you invest in your home will more than repay you. You will have space that radiates harmony, beauty and peace, and these qualities will fill the rest of your life.

3

Finding the Hidden Messages in Your Home

I WOKE UP early this morning. It was still dark outside. My daughter and husband were sleeping. The cat was curled up in a tight ball on the sofa. As I walked by, she opened one eye to glance at me, closed it and went back to her nap. Slowly I walked through our home, room by room. I stopped in front of a drawing of an African bushman made by my daughter when she was seven years old. In another room, I picked up a river stone out of a basket on the floor and held it for a moment. I enjoyed feeling its cool smoothness and imagined that it liked being picked up. I looked at my colourful collection of wind-up toys tucked away in small niches and smiled. I always feel happy every time I look at them.

Nearly half a century of memories are reflected in the objects scattered throughout our home. My grandmother's childhood rattle, the carved wooden lizards we lugged back from Bali, an Indian blanket I got myself to celebrate the completion of a Vision Quest – every object carries a memory. Every object has meaning for me. The rattle connects me to my heritage. The lizards remind me of the magical time

we shared in Indonesia. The Indian blanket carries me back to a special time around a campfire watching the tiny embers of the fire float up to the stars.

As I walked through my home, with the morning's first light softly filtering through the windows, I realised that every part of it had a story to tell. Clusters of family photographs are angled towards each other, subconsciously arranged to gather family members close together. The oversized earthenware pots throughout our house symbolise strength and a connection to the land. All the objects, combined with where and how they were placed in the home, together created a resonant tapestry of memories and associations – a unique signature of energy that whispered of times past, and even of what was to be.

Your home can reveal its messages for you, too. These messages can help you understand who you are and where you are going in life. They can help you look deep into your soul. Whether you are conscious of it or not, you are encircled by personal metaphors, each acting as a secret message. Every part of your home and workplace contains encoded information about you and the other occupants of your space. Examining the hidden messages within your home is like putting together the pieces of a jigsaw puzzle. When the picture is completed you will gain a deeper understanding of yourself.

Deciphering the meanings within your home can carry you into the depths of your soul work. You begin this journey by examining your home and the objects within it. As you discover the significance underlying the organisation of your home, you can then reframe the metaphors in your home to shape your spirit. Your home can become a catalyst for change in your life.

'Shapeshifting' to discover hidden meanings

Although this chapter can offer you some insight about the meanings within your home, ultimately the answers dwell within you. One of the fastest and most accurate ways to discover what the objects and areas in your home mean to you is to embark on an inner journey using an ancient technique called 'shapeshifting'. This is a meditation technique where you shift your consciousness from your own identity into the reality of another form of consciousness. In meditation you can become your home, or an object within it, and then notice the feelings and images which emerge while you are in this state. This is a very powerful technique, and sometimes the results can be quite startling.

I used this method with Jesse, one of my clients, to help him discover the meanings of objects in his home. I suggested that he

> ### Shapeshifting to Become an Object
> Relax. Close your eyes. Imagine that your body is changing shape until it becomes an object in your home. Really imagine how it would feel to be that object. Then notice any feelings or memories that you associate with it.

become very relaxed and then imagine that he was walking through his home and 'becoming' different objects. When he imagined walking into his living room he 'became' the sofa, an heirloom that had been left to him by his grandmother. As soon as he felt his body shapeshift to become the sofa, a memory flashed before him, one that he had completely forgotten. He saw himself as a little boy being spanked by his grandmother *as he leaned over this same sofa*. He felt a rush of immense sadness and a feeling of injustice, for he was being unfairly punished.

When he came out of the meditation, he realised that he had uncovered strong negative associations with this piece of furniture. In his life Jesse had a tendency to feel that he was being treated unfairly. He saw that his subliminal associations with the sofa were constantly strengthening this behavioural belief, and as a result he decided that his sofa needed a new home. Another person might have worked on letting go of the belief while still keeping the piece of furniture, but Jesse did not want to do this. Once he realised the significance that this sofa had for him, he no longer wanted it in his home.

Finding the purpose of the objects in your home

Another technique to discover the significance of the things in your home is to imagine that you are 'talking' to these possessions. Begin by giving each object a personality; then engage in conversation with it. Although this might seem a bit strange at first, it can produce excellent results.

Gabrielle, another feng shui client, imagined talking to a painting of fruit that she had just placed in her bedroom. In her meditation, the painting 'told' her that its purpose was to remind her of the fruitfulness of her life. It said that the ripe fruit was symbolic of her future children. The next day she took a pregnancy test and was delighted to find out that she was two months pregnant. During her conversation with the painting, she tuned into her subconscious mind, became aware of the impending birth . . . and was joyous.

Communicating with Your Objects

Close your eyes and take a moment to relax. Imagine that there is growing within you a wonderful ability to converse with the physical world around you. Now visualise walking through your home and talking to some of the objects there. Choose ones that have a special connection to you. Listen to what each one has to say to you about what they symbolise for you *and what their purpose is in your life.*

In this chapter I will suggest some common meanings for objects in your home and ways to interpret them. However, it is always important to remember that the person who knows best is you.

The meanings of your objects

As human beings we assign meaning to everything in our lives. The meanings for objects in your home may be associated with your feelings about:

- the person who gave it to you
- the person who made it
- the place where you bought it
- the people who have owned it
- the circumstances in your life at the time you acquired it
- the meaning it had for the person who gave it to you
- memories associated with the item
- its colour, sound, smell, touch, etc.
- what it represents for you

THE DEEPER MEANING OF YOUR ROOMS

You can gain a deeper understanding about who you are through examining the rooms of your house, each of which has symbolic significance and represents a part of you. For example, your bedroom often symbolises your inner self and your subconscious mind. If your entire house is neat and tidy, but your bedroom resembles a jumble sale, this could signify that beneath your calm and organised surface there are some deeper issues that you need to work on. On the other hand, if your house is in general chaos, but your bedroom is a sanctuary of peace and harmony, this might suggest that, although you might be juggling a lot of balls in your life, beneath the surface your inner self and sub-conscious mind are on solid ground.

In order to strengthen an area of your life, pay attention to the corresponding part of your home. Here is a list of room meanings which you can use to begin making changes in your life. As always, symbolic definitions need to be interpreted in light of your own experience. Use what seems to fit, and don't be concerned about things which don't apply in your case.

Deeper meaning of your home's threshold

The entrance to your home is very important because it represents the transition point between the outer and inner worlds. It sets the energy for the entire home (and your life). It also symbolises your approach to life. A big door says that you are open to scrutiny from others; a small door might mean that you prefer more privacy. An introverted person should not have a hidden entrance, as this would contribute to feeling even more introverted. Likewise, an extrovert might benefit from an entrance partly hidden from view, one not completely exposed to everyone who passes.

Ideal threshold for the soul The threshold is a sacred area. In past times, the importance of the threshold was often marked by an altar or sacred symbols. In some European traditions, a five-pointed star was carved into the crossbeam of the entrance to represent harmony, health and a connection with the spiritual realms. In Jewish tradition, the mezuzah – a blessing inside a small container – is placed at the front door. Each person who enters the home is thus blessed.[1]

Your front entrance should be inviting and convey a sense of vitality. It should be well lit, clean and free from clutter. If there is a path leading up to the door, it should meander through aromatic and beautiful plants. Place a welcome mat in front of the door. An entrance with these qualities creates a template for your entire home and for your life.

It is valuable to have a transition area just inside the door. In the tradition of feng shui, the front door is the entrance point for *chi* (life-force energy), which enters here and spreads throughout the entire home. Because this area marks the transition from the outside world, to the inner sanctuary of the home, it should be honoured as such on both the physical and spiritual levels. Provide a place to hang up coats and hats and remove shoes. Hang small symbols of welcome or inspiration in this area. A small statue of Hestia, the ancient Greek goddess of the hearth and home, or Janus, the Roman god who guarded the gateway to the home, would be good here.

Deeper meaning of your bedroom

Your bedroom can be a very potent symbol of your innermost self. If everyone sees you as a confident person, but beneath the surface you are frightened and shy, this might be reflected in a dark, dreary bedroom. Adding some lights, opening the windows and using accessories in vivid, clear colours can help create a template of confidence and optimism. A bedroom with many windows and mirrors might be a metaphor for someone who is always giving out energy and doesn't take time to self-nurture. If this is the case, try cloaking the windows with curtains, adding paintings of restful scenes, and creating a general feeling of peace in the room.

Ideal bedroom for the soul   The bedroom should be your personal oasis. In some respects it is the most important room in the home, because it is where you spend the most time. As the bedroom is your gateway to sleep, it should feel cosy, comfortable and deeply restful. Subtle lighting, peaceful colours and comfortable furnishings create the most nurturing environment. Flesh tones such as beiges, browns, creams and lavenders are excellent here because these colours can subliminally represent being nestled in a mother's arms or being held by someone. Earthy shades of rust, salmon, honey and gold are also great for a bedroom as they connect us to mother earth.

You should not have anything looming over you in your bedroom, such as an open beam. There is often a correlation between health problems and beams that cross over a bed. If your bedroom has this feature, either move your bed or, if this is not possible, disguise the beams by draping them with fabric or encourage a climbing plant to grow along the beam's edges.

Nurture yourself through the choice of your bedroom furnishings. Your bed is the place where you renew yourself physically and spiritually. It is the home of your night-time dreams, a place of healing, physical love and deep rest. Choose one which honours the importance of these sides of your life, and deck it in bedlinen which soothes your body and pleases your senses.

Deeper meaning of your living room

The living room is the gathering place for the residents of the home. It symbolises harmonious relationships between household members, as well as your connection to other people and your community. A living room that is seldom used or uninviting can contribute to family members drifting apart. It may also reflect a growing distance between yourself and others.

Ideal living room for the soul   Your living room should be attractive and comfortable, as its purpose is to create community between the members of the household. All decisions about decoration and furnishings should be made with this purpose clearly in mind. What are the interests of the people who will use this room? What activities do they most like to do together? What family traditions would you like to honour here?

Furniture should be grouped to facilitate conversation and make everyone feel welcome and relaxed. A beautiful room need not be overly formal. The living room should say: 'Come in, make yourself at home here.' This is an ideal place to display photos of family members and ancestors, as well as pictures of angels, saints, or spiritual guardians of the family. Awards, mementos of family trips, and artwork made by family members can all be celebrated here.

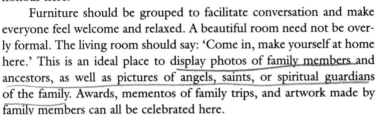

If there is conflict within the family, you can rearrange this room to promote better feelings between family members. Honour each person. Consider their preferences and individuality. Using the objects in the room find a symbolic way to ease the differences between individuals to create a space of joy, community and fun.

Deeper meaning of your dining room

There is no more soulful room in the house than the dining room, where household members gather to nourish themselves. Without consuming food, we cannot go on living. Without a sense of community, we have little desire for life. Sharing meals with loved ones in a beautiful environment is a ritual of such importance that it has been honoured in every culture around the world. A dining room with good feng shui contributes to health and a strong connection between family members.

Ideal dining room for the soul   Ideally a dining room should be a place that is used regularly. Its decor can be modified to reflect the changing seasons. It can be specially decorated for holidays, but even on ordinary days it should always be treated with the respect that its function deserves. The dining table, the focal point, should be placed in a central location, allowing enough room for people to sit down and get up without feeling restricted. Warm colours, especially shades of yellow, stimulate conversation. Red in a dining room will stimulate appetite.

Beautiful dishes and table linens delight the eyes and honour the food served on them. Candles and bowls of fresh flowers or fruit on the table bring harmony and elegance to the simplest meal. They enhance the ritual aspects of eating. Breaking bread together is one of the most ancient celebrations of humanity. In the dining room, we remember our connection to this tradition.

Deeper meaning of your kitchen

The kitchen is the heart of the home. The preparation of food is a holy act, a truly soulful activity, for it reminds us of our place in the great cycle of life. We are dependent on the abundance of the earth in order to sustain ourselves, and in the kitchen this relationship is ritualised throughout the day, every day. This room symbolises your prosperity and financial resources because it is where you connect with what sustains you. The kitchen is also associated with fire, which is an activating force for abundance.

In earlier times the kitchen was the centre of the home because it was where the family gathered to keep warm and talk while food was being prepared. Have you ever noticed how at a party, people will often spontaneously migrate towards the kitchen? Perhaps this is because the atmosphere here subconsciously recaptures a nurturing communal feeling.

Ideal kitchen for the soul   The ideal kitchen is clean, light and airy, and full of free-flowing *chi*. There should be excellent lighting and, if possible, plenty of natural sunlight. Bright and cheerful colours are best for the kitchen, conveying a sense of health, happiness and vitality. Pots of fresh herbs growing by the window, ropes of dried chilli peppers, onions and garlic, bunches of dried herbs and flowers: all are excellent to have in the kitchen. Not only are they beautiful to look at and useful, they also celebrate the abundance of the earth.

Surfaces should be clean and free of clutter to allow for ease and efficiency in preparing meals. Bright pots, beautiful ceramic dishes, old wooden spoons – all of the objects you use to prepare meals should be aesthetically pleasing, well-maintained and full of soul. The things in your kitchen are not only utilitarian. The mood you create in this room will directly affect the health and vitality of all the occupants of the home. The thoughts and feelings you have while preparing food will be evident in the meals you consume. Take time to make the kitchen a place you want to spend time in, a place which radiates warmth and vibrant life force.

Deeper meaning of your bathroom

The bathroom represents cleansing and purification. It is also a symbol for releasing that which you do not need in your life. Since feng shui originated in China at a time when the bathroom was usually an unsanitary place, many of the traditional feng shui associations with this room are very negative. Today the bathroom is often a place of relaxation and cleansing, so usually the negative symbolism is no longer necessarily relevant or appropriate. The bathroom is an essential room in the home and should be honoured as such for the service it provides.

Ideal bathroom for the soul   Ideally the bathroom should be well ventilated, well lit and full of beautiful, healthful colours. Green and blue in particular are good here. Blue represents water, which is the medium for cleansing and purification. Green represents life, new growth and new beginnings. Live plants in the bathroom purify the air and bring a sense of freshness and vitality. If there is sufficient light, plants grow well here because there is always plenty of moisture.

Whenever you clean yourself you are symbolically initiating a new beginning. Use candles, scented bath oils, lovely soaps, soft towels and other objects which speak to you of comfort and health. Pictures of trees, the sea, rivers and lush pastures enhance the bathroom's function as a metaphor for purification and renewal in life.

Deeper meaning of your study

This is the room in the home where you can express your creativity, your productivity and power. If the energy here is blocked or congested, these feelings may be manifested in your working or creative life as well. This is a place where you can give full symbolic expression to your dreams, hopes and ambitions. Work is one of the most sacred ways to express who you are. Making your study a reflection of your true self can have miraculous results in terms of increased productivity and success in all areas of your life.

Ideal study for the soul   It is essential that this area should be free from clutter. *Chi* must flow freely throughout this room, and nothing stops this more than clutter. Your home office or study should convey a sense of refuge. It should be separate from other areas of your home, so that you are free to concentrate on your work. If space limitations make it necessary to have your office in a room that is used by other members of your household, then you can create a sense of privacy and separation through the use of curtains or screens.

Hanging pictures or mottoes or items that symbolise what you want to accomplish, can very helpful in meeting your goals. Be sure to include diplomas, awards and other meaningful representations of what you have already achieved. Also acknowledge sources of support. These

might be personal heroes, your children, your partner or certain friends. Choose furniture and accessories that speak to you of prosperity, abundance, success, and you will find that suddenly you and everyone around you values you more!

Deeper meaning of your basement

A basement almost always symbolises things deeply rooted within you and your subconscious mind. It can also represent desires that you are suppressing in your life. If there is some deep negative programming in your life that you wish to heal, the basement is an excellent place to start working on this. The basement also represents your foundations, being on firm ground in life.

Ideal basement for the soul The basement should be clean, dry, well maintained and free of clutter. If you haven't a clue what is down there, then it's time for a big clean-out. We sometimes think that if we can't see something, it's not affecting us. This is completely untrue. You are affected by all the spaces in your home. Sometimes the areas you can't see are affecting you more than the visible ones, especially if you are resistant to clearing them out, or if there are unresolved issues connected to these areas. Your basement can only function as a strong support in your life after you have cleaned it, repaired it, made it strong and waterproof, and made peace with it.

Install strong shelving as needed. Make sure all tools stored there are in good working order and put away. If your boiler is in your basement, have it serviced regularly. If it is a daylight basement, clean the windows and plant ferns and flowers outside them. This will bring in freshness and the energy of growth. Make your basement a place of security, strength and order to reap these qualities in your life.

Deeper meaning of your attic

The attic symbolises your higher aspirations. In some Asian cultures the altar is placed here because it signifies being closer to the heavens. The attic can also symbolise things hanging over your head, or things that seem perpetually just beyond your grasp. If there are any unresolved issues of this nature in your life, working on your attic can be a symbolic way of approaching the difficulties.

Ideal attic for the soul If your attic is used for storage, everything should be organised. Keep the access to your attic clear, easy to reach and in good repair. Make sure there is adequate lighting and good ventilation, and that your roof is well cared for. Although these precautions are of obvious importance to the health and longevity of your home, it is also symbolically relevant to the health of your soul.

If you have a large attic with natural lighting and substantial flooring, you might want to consider making a special retreat for yourself here. An attic can be the perfect place for meditation, a place to go and get away from it all. A friend of mine has wonderful childhood memories of going up to the attic of his family's Victorian home in San Francisco. He would lie on an old bed up there, reading away many afternoons, listening to the rain on the roof and eating apples.

Deeper Meaning of How You Organise Your Home

When I was in my twenties, whenever I knew that someone was coming to visit I would wait until the last minute and then dash around the house throwing clutter in cupboards or under the bed. Dishes would go in the oven, dirty clothes would be stuffed behind pillows. Looking back, I now realise that my actions revealed an underlying lack of self esteem. I wanted people to see me in a particular way, but right beneath the surface there was a deep sense of unworthiness. As self-respect has grown in me over the years, I have developed new patterns of behaviour. Although I still tidy up before visitors arrive, I no longer approach the problem in my former frenetic way.

How is your home organised? Are you constantly tidying up? Do you never use your best china? Do you hesitate to invite people over because your home isn't smart enough? Or do you avoid entertaining because you worry that people might make a mess or ruin something? Here are some of the ways people organise their homes and what this can mean.

Neat and tidy   A neat and tidy home may indicate an organised, concise approach to life, or in some cases may be related to unresolved issues from childhood. When we don't feel a sense of inner control we sometimes overcompensate by always trying to control our environment. I knew a man who vacuumed his dining room every day, but never allowed his family to use that room because he was afraid they might spill something on the carpet. When I talked with him about his life, he told me that he had suffered a difficult childhood. He never felt empowered as a child. His lack of inner power resulted in his need for excessive external control over the cleanliness of his home.

If you are uncomfortable whenever anything is out of order in your home, you might find that you have some deeper issues that need addressing. As an exercise, it can be valuable consciously to create a bit of mess in your home. For example, you might try doing a creative project and then leave things out instead of immediately putting everything away. Live with the mess for a while and notice the emotions, feelings and memories that come up. Often you can gain insight in this way.

Messy   If your home is perpetually in a shambles, with piles of unsorted papers on tables, stacks of dishes in the sink, and clothing all over the place, this might indicate only that you value neatness less than other things in your life. Many families with small children find that a fair amount of mess is a necessary part of a lifestyle which focuses on the children having fun and being creative. I know one successful, healthy family who live in a house that looks literally as though a tornado has hit it. Once when a family member wanted to show me an article, she had first to dig thorough an enormous pile of yellowed newspapers stored underneath a precariously balanced, old hamster cage, in the corner of the living room. Their house is a mess because their focus in life lies elsewhere. (When you have small children, it is unrealistic to think that you can have a clutter-free home.)

However, sometimes messy homes can also indicate deeper unresolved issues. A perpetually dirty one might be saying: 'My house is out of control because, beneath the surface, I feel out of control.' Some people maintain messy homes as a sort of protective barrier between them and others. On an unconscious level, they use the mess as a reason never to invite others, so that they don't have to get too close.

Note which rooms tend to be the messiest. This can be a clue to the underlying issue. If you feel that the mess in your house is indicative of unresolved inner problems, first clean everything and then notice your feelings. Is it emotionally uncomfortable to live in a tidy home? Watch for any memories that surface. (See section on clutter in Chapter 4.)

Not using the 'good stuff'   Are your lampshades still clad in their original plastic dust covers? Do you have silver or china that you never use? This may indicate that you are a person who doesn't feel worthy of the good things in life. It can also indicate someone who is living in the future and saving their furniture, dishes, or best clothing for some time when everything will be better than it is now. For most people who organise their home like this, the future never comes. Know that you deserve to use your 'good stuff' *now*. Doing so creates a template that says you deserve the best in life. When you start living as though this is true, an amazing shift in your underlying belief system will also begin to take place.

Stockpiling supplies   An accumulation of many unused items in your home can symbolise untapped potential lying dormant within you. This problem is different from not wanting to use the 'good stuff'. Here you may have tools that you purchased for a project that are still in their original packaging. Perhaps boxes of unused stationery, cans of unopened paint, or rolls of fabric, line the shelves of your home. When you start to use these things, new talents and possibilities will also begin to show up in your life.

Stockpiling unused supplies can also be related to fears of the future. It is wise to keep adequate supplies on hand in case of an emergency, such as an extended power failure or even an earthquake; but if you have created a list of emergency supplies, purchased and stowed them away, and yet you still feel a nagging anxiety that you haven't got enough, then you can be fairly certain that you are dealing with unresolved issues about security.

Obstacles everywhere   If you feel as though you are running an obstacle course every time you pass through your home, this can be a powerful metaphor regarding obstacles in your life. Get rid of the clutter. Rent extra storage space if you can't part with it all at once, but be ruthless about clearing out your space. Simplify your living space and you'll find that you encounter fewer obstacles in your life.

Many things out of reach   If you are constantly getting out the ladder or standing on a chair to reach things in your home, this can be a metaphor for always having to strive for what you want in life. It might be related to an approach to life which says: 'Whenever I want anything in life, I have to work hard for it. Things are never easy for me.' When you reorganise your home so that the things you use often are easily accessible, then you will find that you don't have to reach so far to get what you want in life.

Everything on the floor   If you tend to keep many things on the floor of your home, such as baskets of knitting or other projects, stacks of books, cushions and a stereo system, then this may simply mean that you are an earthy, grounded person. You might feel more comfortable being close to the earth. But it could also mean that you are feeling a bit bogged down in life. If this is the case, you need to learn to fly a bit. Try repositioning things off the floor. Put your books on shelves; install your sound system in a cabinet. You will feel lighter and more free, and your spirits will soar.

Very organised   In some cases a home may not always be tidy but it is very organised. This can be a productive and comfortable way of

living, but it may indicate a person who compartmentalises his or her life or who is resistent to change. If your need for organisation is obsessive, there may be deeper issues which need to be addressed.

DEEPER MEANING OF HOME SYSTEMS

As human beings we tend to associate certain phenomena in the physical world with certain human traits and emotions. This applies particularly to the utility systems within our home such as plumbing and electrical wiring. Below are some common meanings for these systems.

Plumbing   The systems in your home can represent different aspects of your life. While it is true that sometimes a clogged drain is only that – a plumbing problem that needs to be resolved by a qualified plumber – nevertheless, there are many times when problems with plumbing can be reflective of deeper, subconscious issues. For example, water is almost always associated with emotions and the subconscious. Clogged drains can represent clogged emotions; they can also represent a sluggish lymphatic system thus indicating a need for more exercise.

A dripping tap can signify a small but constantly irritating emotional situation in life or that you are slowly losing life force. Overflowing plumbing can mean overflowing emotions. Too much water pressure may mean that you are under too much emotional pressure, or you should check your blood pressure. Too little water pressure can indicate that your emotional vitality is waning. A burst pipe can indicate a long-time build-up of emotions, especially anger.

Electricity   If you are having problems with the electricity circuit or the electrical appliances in your home, be sure to get a complete evaluation by a qualified professional. At the same time, however, it is an excellent idea to assess what this might mean in terms of your life, because the electrical systems in your home can be a metaphor for your personal energy.

Additionally, your body is constantly interacting with the electricity in your environment. When you go through a major shift in consciousness – even when the experience is a positive one, such as the release of an old addiction or negative personality trait – this affects your personal electrical system, which in turn affects all the electrical systems around you.

Circuits that become overloaded and light bulbs that constantly burn out can symbolise that you are doing too much and not taking time out for rest and relaxation. This can also mean that you are giving out too much energy and not taking in enough for yourself. Sometimes, too, light bulbs habitually blow out when you are going through a transformational time in your life.

Heating   The heating system in your home can correlate with your reactions to situations and people in your life. If your house is constantly hot, notice if you tend to become overheated when dealing with people and situations. If your home is constantly cold, notice if you are withdrawing from life. If you find that it is hard to maintain a balance of hot and cold in your home, you may also discover that you tend to overreact to a variety of situations in your life. For example, if you are constantly turning the heat up, finding it too hot, turning it back down only to notice a bit later than it is too cold, and so on, this can indicate erratic energy in your life.

Windows and doors   In feng shui, windows are the eyes of the home. They represent your view out into the world. Windows can also symbolise the ability to take in and assimilate information from the world around you. They can also represent your physical eyes. In feng shui, cracked or dirty windows can reflect eye problems or emotional difficulties seeing the world around you properly.

The main entrance door is thought to be the 'mouth' of your home allowing *chi* to enter. It can also represent your physical mouth and your ability to communicate.

Security   Unfortunately, in modern life home security systems are a sign of the times. Alarms that are constantly going off without any provocation can indicate an overreaction to life's situations. This can also indicate an obsessive fear and that you need to take some steps to feel more empowered. Security systems that break down or periodically malfunction may indicate a stronger need for personal borders in your life.

WHAT YOUR HOME'S DESIGN THEMES SAY ABOUT YOU

Whether we intend to or not, we create themes in our homes. It is natural to do this; it's fun and it feels good. A Western theme in a living room, with a deer-horn chandelier and framed posters of cowboys, might make you feel adventurous and exciting. A minimalist theme in a dining room, with a sleek glass table and black lacquer cabinets, might lend sophistication and elegance. Examining the themes in your home

design can provide valuable information about yourself. Usually there are three reasons for the design styles that we are drawn to.

1 *Metaphor*

Often a theme is a metaphor for an aspect of your inner self, or it can symbolise a quality that you desire in life. For example, Charlotte had a very hectic life as an account executive, but as soon as she came home she was filled with an instant sense of peace. Exquisite Japanese calligraphy graced her walls, beautiful shoji screens extended across a corner of her living room, and she had sliding rice paper doors in her bedroom. She told me that the simplicity of Zen Buddhism represented peace and tranquillity to her. The theme of her house provided a metaphor for qualities Charlotte desired in her life.

2 *Ancestral memories*

A second reason we are drawn to a particular style is related to subconscious ancestral memories. Remarkable research has surfaced postulating that there are memories stored in our subconscious mind which did not originate in our present life but are instead a vestige passed down from our ancestors. In my feng shui practice, I have noticed a fascinating correlation between ancestral homes and the types of homes in which people feel most at home. Often a person's present home will contain symbolic components of the homes of their ancestors.

After John's company transferred him to a another city, he found himself looking for a new home. Nothing seemed quite right until the estate agent took him to a Scandinavian-style home. He felt so comfortable there that he made an offer on the spot. Although his paternal grandfather had emigrated to the United States from Norway, John had felt no special connection to this heritage before. Nevertheless, he said that there was something about the simplicity and honesty of the Scandinavian style that drew him like a magnet. It also made him want to get to know his grandfather better and to research his roots on that side of the family.

3 *Past life*

Although the philosophy of reincarnation is not a predominant belief in Western societies, a large percentage of the world's population believes in past lives. The notion of reincarnation accounts for some people being drawn to certain styles of home. Through my work as a past-life therapist, I observed this phenomenon again and again. Often people will make choices regarding their homes based on experiences they have had in previous lifetimes. For example, although Sandra wasn't a weaver and didn't know any weavers, she none the less had collected a number of antique spinning wheels which she displayed in her home. She said that she loved the way they looked, and also that they made her feel peaceful and serene. She later discovered that in a past life she had spun all her own wool.

Often I have found that an individual will be drawn to certain home themes for a number of overlapping reasons. Gina had chosen a Native American theme for her living and dining rooms. She had posters of Native Americans, beautiful Native American wool blankets draped over her sofa, and a large dream-catcher hung at the entrance to her home. When she did genealogical research she found that she had Native American relatives on her mother's side of the family. In a past life regression, she discovered, too, that she had been Native American in a past life. She also felt that using Native American symbols in her home deepened her connection to the earth and nature, and that this was healing for her.

THE DEEPER MEANING OF COLOUR

The colours that surround you have the ability to affect you powerfully in both physical and symbolic ways. Because of this, you can use the colours in your home to change your life. You can repaint your walls, for a dramatic transformation of colour energy, or you can choose new colours for the soft furnishings and accessories.

Research has shown that colour has profound physical effects on us. As we respond to the spectrum of colours, their properties will be manifest in our moods, traits and interactions with others. A preference for warm colours usually indicates an extrovert person, while a liking for cooler colours is usually associated with introverted people. Some colours can cause enzymes and hormones to go through molecular changes. Others can affect the rate of enzymatic reactions or deactivate enzyme reaction.[2]

Dr Max Lüscher, a colour scientist, studied people's colour preferences. He came to the conclusion that individuals' reactions to colour have meaning transcending cultural differences and are rooted deeply within them. He postulated that colour preference could indicate a person's state of mind, as well as possible glandular imbalances.[3]

Choosing Your Home's Colour Scheme

Red activates increased appetite, physical strength, passion, dynamic action, tenacity, excitement.

Orange activates optimism, expansiveness, confidence, sense of community, enthusiasm, warm-heartedness.

Yellow activates the intellect, communication, attention to detail, academic achievement, expression, freedom, sincerity.

Green activates balance, harmony, healing, growth, hope, abundance, replenishment.

Blue activates inspiration, inner peace, spiritual understanding, faith, devotion, patience, composure, contentment.

Purple activates calmness, intuition, psychic awareness, soothing, spiritual perspective.

White activates purification, humility, purity, expansiveness, balance, divine love. Too much white can seem sterile.

Black activates the mysterious, the unknown, stillness, inner realms, being dormant. Too much black can be depressing.

WHAT THE PHOTOS IN YOUR HOME MEAN

The photographs in a home are a gold mine of information about the people who live there. This is because photos bring people and places into the environment of a home in an immediate and symbolic way. When you place photos of loved ones on your mantelshelf, you choose to do so because of feelings that you have about those people, whether they are living or dead, whether or not you have ever known them in your lifetime. Photographs of places you have been to, places you would like to visit, scenes that speak to your soul – all of these bring the characteristics of the place pictured directly into your home. Memories, beliefs, associations, moods and strong emotions will all be connected to and reinforced by the photos in your home.

There is a mysterious alchemy in photos. People in native cultures are often afraid to have their photograph taken because they feel that it will capture their soul. Although this fear is not common in our culture, none the less photos do capture fragments of our lives. They reveal emotions, passing thoughts, ephemeral moments in time. A photo can portray the essence of a person or a situation, and *it will continue to radiate the energy of that moment* into our homes as long as the photo is on display.

The photographs that you have in your home are very important. They are a powerful tool for shifting energy and should not be used lightly. How and where they are placed, who is pictured in them and what was occurring at the time the photo was taken will all have a strong impact on your home.

Symbolism of family photos

Observing displays of family photos often uncovers startling information about the interpersonal dynamics of a household. I once did a feng shui consultation for a couple who owned a very stately home. In my pre-consultation interview, the husband explained that he always felt like a little boy, almost as if he had never really grown up. His wife concurred, and they both said that this had become a problem in their relationship. As I explored their home I saw, hung on a prominent wall, a photo of the husband as a small boy. Directly above this photo was a photograph of the man's father looking rather stern. The juxtaposition of the two photos made the father appear to be looking down on his young son.

I asked the husband about his relationship with his father. He said that his father was very domineering and always treated him like a child, even after he had become a man. I explained that the photographs of him and his father might be serving as a continual affirmation of his negative view of himself. I suggested that he hang a photo showing himself as a man *above* a photo of his father as a child. In this way he could symbolically shift the dynamics of his relationship with his father. In other words, the two photos would act as a visual affirmation of his manhood. Both the husband and wife were keen to do this.

Afterwards they reported that they felt a remarkable change in their relationship. The husband declared that he felt himself beginning to step into manhood. Changing photos on a wall may seem almost too simple a cure to be effective, but the human psyche often responds to symbolic acts instantly and powerfully.

In another couple's home, there were two individual portraits of the husband and wife across from the sofa where they sat most evenings. In these photos, the wife was facing one way and the husband was facing the opposite direction. In other words, they had their backs to each other. When I asked about their relationship, they said that they were contemplating divorce. The wife even said at one point, 'He looks at me, but I never feel he really *sees* me.' They explained that they had invited me into their home with the idea that perhaps feng shui could help their relationship, since they had already tried a number of other solutions without success.

As we walked through their home, I saw a number of other clues which spoke of the increasing distance between them, but none more obvious or poignant than the two photos looking away from each other. I made a number of recommendations, including the reversal of the position of the two photos, which would symbolically affirm their commitment to mutual communication and the relationship. Several years have passed since that consultation, but their relationship has not only endured, it has become much stronger over time.

When placing photos in your home, observe where the people featured seem to be looking. Are they staring at a wall, a rubbish bin, the toilet? I once did a consultation for a woman named Susan who complained that she felt she was always coming up against walls in her life. As we looked at the photos of her displayed in her home, I noticed that every single one was *staring at a wall*. Of course there were also other clues related to these feelings, such as the fact that her front door opened into a wall. In addition to other changes, Susan and I rearranged her photos so that they faced more interesting scenes than blank walls. Whenever someone in a photo appears to be staring at something unpleasant, move the photo to another location.

Clusters of family photos

Clustering framed family photos together on shelves, tables or walls is a subliminal way of recreating ancestral altars. In ancient cultures, pictures or objects representing the family's ancestors were often situated in a place of honour in the home. These ancestral altars honoured the past, which in turn created hope for the future. They were a visual affirmation of the ability of the human spirit to survive.

In current times, gatherings of family photos provide an affirmation of connections between friends and families. They can serve as a reminder that we are part of a lineage that trails behind us and flows before us into the future. They can also serve as a powerful metaphor for the resilience of the human spirit, the continuum of the human family.

Look at the groups of photos in your home. Are the people looking into the centre of the cluster or are they looking away from everyone else? Ideally, in a group of photos everyone should be looking towards the centre rather than away in separate directions. You might consider placing at the centre a small object of meaning or beauty, such as a beautiful stone, to function as a focal point. This object will represent the balance and harmony of the relationships between these people.

A gathering of family photos can also be a powerful affirmation for the healing of relationships. If there are rifts between members of your family, symbolically arrange their photos in a special place in the home. In the centre of this cluster, place an object, or objects, that represents family unity, such as a small figurine of a dove. This photo gallery will act as a constant visual affirmation for peace and unity in the family.

The positioning of each person in a cluster of photos can be important. Arrange and rearrange the photos until you feel a synergetic harmony occurring; this will create a more powerful statement. For example, if two of the people in the photos are constantly bickering with each other in life, then including pictures of both of them in the group will help to heal this discord, but it is best not to place their pictures directly next to each other.

Who's in your home photos

Who is in the photos in your home can be as revealing as where and how they are placed. Rather than having a haphazard scattering of family photos throughout your home, carefully decide which photos you want to display and why. Look at each person and consciously decide how you feel about the photo. Think about the best place to situate it in the home. For example, if your deceased aunt used to be very judgmental of you, you wouldn't want to place her photo above your desk, where it might activate or reinforce self-critical feelings within you.

If you adore your grandchildren, photos of them will be a constant source of joy anywhere in your home. If you have photos of more than one person, notice body positioning, who is standing next to whom, what the expressions on their faces are, what your relationship is with each of the people pictured and what was happening when the photo was taken. All of these factors will help you decide whether to display the photo or not.

If you have photos only of deceased family members in your home, it may imply that you are disconnected from the present. Likewise, displaying only members present in your life now may imply a disconnection from the past. There are times in life when it may be appropriate to sever our connection to the past. However, as a lifelong tendency it can be disruptive to present relationships. Except in cases where past relationships were very damaging, displaying family photographs can be a mark of our ability to overcome past concerns and connect with our extended family in meaningful ways.

What was occurring at the time of the photo

A photograph is a fragment of an experience. It usually doesn't show the mood in the room at the time the photograph was taken; it cannot convey the smell of the apple pie baking in the oven, or replay the Mozart in the background. It is a selective, two-dimensional rendering of a multi-experiential moment. Before placing a photo on display you might consider investigating the circumstances surrounding the moment when it was taken. Even if you don't consciously know what was occurring then, nevertheless there are subtle clues within the picture about the energy at the time. A photo taken with happiness in the air will radiate happiness into a home. A photo taken with confusion or unhappiness in the air will emit these qualities into an environment.

In one consultation I did, I asked Sara about a particular family photograph in her home. Although everyone in the photo was smiling, on an energy level I sensed something very disturbing about it. She explained, 'Oh, that was taken at our last family reunion. It's funny you should ask me about that photo, because just before it was taken a huge fist fight broke out between two of my uncles. Everyone was pretty upset.' Upon further enquiry, Sara said that the event had really disturbed her. I suggested she remove the photo from the wall because, every time she passed it, potentially it was subconsciously reminding her of something painful.

Photos of yourself

Photos of yourself *can influence you more powerfully than anything else in your home*. When you see yourself looking happy and joyous in a photo, this sinks deep into your subconscious mind, programming you for more happiness. A photo in which you look stern or unhappy, or one where you were unhappy at the time it was taken, will be a constant affirmation for unhappiness.

Where to place family photographs

Choosing where to display family photos in your home is important. Ideally they should be placed where you can observe them without rushing. For example, family photos are better clustered together on a piano or bookshelf, where they can be seen and enjoyed at leisure, rather than in a hall or corridor where people are likely to be passing by them on their way to somewhere else. When family photos are displayed in a hallway, sometimes the home's occupants report that although they consider relationships to be important, they just don't seem to have enough time for them. Another unsatisfactory location for photos is along a stairway. This is because *chi* (energy) tends to roll downstairs. Photos displayed here might contribute to jumbled emotions and a lack of harmony between family members.

One good way to help you decide where to place photos is to use the feng shui bagua. The bagua is a grid superimposed over a map of your home. It correlates various areas of your home with aspects of life. By placing photos in certain areas, you can activate the corresponding energy in a person's life. For example, if you want to enhance your career, place a photograph of yourself looking successful in the career area of your home. If you want to strengthen your love relationship, try adding a photo of you and your sweetheart to the relationship area of your home. You can use the same principles to map out areas of a room, or even a desk, according to the bagua. For example, the best place on your desk to display a photo of your beloved would be on the far right-hand corner, which is the relationship section of the desk.

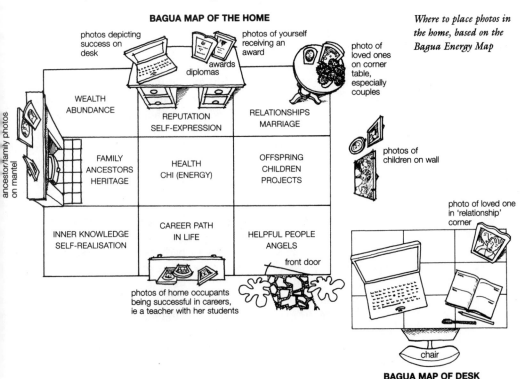

BAGUA MAP OF THE HOME

Where to place photos in the home, based on the Bagua Energy Map

photos depicting success on desk

photos of yourself receiving an award

awards diplomas

photo of loved ones on corner table, especially couples

ancestor/family photos on mantel

WEALTH ABUNDANCE	REPUTATION SELF-EXPRESSION	RELATIONSHIPS MARRIAGE
FAMILY ANCESTORS HERITAGE	HEALTH CHI (ENERGY)	OFFSPRING CHILDREN PROJECTS
INNER KNOWLEDGE SELF-REALISATION	CAREER PATH IN LIFE	HELPFUL PEOPLE ANGELS

photos of children on wall

photo of loved one in 'relationship' corner

front door

photos of home occupants being successful in careers, ie a teacher with her students

chair

BAGUA MAP OF DESK

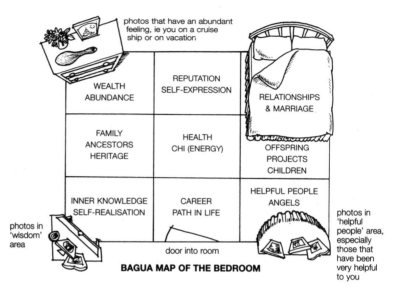

photos that have an abundant feeling, ie you on a cruise ship or on vacation

WEALTH ABUNDANCE	REPUTATION SELF-EXPRESSION	RELATIONSHIPS & MARRIAGE
FAMILY ANCESTORS HERITAGE	HEALTH CHI (ENERGY)	OFFSPRING PROJECTS CHILDREN
INNER KNOWLEDGE SELF-REALISATION	CAREER PATH IN LIFE	HELPFUL PEOPLE ANGELS

photos in 'wisdom' area

door into room

BAGUA MAP OF THE BEDROOM

photos in 'helpful people' area, especially those that have been very helpful to you

Where to place photos in the home, based on the Bagua Energy Map

Photos in the bedroom

Because the bedroom is such an important room for the soul, it is wise to be very careful what photos you include here. There is nothing that dampens your sex life more than a picture of your mother-in-law directly overlooking the bed. If you place photos of yourself and loved ones in your bedroom, make sure you pick those with very positive associations, because their energy will be with you during the night, and will be subliminally implanted in your subconscious mind while you are sleeping.

One of my clients complained that all the men she met were only interested in sex. When I looked in her bedroom, I saw she had beefcake photos of men plastered on the walls. I suggested she replace them with romantic photos, to achieve the kind of relationship she desired.

Photos of nature

There are very few things more uplifting or inspiring than a beautiful scene in nature. Nearly everyone has wonderful memories of a favourite time in the mountains, near the sea, or perhaps overlooking an endless plain of windblown grass, where they felt at one with nature and the Creator. Photos of these kinds of scenes can instil this feeling into the heart and soul of your home.

Fertile landscapes invite a feeling of abundance and prosperity into a home. A photo of a rose can invoke feelings of love. A photo of a waterfall can bring a sense of freshness and vitality, while a mountain lake can generate a feeling of tranquillity and peace.

Mountains In the tradition of feng shui, as in life, it is essential to feel that you have a strong base of support. When you feel supported, you have the courage to go out and realise your dreams in life. In feng shui, the back of the home is associated with this sense of support, so this is an excellent place for a photo of a strong majestic mountain facing into the home. This will create feelings of strength and groundedness for all members of the family. You might also consider putting a photo of a mountain behind your chair at work, so you symbolically have support the size of a mountain.

Water Water represents flow, emotions, life force, purification and healing. The soul needs the refreshing qualities of water as much as the body does. To bring these qualities into focus in your life, consider placing photos of water in your home. Water photographs can be used to strengthen a particular bagua area anywhere in the house. For example, in traditional feng shui water is associated with wealth, so the placement of a photo of a stream, river or lake in the wealth sector of the house can help increase prosperity.

A word of caution: if you have experienced many emotional crises in your home, or if fellow occupants seem to be continually dealing with emotional issues, the use of water photos might exacerbate these tendencies. It might be better to remove existing photos and paintings of water for a while. I was recently called into a home where there had been a number of family crises, including the death of a close family friend and the loss of employment for the head of the household. One of the teenagers in the home told me that it had been six months since she had had a day without tears.

When I asked when the period of emotional crises had begun, I was told that it had started after the home was remodelled the previous year. This renovation had included the installation in the living room of a large picture window, which overlooked a lake in front of the property. In addition there were *seven* pictures of water scenes in this same room, including a very large painting of boats on the sea.

The expression and cleansing of the emotions is an essential part of a healthy life. But, as in all areas, balance is the key word. For this family, moving away from the world of emotion and back towards a feeling of groundedness was very helpful. They continued to enjoy the beautiful view of the lake in front of their home, but they chose to redecorate using colours, materials and motifs that all celebrated the element earth, rather than water.

Fire A photograph of a blazing sunset or a single candle's flame will invite the Spirit of Fire into a home. This can help bring vitality, life-

force energy and activity into the soul of your home. Photos of fire are great to display if your life has become sluggish, or when you want to begin new projects. Using photos of fire in an area associated with the bagua is an excellent way to ignite the qualities represented there. However, if you find that there is too much anger, agitation or irritation in your home, fire photos will fan the flames of dissent, so remove them until you have restored a sense of calm and harmony to your life.

YOUR HOME AS A CATALYST FOR CHANGE

Your home can be much more than a mere shelter and a repository for your belongings. It can be a magical place where dreams are conceived and realised, where relationships grow and blossom, where problems are tackled and resolved, where each member of the family can be cherished and honoured. Ideally your dwelling is a place you want to come home to, where you invite guests, express yourself and feel nurtured by those you love. Home can be heaven on earth, a refuge for the soul.

Learning what your home is saying to you, and about you enables you to create the home of your dreams. Unravelling the mystery of the messages that surround you in your environment can dramatically promote your success in the material world, but more importantly it can support your spiritual growth. The objects in your home, the metaphors and symbols within it, can be used to transform your life. Feng shui offers a set of tools which can help your house to come home to itself, so that everyone who lives there feels energised, full of love and joy.

4

Clearing Home Issues

LAST YEAR I decided to visit one of my childhood homes. I was nervous. What if it had been torn down and replaced with a concrete block of flats? What if it was really a rundown little hovel, instead of the wonderful house I remembered? As we drove closer to it, I was surprised that I could still find my way there, through all the new suburbs and shopping malls that had grown around what used to be a sleepy little town.

We drove up a hill, rounded the corner, and there it was. It was an overcast day but, as we approached, a shaft of light illuminated the house of my childhood memories. It looked the same . . . a little smaller, a little older . . . but the same. I was flooded with memories. I remember spending a spellbound afternoon watching a spider create its web. I remember playing on the swing that hung from a tall oak tree in the back garden. I used to twist myself round and round and then let go and untwirl with delight. I was also engulfed with some of the dark and disturbing memories that occurred while I lived in that home. As I sorted through what had occurred there, pain was ignited, but wisdom blossomed.

'AT HOME' WHEREVER YOU ARE

When I began working in the feng shui field I became aware of the importance of helping my clients to resolve inner issues, as well as providing them with feng shui information. In my consultations, I realised

that beneath people's interest in using feng shui to increase their prosperity or career opportunities, often there were much more intimate desires. Again and again I found individuals wanting to create spaces where they felt truly 'at home'. In the deepest sense they yearned to feel at home, wherever they were.

Ultimately, I developed meditation methods for working with my clients that I call Synchro-Alignment™ techniques. These are special clearing processes designed to synchronise a client's inner aspirations with the outer structure of their home. The results have been quite remarkable. Here is an example of how the process works.

One afternoon I went to a client's home for a feng shui consultation. When I asked Christine what results she desired from our work together, she said that she and her husband had been having difficulty conceiving a child. They had gone in for testing and there didn't seem to be any medical reason for their infertility. She had heard that feng shui was sometimes helpful in cases like this, so she had decided to call me.

I explained that there were ancient feng shui techniques that could help create an environment conducive to pregnancy. I also suggested that there could be other issues that she might want to address, and asked her if she was willing to go on a short guided Synchro-Alignment™ meditation with me. She agreed, so I asked her to close her eyes and relax. I then requested that she say the word 'pregnant' a few times and tell me what she felt as she said it.

As she said the word 'pregnant' she began to cry. I asked her what she was feeling and she said, 'I feel scared.' I enquired if she noticed any memories that might be associated with these feelings. Suddenly she said, 'Oh! I'm seeing myself as a small child. My mother is talking to me. She's telling me that she had a really difficult birth with my brother . . . Oh no! She's saying that she hopes *I don't ever get pregnant.* She doesn't want me to have to go through what she went through, because it almost killed her!'

Gently I asked Christine to open her eyes. After taking a few minutes to compose herself, she said that she had completely forgotten that childhood memory. As we talked, she realised that she had internalised her mother's remarks. Christine had a subconscious fear about pregnancy and labour that potentially was blocking conception. She was excited to discover a possible cause of their infertility. We spent the rest of the time going over feng shui suggestions to increase the likelihood of pregnancy. A short time later the couple were delighted to report that they were expecting a child.

There are times when feng shui is not enough. You have to get to the source of your blockage in order to change your life. For example, George came to one of my public feng shui lectures because he was angry about feng shui. He publicly announced that it didn't work, explaining that he had previously hired a feng shui practitioner because he wanted to get his career off the ground. Yet every project he started after this consultation had failed. He felt he had been cheated. I asked, 'George, are those the first projects that have failed in your life?' He said, 'It always happens to me. I fail at everything I do.'

Through talking to George I realised that he had such a strong subconscious belief that he was a failure that it dictated the circumstances of his life, and no amount of feng shui alone was going to shift it. I suggested that he get to the source of his inner belief about himself, so he could release it, while at the same time using feng shui to enhance his career.

The power of the subconscious mind is remarkable. By reprogramming it to release negative inner messages, you can change your life. And when these inner changes are supported by doing feng shui at the same time amazing results can occur. In this chapter I will share with you some of the processes and techniques that have produced the greatest results for my clients.

How Your Childhood can Affect Your Present Home

It is a well-known fact that often present-day problems have their source in early experiences. Because so many of these experiences occur in the homes of our childhood, these homes often provide a kind of psychic context for the rest of our lives. It is here that our first definitions about homes are formed, and *we will implant these definitions in every single home that we live in.*

I was in Norway giving lectures on feng shui. During a break, a woman from the audience approached me with a question. She told me that shortly after moving into her current house, construction workers had started on the house next door. She found the noise from this project very aggravating, and wanted to know what feng shui she could do to get them to stop.

Although there are feng shui cures for neighbourhood irritations, I wanted to find out more about her situation, so I asked her if she had ever been in a similar situation before. She answered, 'Yes, neighbourhood construction started up after I moved into my last two houses as well. I hate construction!' I looked into her eyes and softly asked, 'What

was your father's career?' With a puzzled look, she replied, 'He was in construction, and so are both of my brothers.' I then asked her about her relationship with her father. She said that it wasn't very good.

I suggested to her that, on a subconscious level, she had been drawn to houses in neighbourhoods with construction plans as a result of unresolved issues with her father. I added, 'On some level, the construction noise in your life is a blessing, because it gives you a chance to bring these issues to the surface, where they can be healed.' I gave her the name of a therapist in Oslo, and suggested that she do some inner work on her relationship with her father. I also offered her some feng shui suggestions to help her feel more at peace in her neighbourhood.

Our childhood homes, and the experiences we have had in them, form a very important reference point for our present homes. This is because our memories are tied to specific locations. Time is very abstract, so most of us measure the passing of the years through memories of specific events that occurred in the places we have lived in childhood. They remind us of where we have come from, and help us to understand the forces that have shaped us. *They form a template that is repeated again and again in our adult homes.*

Your present house might appear to be completely different from your childhood home, but very often there will be compelling symbolic representations of the same features that were present in your early years. For example, Joshua was very lonely as a child. Although he had brothers and sisters, he always felt unconnected to his family. His bedroom was in a separate part of the house from his siblings', and this reinforced the separation he felt.

Joshua's present home looks completely different from the one he grew up in. However, some of the emotional issues left over from his childhood have been recreated in his adult home. During our work together, he told me that he still felt lonely and that he was isolated from his wife and children. In the evenings, when everyone else sat on the couch to watch television, Joshua sat apart in his reclining chair, several feet away. He also had a combination shop/study, which was located in a small building separate from the main house. Most of his time at home was spent in this shop, increasing his sense of isolation from his family. Walking around his home, I noticed a collection of family photos on the piano, but Joshua's picture was off to one side, by itself. Imprinted in his present home, again and again, were symbolic re-enactments of his childhood experiences.

We decided to use Joshua's home as an affirmation for the life changes he desired. We addressed his childhood issues and at the same

> ### *Clearing Childhood Home Issues*
>
> Close your eyes. Relax. Visualise your body shape shifting to become the body you occupied as a child. Now imagine exploring your childhood home (or homes). Notice your feelings, memories, attitudes. As you continue to explore your home, ask yourself how you feel about it, if you like it, if there are any places in it that you don't like, or any places that bring up bad memories for you.
>
> Now imagine that you are in your present home. As you journey through your house, notice if there are any places that have the same feeling as your childhood home. If you find a negative association, then you can choose to explore and change this area.

time made changes in his home based on feng shui principles. As a result of these processes, he decided to turn an unused bedroom into a study for himself, so that he could do his work closer to his family. The grouping of family photos was reorganised to include him at the centre. We rearranged the living-room furniture so that his chair was an integral part of the seating plan for the whole family. I also asked Joshua to devise a Vision Seed Map (see end of chapter) to help him visualise being more connected to the people he loved. He created this using pictures and photos that symbolised loving relationships and family unity.

Healing childhood home issues allows you to create a home that will support who you want to be now, not who you were conditioned to be at an earlier age. When you live in a home that reflects unresolved childhood issues, then those issues will be continually reinforced in your present-day life on a subconscious level. This unfortunately can set up a very powerful cycle, which will be broken only when you become aware of, and deal with, home issues from your past.

HOW YOU ARE AFFECTED BY YOUR ANCESTORS' HOMES

One of the areas of my feng shui work that I have found particularly fascinating is the exploration of ancestral homes. It may be an area that you might like to explore for yourself, because the homes that your ancestors lived in can have an enormous effect on you, *even if you are not consciously aware of what those homes were.*

Within each of us are genetic memories. Current research supports an idea that native people have long understood to be true, that within each of us is an ancestral memory that connects us to our heritage and lineage, even if we are not knowingly cognizant of it. It is valuable to research your roots and find out where your predecessors came from. This can offer valuable clues for you regarding your present home.

If you have never felt at home in your abode, it could be that there is a genetic memory tugging at your soul. If this is so, try introducing some aspects of the homes of your ancestors into your present dwelling and see if you feel a difference. For example, if your Irish ancestors lived in stone houses near the sea, and you have never felt at home in your weatherboard house in a woodland valley, consider placing an arrangement of stones in your home as a way of subliminally activating the energy of the stone homes of your ancestors.

Sometimes there will be one side of your ancestry that plays a stronger role in determining the environment that is the most nurturing for you. The type of landscape where I feel truly at home, and where my spirits fly, is high rolling hills, punctuated by rock, outcrops and occasional copses. Although I feel a strong alignment with my Native American roots, I feel most at ease when I'm in a landscape similar to that of my Scottish ancestors. During my visit to Scotland, the land formations made me feel so much at home. I fancied I could sink roots into the earth.

CLUTTER

When clients come to me wanting immediate results, I almost always tell them to clear their clutter. *Clutter-clearing is modern-day alchemy.* It is one of the fastest ways to completely transform your life. It can work in seemingly magical and mystical ways. Your health improves, your abundance levels increase and relationships improve by clearing clutter.

I'll give you an example from my life. Although most of my home is fairly well organised, one matter that has been in complete disarray for years has been my photographs. For twenty years I have been taking photographs and then tossing them into boxes. These boxes contained a jumble of scenes, people and time periods. Photos from the 1970s were mixed with ones from the 1990s. Packets of negatives had become separated from the corresponding photos. It was in such chaos that in recent years I hadn't taken many photos, probably because I subconsciously knew more would only worsen the mess.

Over time, the prospect of organising my photos came to seem like

Everest to a novice climber. When I finally tackled the task, it took a week of sorting and labelling . . . and during that week the most remarkable thing occurred. People that I hadn't heard from for twenty years began to call. Old unresolved rifts almost magically began to heal. It was miraculous. As I focused on the photographs and put them in order, it was as if a balancing and ordering of all my past relationships occurred simultaneously. It seemed that focusing attention on the people in the photos sent a shining beam of light to them, and they responded by contacting me without knowing why. This is the power of clearing clutter.

Because objects are invested with symbolism, clearing things out of your home has a direct effect on your psyche. You are shifting the energy of your environment, which will in turn have an effect on your life. In other words, sooner or later you will experience the consequences of clearing the debris out of your life.

What is clutter?

Clutter is an accumulation of things that impede the flow of energy in your home. Clutter is sometimes tied to identity. It can make a statement about who you are, and can represent aspects of your life.

Examples of Clutter
- Any object that you don't love or use
- Half-finished and never-started projects ✓
- Anything that has been broken for a long time or has parts missing ✓
- Unwanted gifts that you keep 'in case the person visits' ✓
- Things which 'might come in useful some day' but which you know in your heart never will ✓
- Personal letters and old Christmas cards from people you can no longer remember
- Empty pots from plants that died or were transplanted
- Collections of recipes for dishes you will never get around to cooking
- Stacks of expired coupons
- Partially used old make-up ✓
- Piles of magazines and newspapers you will never get around to reading
- Bottles of expired pills and potions
- Clothes that don't fit or you don't like
- Odd socks and worn-out shoes

A useful phrase when deciding whether or not something is clutter is: 'Use it, love it or get rid of it!'

'As-soon-as-I-get-rid-of-it-I-need-it' syndrome

After an episode of clutter clearing, it is common to find that you need something that was given away, *even if you didn't need it in the previous twenty years*. There is a reason for this: the subconscious fear that makes you hold on to the object in the first place is so strong that it wants to gain validity in your eyes. It is like a sub-personality inside you that desperately wants to be right. Sometimes I can almost hear the voice of this sub-personality saying, 'See, I told you not to throw that away, didn't I? Now you're in a real pickle. I told you so!' However, being aware that this is a common response will make it less likely to happen.

Why people keep clutter

There are many reasons why people keep clutter. One of the most common ones is fear of the future. Although you might not need a particular piece of clutter (and haven't needed it for years), you might be afraid to get rid of it because a need for it might arise in the future. By thinking this way, you create your own need and stop trusting that the universe will provide for you. This belief becomes self-perpetuating, because fear of the future tends to create a fearful future.

If you believe that all your needs will be met in the future, they usually will be. What you expect in life often becomes reality. A person who expects to have a bad day is usually not disappointed, while someone anticipating a good day is usually rewarded. If you are holding on to junk because you are fearful about the future, get rid of it! Trust that you will be exactly where you need to be in the future. No matter what your reason for keeping clutter, it clogs the energy in your home, your body and your life.

Common Reasons People Collect Clutter

- It represents security – it's a cushion against life
- Out of habit
- It's an inherited pattern of behaviour
- Out of fear about the future
- It's 'evidence junk' (e.g., the blue ribbon that is evidence that you were a fast runner at school)
- It represents unfulfilled dreams
- For sentimental reasons
- It represents self-esteem
- Feeling a responsibility to take care of their things
- 'It's been in the family a long time'
- Fear that they will not be liked or respected without it

- 'It might be worth something some day'
- 'They don't make these any more'
- They were brought up during hard times
- 'They don't make these the way they used to'
- 'It's perfectly good'
- 'Nobody else will take care of it'
- It would hurt someone's feelings if they got rid of it
- For spare parts
- They might need it some time

What is clutter to one person may not be to another. If you love it or use it, it is *not* clutter. Also, something that is clutter in one part of your home might not be clutter in another part.

'I-am-my-house' syndrome

When we don't want someone to visit because our house is messy, or when someone drops by unexpectedly and we apologise for the mess, we are identifying with our home. Sometimes this form of identification can be extreme.

I arrived at a new client's home for a feng shui consultation. I saw her in the window as I approached and we waved to each other. I waited at the front door, expecting that she would soon open it. A minute went by. I thought that maybe she was waiting for me to ring the bell, so I pushed the buzzer. I continued to wait. There was still no response. Finally, I knocked loudly and she opened the door.

Later in the consultation, I alluded to her delayed reaction in opening the door. She explained that she hadn't come right away because she had been straightening her house. I looked at her. Her hair was dishevelled, her tights had runs in them and the seam of her dress was coming undone . . . but her house was neat. I realised that she more strongly identified herself with her house than with her physical body. Her home was her main identity in the world.

There is nothing wrong with being proud of your home. This is natural. However, from a spiritual prospective, *you are not your home and your possessions*. You have these things. They influence you, but they are not who you are. When you are clearing out clutter, notice how much of your identity is attached to the objects in your home.

Why clutter is a problem

Clutter affects the flow of life-force energy throughout your home and it can bring the entire home energy down. It's easy to feel bogged down and tired in an environment that is bogged down with stuff. In addition, clutter is often connected to emotional issues from your past. Your energy goes down every time you walk by that piece of clutter that subconsciously reminds you of a failed marriage, a lost dream or a wrong life choice. There are strands of energy connecting you to every object that you own. If there are negative associations connected to your clutter, these energy strands drain your life-force energy and cause it to congeal and clog.

The Effects of Clutter

- Makes you feel disorganised and/or like a failure
- Limits you (think of all the things you could do if you weren't taking care of all your possessions)
- Creates chaos in life
- Can be depressing
- Makes you feel physically and emotionally heavy; it might even manifest as excess body weight
- More 'stuff' often means more to trip over, more to lose and more to feel guilty about neglecting
- The more stuff you have the more you are in service to it. Do you own things or do they own you?
- Can make you feel as though it is difficult to breathe and can make you feel exhausted
- Keeps you emotionally bound up with the past and the future, so you can't stay in the present
- Makes every task take longer
- In the basement, can affect you on a subconscious level
- In the attic, can limit possibilities
- In hallways, can restrict arteries both physically and emotionally; it can clog the body and lymphatic system
- On the floor, can pull your energy down
- Above you, can represent problems hanging over you
- Under the bed, can affect sleep

Clutter is Expensive

This is important to remember. It can seem economical to keep things that you *might* possibly need at some future date. However, the following considerations show what clutter is costing you in terms of time, energy and money right now:

- You waste time and energy when you frantically look for lost items or try to clean around piles of things.
- You waste money when things are bought and never used, or when duplicate items are bought because the originals are buried under clutter.
- It costs money, time and energy to maintain and store clutter.

Clearing your clutter

Clearing your clutter can be a spiritual experience. Often our identify is so tied to our things that when we let go of them, it can feel like a spiritual death of the ego. Throwing away clutter might feel like throwing away a part of yourself. We tend to hold on to things tenaciously. The older we get, the more possessions we accumulate. These things give us a sense of permanence, yet life is impermanent. Accepting this connects us to the great cycle of life. The cycle of birth, death and rebirth is a cycle of impermanence, as is the cycle of the seasons. Out of fear, Western culture resists the transitory nature of life, and thus we lose part of our connection to the sacredness of life. You came into this world without possessions and you will leave it the same way. You have possessions, but they are not who you are.

De-Clutter Session

Start small. Choose one drawer, one cupboard or one small room. Decide how much time you are going to spend de-cluttering. Set a timer for half of the allotted time. Begin sorting things into categories (see below). When the timer goes off, reset it for the remaining time so you can finish what you've started.

Obtain three boxes and label them:
1 Keep/Relocate/File
2 Discard/Donate/Give away
3 Unsure

Ask yourself about each item:
- Does this make my energy go up, down or stay neutral?
- Why am I keeping this?
- Do I really need this?
- Does this really fit who I am?
- Will the freedom I gain by getting rid of this outweigh any possible regrets I may have about parting with it?

If you decide to keep something, put it in the Keep/Relocate/File pile. If you are ready to release it, put it the Discard/ Donate/ Give away pile. And if just aren't sure, put it in the Unsure box. As soon as the timer goes off, put everything away and clean up. Then schedule a time for a friend to go through with you the things in the Unsure box. Ask your supporter to help you stay focused on the task, rather than on your stories and feelings about the items. It's human to reminisce about things, but remember to stay focused on your intention of de-cluttering your life.

When you practise trust and let go of things that no longer suit you, you open a space for what is exactly right for you now. If, out of fear, you hold on to what you have, then you are not open to receive wonderful gifts that are coming your way. Confronting the clutter in your home frees up energy for living in the present. When you unclutter you house, you unclutter your life and your soul. This doesn't mean you need to get rid of everything from your past, or that you shouldn't be prepared for the future. It does mean that there should be plenty of space and energy available for the here and now.

Clearing your clutter is one of the quickest ways to change your life, but proceed carefully. *Clearing too much clutter too fast can cause a healing crisis.* We are so attached to our stuff that sometimes when clutter leaves our home it can feel like losing part of ourselves. Doing too much too quickly can be like an emotional purge. It would be like someone who has eaten a junk-food diet all their life suddenly switching to a diet of only raw foods. This person might feel sick and very out of sorts, because the new diet stirred things up too quickly. However, if you go slowly and carefully, your entire life can change softly, easily and magically. Below is a Synchro-Alignment™ meditation exercise that I have done with my clients with excellent results.

Vision seeding

As you clear away some of the internal and external debris and blockages in your home, it becomes easier to bring about your dreams, sometimes in an almost mystical fashion. If you aim an arrow at a target but there are scrubs and tall weeds in the way, it is difficult to hit your mark. But once the area is cleared, your ability to hit the target is greatly enhanced. Resolving blockages allows you to direct your intention clearly and thus realise your dreams more easily.

De-Clutter Meditation

Close your eyes. Relax. Visualise walking through your home, room by room. Imagine that you are highly sensitive to energy fields. You can sense the energy around each object in your home. As you approach each thing, notice whether it raises your energy, lowers your energy or is neutral. When you come out of the meditation, make a note of the objects that lower your energy and decide if you want to keep them or not.

A powerful way to make your desires for your home manifest is by creating what I call a 'Vision Seed Map'. Doing this gives a visible form to your intention, which can act as a point of distillation and focus to bring your dreams into reality. It's a lot of fun, too. You are mapping out your future. Every client who has done this process with me has had wonderful results after creating the map.

Creating a Vision Seed Map

Materials:
- One large poster board
- Scissors
- Glue
- Stack of old magazines that have photographs in them – home and garden-type magazines are particularly helpful
- Photograph of you and your family or household members

Process:
Go through the magazines and cut out any image or any word that makes you feel good or that gives you the *feeling* that you would like to achieve in your current, or in a future, home. Don't be concerned by any thoughts that it's unlikely you will actually have that particular thing . . . you are creating a feeling. Include pictures of the people who are important to you, who will be sharing your vision with you.

When you have collected your images, stick them to the poster board with glue in a design that feels right, thus creating a collage of your hopes and dreams.

Then place or hang your Vision Seed Map somewhere where you will see it frequently, so that it can begin to programme your subconscious mind to help you achieve your dreams.

5

Using Your Intuition to Heal Your Home

IT WAS A COOL autumn night. A chill crept through the small pine-covered island nestled in an archipelago off the coast of British Columbia. I was on one of the most beautiful islands in the world. It was like a green jewel encircled by Orca whales, sea otters and huge purple starfish with colours so bright that they had seemed to sing as they clung to the rocks in the setting sun. The hour was late and I looked forward to snuggling into the warmth of my bed in my small cabin.

Suddenly a voice rose up within me, saying, 'Go to the dock.' My rational mind whimpered, 'But it's cold. It's late.' I heard again: 'Go to the dock.' Reluctantly, I surrendered to my intuition and walked through the woods. When I arrived at the dock, I looked across a luminous phosphorescent sea and saw a remarkable display in the night sky. Overhead was a startlingly beautiful cascade of soft wavering light. It was the aurora borealis, waxing and waning like an ethereal curtain across the dark expanse of the universe. It was mystical and wondrous. And I would have missed it if I hadn't listened to my intuition.

How do I explain the inner voice that spoke to me? How can I explain the northern lights appearing at just that moment? I believe there is at work in the world a natural force that is deeper than logic or physics. It dwells inside us as the great mystery spoken of by our ancestors; it speaks to us of wisdom and natural knowing. It carries the voices of our forebears and the nudgings of our higher self. In its purest form it is a message from the Creator – it is our intuition.

Your intuition helps keep you in balance throughout your day. It pushes you to be at the right place at the right time. It can also help you arrange a home that suits your soul. However, in order to activate your intuition for home design, you will need to surrender your judgment about the placement of things in your home. You will have to give up ideas about what is right or wrong.

When we let go of our beliefs about how things should be, about what is right and what is wrong, then we enter into what a Japanese monk friend of mine called 'dono-mind'. He meant to say 'don't-know-mind', but with his Japanese accent it always came out 'dono-mind'. In Zen Buddhism this is called 'beginner's mind', which is a state of natural intuitive knowing that dwells beyond prescribed rules and belief systems.

'Dono-mind' is a divine state where you realise you don't know everything and where you are receptive to receiving inner guidance and wisdom. When we have 'dono-mind', we are open to messages from our higher self, the universe and the Creator. We aren't preoccupied with rearranging reality to fit into our preconceived belief systems. We aren't trying to figure everything out. We are in a state of natural knowing.

Feng shui has precise rules. These rules have been around for a long, long time because they usually work. Yet even within this ancient, highly valuable system, there will be times when your intuition regarding your home will ignite more results than a 2,000-year-old tradition.

Caroline had taken a number of feng shui and interior-design courses, and had rearranged her home and business space accordingly. She called me because she also wanted the opinion of a professional consultant. She said, 'I'm frustrated, Denise. I've done everything right. I've followed all the feng shui rules. My home looks different, but somehow my life isn't any different. Nothing has changed. What am I doing wrong?'

I told her that sometimes the answers to our deepest questions are held inside the subconscious mind. I asked her if she would like to embark on a short guided visualisation. She consented, so I asked her to close her eyes, become very relaxed and imagine that she was walking around her home looking at all the feng shui changes that she had made. I asked her how she felt looking at them, and she said: 'I'm

angry.' I asked her to go into the anger and tell me what she saw. Suddenly she explained, 'I'm seeing my father. He's telling me what to do.' I asked, 'How does that make you feel?' 'Angry!' she retorted. 'I'm *not* going to follow his rules.'

I gently brought her out of the guided meditation and we talked about what she had experienced. She realised she was subconsciously angry with her authoritative father, who used to give her specific rules to follow. *And she had equated his rules with* all *rules.* In other words she had followed the rules of feng shui and interior design, but since she was still subconsciously rebelling against her father, her rebellion dictated that she wouldn't get any results from the rules that she implemented.

I said, 'Let's get rid of all the rules for a moment, and reach inside you to find out what your soul wants.' I once again asked her to close her eyes and become very relaxed. I said, 'Imagine that your soul is going to design your home to give you exactly what you need. There is nothing that is right or wrong . . . Just imagine whatever your soul desires.' After a short while Caroline began to get very clear about how she wanted to arrange her home and business in order to nourish her soul. When we had completed the exercise she was radiant. I received a joyous phone call a week later. After she had rearranged her house in accordance with the intuitive information received during the meditation, wonderful opportunities began to flood into her life.

I have found that the greatest feng shui results occur for my clients when I actively involve them in the feng shui process. To do this I help them activate their intuition to get in touch with their deepest desires. This helps feng shui take hold in their lives. One of the main ways I do this is by taking clients on guided meditations (Synchro-Alignment™ processes), because these techniques help 'synchronise' a person's soul with their outer environment. Anyone can use these kinds of techniques to activate their intuition and balance the energies in their home.

In this chapter there are suggestions for using your intuition for home design. There are visualisation techniques and dowsing techniques you can do yourself to tap into your natural knowing. The stronger your intuition, the more powerful the results you will obtain. There are three things that are essential for activating your intuition:

1 Trust in yourself and your intuitive sense.
2 Be willing to be wrong.
3 Practise your intuitive skills.

1 Trusting your intuitive sense

Although we live in a technological age that prizes logic and disparages intuition, still there is a part of you that is intimately connected with the world of invisible energy around you. Even if you have consciously forgotten this connection, you can still tap into it. Many people have sensed that something is about to happen seconds before an accident. Or perhaps they receive a clear image of who is calling just as they reach to pick up the phone receiver. Other people have these same sensations when they see a meteor shooting across the sky – a sense of wholeness, a precognitive awareness of what's really important in life. The feelings and sensations that arise within us at these times come out of the place where our inner voice speaks to us. This voice is constantly giving us guidance and information. To hear it you must first place your trust in it. Even when it doesn't seem to make sense to your conscious mind, pay attention to this voice. Listen to what it is telling you. Trust it.

2 Be willing to be wrong

One of the greatest barriers to trusting your intuitive voice is your fear of being wrong. To develop your instinctive knowing, let go of your need to be right. When I teach dowsing, I've noticed that the students who get the best results are the ones who don't give a hoot whether they are wrong or not. The person who is frightened of failing will sub-consciously restrict the free flow of the intuitive mind. Be willing to fail. Embrace your failures! Every time you fail, you learn something. When you are wrong you connect with 'dono-mind', beginner's mind, the place where you are ready to learn, to listen, to receive.

3 Practise your intuitive skills

Developing your intuition is no different from learning any new skill. You need to practise in order to get better. There are lots of easy ways to practise using your intuition. For example, when you are waiting at traffic lights, guess how many red cars will pass the other way before the light turns green. You won't always get it right, but, when you do, *notice the feeling that you have* and notice any accompanying symbols or physical sensations. Emotions, physical sensations and symbols are inner indicators that highly intuitive people use in order to find answers to their questions. Sam, who is highly intuitive, always gets a particular sensation in the centre of his chest when his intuition is focused and clear. As you practise, you can begin to recognise

your own inner signals. This will help you decipher what is true intuition.

In one exercise I ask my students to hold an object, such as a pebble, and to imagine forming an energy connection with it. I then hide the pebble and tell them to imagine they are tracing their energy cord to it to locate it. With practice, usually their ability to 'find' hidden objects increases. You could do this exercise by asking a friend to hide an object for you.

Here is another intuition exercise. On page 177 there is a drawing. Without actually turning to this page, close your eyes and *imagine* that you are turning to this page to see what is on it. Now, turn to page 177. If you got it 'right', notice how your body felt. Being aware of how your body feels when you are accurate is a good indicator for future intuitive hunches. Doing this exercise can help increase your intuition. You may want to try it with other books.

Using Intuition to Decipher the Energy in Your Home

Your intuition can be a powerful ally in helping you to create an ideal home for your soul. You already know what you need in order to feel nourished by your home. Using your intuition allows you to uncover this knowledge. Sculptors use their intuition to create great works of art. They have an image of the beauty that lies hidden within a block of inert stone. Using their intuition they slowly remove whatever is covering this up. Similarly, your intuition will help you discover the beauty and the energy which lies dormant within your home.

How to discover draining energy

Every object in your home will either increase or decrease your energy level, or it will have a neutral effect – neither expanding nor diminishing your energy. Some objects uplift your energy because of the positive associations that you have with them. Seashells that you brought back from your holiday might restore your energy every time you look at them because they subconsciously activate happy memories of splashing in the sea under a brilliant sun. Other things will expand your energy because they please your senses. An elegantly proportioned, cobalt-blue vase sitting on a windowsill where light streams through it might make your spirit soar every time you pass

Discovering the Energy Drains in Your Home

Relax. Close your eyes and imagine that you are slowly walking through your home, room by room. In each room stop and tune into the energy there. Hold or touch each object in the room. Notice if your energy goes up or down, or stays the same. Take special note if you find your energy plummeting when you touch an object. Pay attention to any place where you feel your energy diminish. Use your intuition to see if you can discover the reason for the energy drain. Let your mind travel freely. Be open to: memories, associations, fears, smells, even things which might at first seem unrelated. Once you have come out of the meditation, take time to write down immediately everything that you have discovered. Make whatever changes in your home that feel appropriate.

it. Some objects have wonderful energy because of the meaning that we assign to them. The thimble that your mother used when she made your wedding dress might subconsciously symbolise her love for you.

It is usually obvious how you feel about many things in your home. You either like them and feel energised by their presence, or you dislike them and sense a negative energy from them. However, there may be objects which can be affecting you on a *subconscious* level. They may be draining your energy without you knowing it. These objects might be affecting the way you feel about your home or space at work, and it is very important to identify them.

Whenever you discover that something in a room is lowering the energy level there, as soon as you remove it or change its location in the room, almost everyone will immediately be able to notice a difference. The room just feels better. Your intuition can guide you in locating problem areas in your space. It can also help you find solutions to these problems. Above is an exercise to help you determine the energy of objects and areas in your home.

Finding the right place for your objects

Everything in life has an optimal place – the place where it seems to fit best, where it belongs, where its energy can shine. Sometimes an object that seems to be an energy drain is not: it is simply located in the wrong place. When it is moved to another area, it actually functions as an energy enhancer. The following is an exercise to help you find the ideal place for every object.

> ### *Finding the Right Place for the Objects in Your Home*
>
> If the object is small enough to hold in your hand, carry it from room to room. When it is in the wrong place, it will feel heavy, and you will feel tired. When it is in the right place, it will feel much lighter and you will feel lighter. In the case of objects too large to carry, close your eyes and *imagine* them in each room in your home. Notice the rooms or areas where things seems to glow, and be aware of areas where the life force of an object seems to diminish. If there is no place in your home where an object seems perfect, where its life force shines brightly, then perhaps it would be better not to have this item in your home at this time.

MEETING THE SPIRIT OF YOUR HOME

When we develop a personal relationship with the objects in our life, they work better. When you connect to the personality of your home and name it, you create a stronger energy field around it. Anything that you name and relate to in a personal manner will emanate more life-force energy than an unnamed object. This was common knowledge in ancient cultures where weapons, cooking utensils and tools were named. In ancient metaphysical traditions, to know the name of something was to form an intimate connection with it. Finding the name of your home and meeting its spirit guardian can give you valuable information and increase the harmony there.

When Germaine did a meditation journey to meet her Spirit of the Home (see exercise below), a kind old man with a twinkle in his eyes greeted her at her front door. In the course of her 'conversation' with this Spirit of the Home, he told her about a pipe by her washing machine that was potentially a problem. She normally never thought about her plumbing, but since she was going on holiday, she called a friend who was a plumber to look at her pipes. The plumber explained,

> ### *Meeting the Spirit of Your Home*
>
> Close your eyes and imagine yourself at your front door. The door is closed, but you can feel the approach of the Spirit of Your Home. Visualise the door opening and imagine that you are meeting this Spirit. (For some people this might look like a person or animal, for others it may be a light, a voice, or a felt presence.) Spend time getting to know your Home Spirit. Ask its name and if there is any information that would be valuable for you to know.

'It's good you had this checked. This hose behind your washing machine is old and nearly worn out. Because your washing machine is on the second floor, you could have had a major flood, causing damage to this floor and the ceiling of the room below.'

Your home and the changing seasons

Living in our modern well-insulated homes, it is easy to forget the impact of the seasons on our lives. Nevertheless, we are greatly affected by these changes in light and weather because the seasons form the grid-work of a powerful cadence of energy that ebbs and flows throughout our planet. Your home is always in direct contact with nature's cycles. Spring rains run down its roof. The warmth of summer days causes its walls to expand. The winds of autumn rattle the windows, and the cold of winter causes the timbers to shift. These outer changes are obvious, but there are deeper seasonal influences affecting your home as well. You can become aware of these more subtle effects by embarking on a meditative journey to become your home throughout the seasons.

When Wendy visualised herself as her home going through the seasons, she had a remarkable realisation. She noticed that she felt constricted and wanted to open the windows and doors to let in fresh air. Many of the windows in her home were jammed, and she ordinarily opened the others only on rare occasions. As a result of her meditation, Wendy decided to air her home regularly and to prise open the windows which were stuck. After doing this she immediately felt better, but something else unexpected happened at the same time. Wendy did her sales work from home, and from the moment she began opening her windows, her business began to flourish. Amazing opportunities came into her life. (Sometimes doors and windows can be metaphors for allowing more energy into your life.)

Experiencing the Seasons

Still your thoughts. Close your eyes. Imagine that your body is 'shapeshifting' and becoming bigger until you become your home. Notice how you feel. Take a moment to be aware of the connection between you (as your home) and the outdoor elements. Feel the air and water and the sun and earth around you. Imagine yourself going through a day and a night. Notice how you feel. Now speed up time and experience an entire cycle of seasons. Imagining yourself as your home over many seasons can connect you to the elements of weather, and help you to see how you and your home change over time.

Your present home in the future

The energies in your home help shape your destiny. Your home may be supporting you on your path at present, but what is helpful to you now could actually limit your growth later on. Conversely, you may have a home that is currently restricting your energy but in the future will be a template for greater strength for you. Here is an exercise to give you information about you in your home in the future.

Envisaging Your Home in the Future

Relax and close your eyes. Imagine that you are sitting in a comfortable place in your home with your eyes open. Take a moment to notice how you feel about your home right now. Now imagine that a whirring sound completely surrounds you. When the whirring noise stops, imagine finding that one year has gone by. How do you feel in your home now? The whirring sound takes you forward another year. Notice how you feel at this new point in time. Continue to go forward in time. At each stop, imagine walking around your home, or outside in your neighbourhood. What do you find inside and outside your home over the years? Do you like what you see? Do you want to stay in this home over time? Are there things you don't like now that are going to be helpful to you in the future? For example, if you have teenaged children at home now, things may feel a bit cramped, but in five years they will have moved out and your home will be the perfect size for you then. Or you may love living in the city now, but as you walk around your neighbourhood ten years in the future you realise you are going to need a more rural setting to nourish your soul then.

CHOOSING A HOME

Because our dwellings have such a profound effect on every aspect of our lives, choosing where we will live is one of the most important decisions we ever make. Your intuition can provide invaluable assistance in helping you find a home that will shelter your soul. A method you can use to find your new home is one I call 'dream-hunting'. In native cultures, the best hunters found their prey by dreaming. As strange as this may sound, dream-hunting has worked for thousands of years. Through dreaming the hunter was able to tap into his intuition to pick the best locations for the hunt the next day. In his dreams he was also able to prepare himself mentally, physically and spiritually for the ritual of the hunt. Medicine men and medicine women also used these techniques to decide where and when to move. You can apply dream-hunting techniques to help you find your new home.

Dream-Hunting for Your New Home

Before going to bed, programme yourself to find the location of your new home by affirming again and again that your dreams will show you the way to your new location. When you first awaken in the morning, write down any memories or fragments of images from your dreams. Look for clues. The language of dreams is usually symbolic, rather than literal. For example, a dream of roses gleaming with early-morning dew may remind you of your trip to your aunt's home last summer. This in turn may bring to consciousness your soul's longing for a home with a nice garden. You may have actually turned down a home that could have been perfect for you, because you had not realised that the garden surrounding the home is perhaps more important to you than the actual qualities of the home itself. Observing the clues provided by your dreams in this way will be like a treasure map helping you to find and recognise your ideal home when it shows up in your life.

Once when I was teaching a weekend seminar in Germany, two women on the course told me that they were looking for a new place to locate their healing centre. They felt discouraged because they had been looking for three years without success. We discussed the possibility of using their dreams to find what they were looking for. I suggested that before going to sleep that night they focus on their desire to find the perfect location for their centre.

The next morning, when I asked about their progress during the night, they excitedly told me they had both seen in their dreams a perfect place in a residential area of Hamburg. One woman had seen it more clearly than the other, but both were sure that this was the place for them. I received a letter a few weeks later explaining that when they had gone to this area of Hamburg they had indeed found the ideal place for their centre. At the time of writing, they were in the process of purchasing it. A number of people have found their new home using this method.

WITHDRAWING YOUR ENERGY WHEN YOU MOVE

Anne scheduled a feng shui appointment with me because her home was up for sale and wasn't attracting any prospective buyers. She had heard that feng shui could help sell a house and had decided to give it a try. While we talked, I noticed that she didn't seem particularly upset that no

offers had been made for her house. She actually related this information quite happily, so I asked her if she really felt ready to leave her home. She answered, 'Oh, yes! Absolutely! I need a much smaller place.' But when we did a meditation where I asked her to imagine moving away from her home, she began to cry. She said, 'I'm so sad. This is the home where my children grew up, and I hate to leave it behind.'

After the meditation Anne said she hadn't realised that a hidden part of her was reluctant to move. We talked about the ambivalent nature of feelings. I said that she would take her memories of this place with her, wherever she went. She told me that she was looking forward to the freedom of living in a smaller place but that until she had acknowledged her sadness about leaving this house she hadn't been ready to let go.

Very often people have trouble selling their homes because they subconsciously remain attached to them. When this is the case, there will sometimes be an energy barrier preventing prospective buyers from imagining themselves living in the house. This happens *because the energy of the home-owner is so evident throughout the home.* There seems to be no room for a new owner. Even if on the face of things the house has everything they want, prospective buyers will decide against going ahead, because it doesn't feel right. If you are going to sell your house, it is essential to withdraw your energy from it.

After Anne and I talked about her dreams of a new beginning in her new home, I suggested that we do another meditation exercise to withdraw her energy from her current home. I also suggested she say goodbye to each of the rooms, one at a time. The psyche responds to symbolic acts and this is an excellent way to withdraw your energy from a space.

Anne called the next week to report that after she had withdrawn

---

Withdrawing Your Energy from Your Old Home

Relax. Imagine that you are walking into each room in your home and that you carry a large basket with you. In each room allow memories that took place there to emerge for you. Any memories that you desire to carry with you can be symbolically placed with love into your basket. Memories which you wish to leave behind can be blessed and released to the winds of time. As you leave each room, imagine yourself physically drawing your energy away from the house and back into your solar plexus. As you do this, know that you will be carrying a basketful of wonderful memories from your old home to your new one.

her energy, she had sensed immediately a difference in both herself and her home. I was not surprised when she added that she had also received an offer. Her voice was full of excitement about the new chapter which was now opening in her life.

Moving into Your New Home

Rooting your energy in your new home is just as important as withdrawing your energy from your old one. Doing this takes time. Probably everyone is familiar with the sense of dislocation which is a part of moving house. When you wake up in the night you may wonder for a moment where you are. When you go to sit down after work, the environment may seem less comforting than your old home. But this strangeness is also full of possibilities. The fact that you are starting afresh somewhere different means that you are also free to create new patterns there. You have the opportunity to decide exactly what you want your home to be like, and then to make that happen. Here are some energy exercises to help you plant your spiritual roots in your new location, and to make your new home a haven for your soul.

Planting Your Roots in Your New Home

See yourself in your new home. Visualise your soul communicating with the land your home rests on. Even if you live in a flat, its foundations go down into the earth. Introduce yourself to the land. Tell it your name and that you are grateful for the firm base of support it is providing for your home. Listen to the land. Let it speak to you, heart and soul, of its history, its wisdom, its ancient and sacred bounty. Know that the plot of land underlying your home is like no other, and that it is connected to the entire earth. It supports and sustains you.

To call Spirit into your home you can perform a Blessing Ceremony. (See my book *Sacred Space.*) Blessing ceremonies come from an ancient tradition which acknowledged the importance of establishing a spiritual relationship with your home. There is no better way to begin your life in your new home than by dedicating it to Spirit. A blessing will invite a harmonious energy into your life there from the very beginning. It can be performed in a public way by including family members and/or friends, or it can be a private affair just between you and the spirit of your home.

Calling Spirit into Your New Home

Light a candle in your new home and focus on your desire to have a loving spiritual energy in your home. Imagine a radiant light entering your front door and flowing through every room. Then take a bell and ring it in every room to invite beneficial energy into your home.

If you are doing a Blessing Ceremony involving other people, you might want to let all the participants write their hopes for the home on pieces of specially prepared paper. Have a period of quiet when all hold their intention in their heart and clearly visualise the home filled with harmony and joy. If your home includes a fireplace, place the wishes in a fire, saying the blessings out loud. Alternatively, the blessings could be gathered together and kept in a small, covered basket. Either way, know that the loving energy of the ceremony will continue to radiate in the house as long as you live there.

DOWSING

Dowsing is one of the best ways that you can activate your intuition regarding your home. I learned about this remarkable tool years ago, from my favourite uncle. One hot Oklahoma summer afternoon, I stood in a field with Uncle Wade, who was from the Cherokee side of the family. The sky was a vivid shade of blue that I see only in Oklahoma. He handed me a split branch and said, 'Here, Denise. This is a dowsing rod. See if you can find the underground water in this field.' Although some people assign mystical significance to the practice of dowsing, my relatives believe in it for practical reasons.

I was nervous. I really wanted the approval of my uncle. In trepidation, I held the Y-shaped branch, waiting for something – anything – to happen. Suddenly it seemed to twitch and I exclaimed, 'It's moving!' He calmly replied, 'Just let it lead you. Don't think about it, just let go.' I scrambled across the field, following the 'lead' of the branch. My uncle watched, first with a look of uncertainty and confusion, then with a smile of approval. He said, 'Denise, you didn't find the underground water.' I was crestfallen. 'But you followed perfectly the underground electrical wires.' And he proceeded to show me where the wires came into the land. It was then that I learned I had a talent for dowsing for electrical fields.

Dowsing for residual energy

Often when we move into a new home we inherit the residual energies left by previous owners. Dowsing is an excellent way to activate your intuition, and it can be a remarkable tool for diagnosing any residual energy in your home. I was once called into the home of a family who had been experiencing emotional difficulties dating from the time they moved into the home. Using a pendulum as my dowsing tool, I slowly walked through the house. When I came to the boys' bedroom, the pendulum began to swing back and forth erratically.

Through investigation I learned that this room had been the bedroom of the couple who had previously owned the house. They had sold it following an acrimonious divorce, and their bedroom had been the location of their worst fighting. I cleared the entire house, focusing my energy especially on the boys' bedroom. (See *Sacred Space*.) The family later told me that they had all immediately felt much better, and that, despite occasional differences, harmony was once again the prevailing theme of their home life.

Dowsing to determine the best place for your bed

From a feng shui perspective, your bedroom, and particularly your bed, is the most important place in the home because it is where you spend the most time. Your bed is also the place where your body rejuvenates, so it is essential to create a healthy flow of energy here. through auspicious placement of the room's furnishings.

I was called to the home of a young woman who was having difficulty sleeping. She had tossed and turned restlessly every night since moving into her new home. Sleeplessness is often related to external annoyances, such as the noise of heavy traffic or a barking dog, or internal worries about work and relationships, etc. But in this case, the woman's insomnia did not appear to be caused by any of these factors. I used my pendulum to determine if her bed was situated in the best spot in the room for it. I received a very clear 'no' answer. Upon further investigation, I discovered that her night-time unrest was being caused by subtle electrical energy emanating from water flowing underground in the earth directly beneath her bed. (Underground water can generate a natural field of energy which may be disturbing to some people.)

I then used a dowsing rod to determine where the energy from the water was flowing through the bedroom. We moved her bed a few feet to one side in order to avoid this stream of flowing energy. She phoned the next morning to tell me that she had had a great night's sleep. She has continued to sleep well ever since.

Why dowsing Works

The art of dowsing has been used for thousands of years. Prehistoric rock paintings in Algeria depict early dowsers, and research has uncovered evidence suggesting that the ancient Chinese and Egyptians used dowsing. The first written descriptions of dowsing appeared in the Middle Ages. One striking example can be found in a book called *De Re Metallica*. This book, first published in 1556, contains a number of wood-block illustrations showing various stages of dowsing with a forked branch.

Although there are many schools of thought regarding why dowsing is successful, practitioners of this ancient art all agree on one point: it works. One explanation for why dowsing for water has been so successful over the centuries is that the dowser is able to detect subtle electromagnetic fields emanating from underground water. There may be a scientific foundation for this theory, because flowing water does create a natural electrical field. (See Chapter 10 for more information about this.) However, this explanation fails to explain why map dowsing works. (Map dowsing is a method to find water, oil, ley lines, minerals, etc, by using a dowsing rod or suspended pendulum over a map.)

Many dowsers believe that dowsing works because they subconsciously tune into the stream of wisdom accessible at the level of the collective unconscious of all people. The dowser receives information from this source, causing muscles to twitch, which in turn causes the rod to turn or the pendulum to swing. In other words, the body of the dowser becomes a receiving station for energy flows. The dowsing tool acts as an amplifier for the information received. It is important to note that all dowsing is affected by the subconscious beliefs of the dowser.

PENDULUM DOWSING

You can learn to dowse. Anyone can, because dowsing taps resources available to all. There are many kinds of dowsing, but I suggest starting with a pendulum, because it is one of the easier methods to master. It is especially useful for detecting home energy fields. Here are the steps to follow to begin dowsing:

Create or obtain a pendulum

Any weight attached to the end of a cord or chain can be used for pendulum dowsing. If you are purchasing a pendulum, find one that both looks and feels good to you. Try it out before you buy it. Pendulums are made from stones, crystals, lead crystals, wood and metal, and can be very beautiful. The best pendulums are symmetrical in shape with a point at one end, but other shapes will also work.

Before you begin to work with your pendulum, you will want to energise it. You can do this by holding your hands over it and imagining that light is radiating out of your hands into the pendulum. Energising your pendulum will almost always improve the way it works for you.

Hold the cord or chain firmly between your thumb and index finger several inches from the pendulum (a comfortable range is between three and twelve inches), so that it can swing freely and smoothly. Pressing your elbow firmly against your body or placing it on a table will help steady you and ground your energy.

How your pendulum provides answers

To get accustomed to using the pendulum, ask it a question to which you already know the answer. This will help you decipher movements which indicate 'yes' or 'no' to further questions. For example, if you ask your pendulum 'Does the earth revolve around the sun?' and it swings in a direction perpendicular to your body in response, then you will know that this movement indicates 'yes' for your particular pendulum. Usually, although not always, when the pendulum swings perpendicular to the front of your body it means 'yes', while a swing parallel to your body means 'no'. Clockwise swinging usually means 'yes', and anti-clockwise means 'no'.

To familiarise yourself with your pendulum, it is good to practise by asking very simple, straightforward questions such as: 'Am I male?' or 'Is it daytime?' When it is clear which movement indicates 'yes' and which 'no', you can ask your pendulum questions about other things you would like to know. However, before seeking information from your pendulum, you should always ask the following questions of yourself:

'Can I?' This question relates to whether or not you have the pre-requisite knowledge necessary for receiving the answer you seek. For example, if you are asking about ley lines and you don't really know what they are, then the pendulum will be of limited use to you in dowsing for them.

'Should I?' This question asks you to consider carefully whether or not it would be in your best interests to receive knowledge about this issue at this particular time. It also asks you to consider if it would be helpful for everyone concerned. Sometimes we are not ready to receive the answers to our questions.

If your answer is 'yes' to both of the above questions, then you are ready to go ahead and use your pendulum for dowsing. Remember to ask simple, clear questions. Experienced dowsers have mastered the skill of asking questions in a concise manner. The way you frame your question will determine how useful the information you receive will be.

Once you have begun, don't worry if the pendulum doesn't respond immediately. Sometimes beginners become so afraid of getting a wrong answer that they 'freeze up'. Consciously release the idea that you need to be 'right,' or even to receive an answer. Completely clear your mind. When your own thoughts are quiet, you will function as an antenna, accessing your own subconscious and the collective unconscious. Dowsing is not a force that can be controlled. You are a channel. Sometimes answers will flow easily through you; sometimes nothing will come at all. Let go. When you are relaxed and enjoying yourself you will be able to achieve much better results. And, as with most skills, you will get better with practice.

In the case of an unmoving pendulum, it sometimes helps to hold it in your hands for several minutes, or rub it in one direction, or breathe on it. These techniques often increase the responsiveness of a pendulum.

Trust your first reaction

Usually your first response is best. When you have practised with questions to which you know the answers, progress to ones you don't know the answers to but can find out. When asking a new question, stop the pendulum completely and start again. The more practice you have, the more accurate your ability will become and the more your confidence will increase. Once you have gained confidence about your dowsing abilities you can begin to apply this skill to feng shui.

Degrees of truth

Sometimes an answer isn't either 'yes' or 'no', but rather is expressed in terms of degrees, or percentages, of rightness. For example, if you are dowsing about where to locate a shed on a building site, you might find that one area would be 75 per cent good, while another would be 90 per cent good. So although both would be fine places to build your shed, one site would clearly be better than the other. To determine the degree to which one outcome is better than another by dowsing, you can use the following method.

Pendulum Dowsing for Degrees of Truth

Draw a half circle on a piece of paper with the flat edge aligned parallel to you. Divide this half circle into two equal halves and then divide each half into four segments (see illustration). Write 'Yes' on the left-hand side and 'No' on the right-hand side. Hold the pendulum directly over the chart and ask your questions. The pendulum will swing somewhere between 'Yes' and 'No', and the angle of its swinging will give you the degree to which your answer tends towards positive or negative. This method is especially useful in situations where there is unlikely to be a simple yes or no solution.

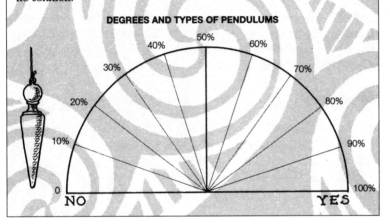

DEGREES AND TYPES OF PENDULUMS

Dowsing in the home can help you:

- Locate stagnant energy
- Discover residual energy from previous tenants
- Find the most auspicious area in your home for your health
- Learn the best method for clearing stagnant home energy
- Find out if, and where, there is underground water
- Locate the best position for beds
- Decide where to place furnishings
- Decide where to plant your garden, and which plants to include

Dowsing in your workplace can help you:

- Locate stagnant energy
- Identify the best location for cash register
- Decide the best position for your desk
- Decide where to place furnishings and products

ROD DOWSING

A dowsing rod is sometimes called a divining rod. The words 'to divine' mean to perceive something through inspiration, intuition or reflection. This definition has become somewhat unfamiliar in recent times, but it is a very good description of dowsing. Rod dowsing is commonly used in feng shui practice to detect underground water, geomagnetic lines, ley lines or earth grid lines – all of which influence the energy of a home.

Create or obtain a dowsing rod

Dowsing rods can be made from any kind of metal, from coat hangers to welding rods. They are usually made in either an 'L' or a 'Y' shape. There is no regulation size, but about five inches by thirteen inches is a good dimension for an 'L'-rod.

DOWSING RODS

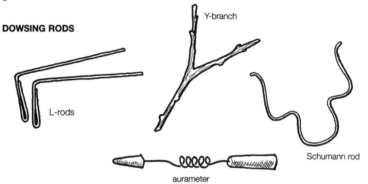

Divining rods can also be made by cutting a forked branch from a tree. Some dowsers believe that some trees are better for this purpose than others, but any tree branch will work. Professional dowsers sometimes use a dowsing rod called the Aurameter. Others prefer the Schumann rod. (See Resources at the end of the book for more information about these.)

Using Y-shaped dowsing rods

Hold the rod by its shorter ends, one in each hand. Hold these loosely in your fists so that nothing is preventing them from swinging freely. With your elbows held close to the sides of your body, the rod should be about the level of your solar plexus. When the dowsing rod picks up energies emanating from the earth, it will swing in the direction of the energy flow.

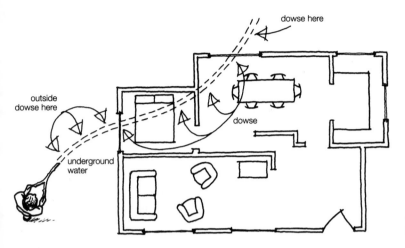

dowse here

outside
dowse here

dowse

underground
water

*A man walking over
energy line with rods*

When dowsing a house for earth energies, first walk around the perimeter of the land on which the house is situated. Note your findings on a drawing or map of the land. Remember that your intention will be reflected in your dowsing. For example, if your intention is to dowse for water, then when your rod moves, it will be in response to the flow of water. After you have dowsed along the perimeters of the house site, dowse again outside the edges of the house itself. Again mark on your map what you find. Finally, walk through the house with the dowsing rod and mark your map accordingly. Compare the map of your findings outside the house with what you observed inside. Particularly note whether any lines of energy flow cross the entire house.

A Synaesthesia Approach to Home Design

Modern human beings usually see the world as a conglomerate of separate objects. We experience sound as separate from light, light as separate from smell, smell as separate from touch, and so forth. But in actuality every taste has a colour, every colour has a sound, every sound has a smell, and every smell can be touched. Ancient people understood that all aspects of reality merge into one universal flow. Mystics, shamans and other people who have had peak experiences talk about this melding of the sensual world around them. Their experiences, in some ways, mirror a medical condition called synaesthesia, which affects only ten people out of one million.[1]

Neurologist Richard Cytowic became fascinated with the phenomenon of synaesthesia after a man he knew described how he had always perceived tastes as being linked with the images of shapes in his mind. For instance, he experienced sour flavours as having many points, and bland ones as being rounded. A cool mint flavour produced images of tall columns in his mind. This man's experience led Dr Cytowic to do extensive research on this syndrome, where people experience sensual perceptions as blended, rather than separate sensations. He discovered that some people with this condition can perceive colours through their fingers while blindfolded; others hear colour or taste sound.

Dr Cytowic monitored the brains of synaesthetic people while they were experiencing various sensual phenomena. The results of his inquiry were startling. Usually when the brain is stimulated by incoming sensual information, blood flow *increases* to the cerebral cortex. However, when a synaesthetic person is seeing sounds as colours, for example, their blood flow to the cerebral cortex actually *decreases* far below normal levels. Blood flow increases instead to the deeper and more primitive limbic area of the brain.[2] Cytowic eventually concluded that people with synaesthesia have direct access to a capacity of the brain *which is present in everyone*, but of which most of us are unaware.[3]

While the medical syndrome of synaesthesia is very rare and cannot be consciously controlled by the people who experience the world in this way, none the less it has great relevance for all of us as it gives us a unique approach for designing our homes. Even if you only imagine that you can smell colours, taste sounds and touch music, your appreciation for the world which surrounds you will be enormously expanded by doing so. You will experience life as being more connected and you will deepen your intuitive abilities.

To give you an example of how this can work, imagine that you are out shopping and find a beautiful antique. It looks great and you think you know the perfect place for it in your home. But before you buy it, focus your awareness on it and listen, *really* listen, to the sound of it. Not just with your hearing, but with your entire being. As you quieten your mind and open yourself to your intuition, you may tune into unexpected realisations. The antique looks good, but might have an unharmonious sound. You might sense a kind of jangly sound, or sense a bitterness if you could taste it.

So even though this object remains beautiful, you know that it is probably not right for your home after all. You sense that it will not contribute to the harmonious energy there. Your rational mind identified it as something good, but when you sensed with your intuition – with the sum of your conscious and unconscious awareness – you realised that there were underlying qualities there which would not enhance the energy of your home.

At the close of this millennium, science, art and mysticism are coming closer and closer together as we realise that no part of reality is disconnected from another; that the good of each is dependent on the good of all. When we tune into the world through our sensual knowing, we can sense this reality. When we create our homes from this perspective, we will have places that offer so much more than mere shelter; places where we can know that we are one with all things.

6

Instinctive Feng Shui

A FEW YEARS AGO I was giving a talk at a bookstore in Houston. I kept noticing a woman at the back of the room who was half hidden by a book shelf. Her dark eyes shone behind her oversized glasses, and the expression on her round face spoke of shyness. As she listened she kept twisting a strand of hair which had escaped from the neat bun at the back of her neck.

At the end of my talk she slipped to the front of the room and quietly said, 'I really want to have my home feng shuied, but I can't afford to hire a practitioner.' I had a few minutes to chat, so I said, 'Let's sit down for a moment. Maybe I can help you.' I began by asking her about her goals and what she dreamed of doing with her life. She looked surprised and said, 'What does that have to do with feng shui?' I explained to her that you can't separate homes from the people who live in them. I said that before she made any changes in her home she need-ed to be clear about what she wanted in life, so that the changes made would be supportive.

She started to cry, saying, 'I don't know what I want.' I told her that even when we don't consciously know what we want, deep within our subconscious minds we actually do. I suggested that we do a quick exercise together. I asked her to close her eyes and imagine herself being really happy and then tell me what she saw. After a few moments she said she saw herself in a loving relationship, holding a child in her arms. She explained that she had never been in a relationship, because she was so shy and didn't believe this was possible. I told her to just set that aside for a moment so that we could continue with the exercise.

I then said, 'Imagine that you are walking into your home *while experiencing this same loving, contented emotion*. While holding this image in your mind, imagine what you can rearrange in your home to make you feel this same way.' I was quiet and held her hand as she took the time to do this. After a few minutes, she opened her eyes and asked wonderingly, 'Can it really be this easy?' Her face was glowing, and I assured her that sometimes it really is this easy. I encouraged her to go home and make the changes she had seen in her meditation. Then I left to catch my plane.

A year later, I had forgotten about this brief encounter when I opened a letter that contained a photo of a very happy-looking couple. I was delighted to recognise the same young woman. In her letter she said that never in her wildest dreams could she have imagined finding such a wonderful partner. She went on to describe the changes she had made in her home, adding that shortly after this she had met the man who was now her husband.

Not everyone will be able to afford (or have access to) the services of a feng shui practitioner. However, you can use the power of your own intuition to discover changes you need to make in your home. This chapter will show you how to do this.

AWAKENING YOUR FENG SHUI INTUITION

Your ancestors knew how to live in harmony with the land. They intuitively found the best place to site their homes, just as they instinctively sensed the best location for the front door. Although we may have consciously lost this instinctive ability, it can be reawakened with you.

A baby bird just out of its shell will duck when a hawk flies overhead, but will be completely unconcerned when a pigeon flies nearby. It is an instinctual reaction. You also have instinctual abilities and you can use these instincts to arrange your home in a way that is beneficial to you and all who live in it. This ability arises out of your ancestral memories and recalls the experiences of generations of your forebears who lived close to the land. It is part of your heritage.

When you analyse the energy patterns in your home, rather than breaking them down into little parts, you will instead see how they are woven together into an intricate web of pattern and rhythm. This way

Connecting to the Essence of Your Home

Close your eyes and relax. Imagine that it is late at night and you are walking through your neighbourhood. The lights are off and people are sleeping. As you stop in front of each house, you use your inner sight to look through the walls. Inside each home you can perceive a luminous glowing there. You are sensing the 'seed energy' or core essence of that home. The seed energy of each dwelling may look different; one may look like a blue light, another may be a radiant symbol such as a star, another may be undulating golden light. As you approach your home, imagine standing in front of it and noticing that within its walls is a luminescent light – its seed energy. Now visualise a strand of energy flowing from you to the essence of your house. This deepens your connection with your home and helps to make it a more nurturing place for you.

you will begin to form a clear idea of what the 'seed energy' of your home is like.

The 'seed energy' of your home is like the theme of a piece of music. It is a recurring motif that will keep appearing again and again. Even though each time it is heard it may be slightly different, there will still be easily recognisable characteristics that give artistic unity to the piece as a whole. The seed energy of your home captures its essence. When you connect with this energetic essence, you feel more 'at home' when you are there. Every time, you connect with the true essence of something, you deepen your connection to it. Above is a simple exercise you can do which will help you to comprehend and connect with the seed energy in your home.

Communicating with your objects

When you first begin to use intuitive methods, they can seem strange or even bizarre. However, when you buy something for your home because it intuitively 'feels' right, you will almost always gain more joy from it than from something you logically decided was best for your home.

Susan engaged in a 'conversation' with an old rocking chair that she was thinking about buying at a flea market. The rocker 'told' her that it had spent many happy years in a large family. Susan saw an image of a child pulling it out to a spot under a big willow tree in the garden on a hot summer day. She said that these associations with the rocker made her feel good about bringing it into her home. After doing so, she asked it where it would like to be placed. The rocker 'chose' a sunny corner next to a south-facing window. As eccentric and madcap as this method sounds, Susan said that using her intuition regarding the furniture and objects in her house brings a special energy into her home that wasn't there when she relied on her logical mind for domestic purchases.

If it feels good, it's good feng shui

Feng shui can be very complex. Confusion can arise when different schools of feng shui disagree with one another. However, there is a simple rule of thumb you can use when in doubt: 'If it feels good, it's good feng shui.'

This rule is easy to apply anywhere. If you walk into a shop and it feels good, the chances are it has good feng shui. If you walk into a restaurant and it doesn't feel good, you will often find that it has bad feng shui. The problem with assessing the feng shui in our own homes is that we are so used to living in them that we are often unaware of whether they feel good or bad. One way to overcome this obstacle is to walk into a room and close your eyes. Take a moment to still your thoughts and then notice how you feel. As you do this throughout your home, you will usually be able to tell which rooms have good feng shui and which ones need some work.

Ultimately feng shui should be about living in harmony with your environment rather subscribing to rigid rules. There are no Feng Shui Police to come banging on your door in the middle of the night if you don't have bamboo flutes hanging from your beams. Some rules of feng shui that are very appropriate to Chinese culture don't work as well in Western homes without a bit of practical translation. For example, in some parts of China the number four is considered to be very unlucky because it sounds similar to the word for 'death'. So in traditional feng shui the number four is usually avoided. This number does not have the same associations in Western cultures. A chrysanthemum may symbolise one thing in one part of the world but something completely different elsewhere. It is always important to evaluate whether or not a particular rule or symbol makes sense in your case. Your home needs to feel good to *you*, because you are the one who will be living there.

Looking for the good in your home

It is so easy to be judgmental about our home. We often look at it and see first and foremost what is wrong with it. Because of this tendency, I have found it very useful to approach the evaluation of homes from the perspective of Mother Theresa. When I think of her entering a home, I imagine that she would do so with great love in her heart. No matter how much clutter was about or how many things needed repair or attention, I'm sure she would feel great compassion and look for the strengths in the place. She would find good in the people who lived there and be able to make recommendations in a way that supported them. If you tend to be very hard on yourself, using this image can help you to approach your home in a loving, non-judgmental way.

The most powerful way to relate to other human beings is always to look for the best. When you do, they will usually fulfil your expectations by acting their best. Homes are no different. When you start by looking at your home to see what is truly special about it, you will be able to make necessary changes with a completely different spirit than if you begin by searching for weaknesses.

Each house, like every person, has special qualities. The more you emphasise the positive in your home, the more positive it will become. Notice how the kitchen window catches the afternoon light in a beautiful way, or perhaps there is a magnificent tree growing just outside your bedroom. The golden oak of a stair banister may bring brightness to an otherwise dull corridor. When you pay attention to what is best in your home, you will begin to see these same qualities showing up in other areas of your life.

One potential pitfall in feng shui is to dwell on what is wrong with a building rather than observing what is working well there. This is illustrated by an experience I had many years ago when a young adult, I decided to enter therapy. I chose a therapist with outstanding credentials, but during our sessions we usually focused on what was wrong with me. Even though her observations about me were probably right, I began to feel worse and worse about myself, so I decided to switch therapists. The second therapist wasn't as well known, but from the moment I stepped into her office she saw what was good about me. She pointed out my potential and many strengths that I hadn't considered.

This wonderful therapist also saw some areas that needed attention, but she let me know that by working together we could easily overcome those issues. We did, and so I began to heal and to grow exponentially. She saw the good in me. She believed in me. When you recognise the good in something it will blossom. This is especially true about your home.

In some feng shui practices there is a tendency to dwell on the house and not on the people You cannot separate dwellings from the people who live in them. When you see the good in one, it will be reflected in the other. Improvement in a home creates a template for improvement in a person, and vice versa. When you find the good in a home, you are creating the right conditions for the people who live there to find the good in themselves.

A place should look like itself

There is a rule in feng shui which says that a place should look like itself. I first heard this from my friend Angel Thompson, who is an author and feng shui teacher. The look of a place should be consistent with its function: a gym should look like a gym – it should be light and bright; a bar should look like a bar – it should be dark and relaxing. When the way a place looks is consistent with its core essence, then there is a feeling of harmony and rightness there. A house with lots of children shouldn't be perfectly neat with precious glass objects at waist level. It should be comfortable and childproofed. A thatched cottage furnished with sleek stainless steel and modern glass would feel strange and unharmonious. Likewise, a high-tech apartment kitted out with chintz, lace cushions and Dresden china would not be pleasing. People look more beautiful when they wear clothes that are suited to their bodies and personalities. When this is the case, they feel at ease and seem to glow. The same is true of homes. Harmony and beauty are two sides of the same coin, and harmony cannot grow out of inconsistency.

If it's not broken, don't fix it

'If it's not broken, don't fix it' is always a good maxim to remember when considering whether or not to make a change in your home. I once received a call from a man who was very upset because he and his wife had just completed a feng shui course where they learned that the wealth area of their home had bad feng shui. They were thinking about knocking down a wall and building an extension to their home to rectify this problem, but they were calling me first to get a second opinion. I asked, 'Are you having financial problems?' He answered no, and added, 'In fact, ever since we moved into this house our finances have been great.' I then asked if they liked their home the way it was. He told me they were both very happy with it. My advice to them (and to anyone considering a feng shui cure) was: *'If it's not broken, don't fix it!'*

There can be so many influences on the energy of a home or workplace that, even if one area doesn't seem to have good feng shui, there may be fifteen other subliminal elements balancing that area. This process is like the homeostatic capacities of the human body, where, for example, if someone loses a spleen, then part of that organ's function will be taken over by the bone marrow. The health and functioning of the body is maintained by this compensatory action. In your home or office, if things are going well you can assume that the energy is balanced there.

Only change the feng shui in your home or workplace if something *isn't* working for you. Otherwise, changes in your environment can produce a domino effect, as the balance between unseen influences is shifted in your home. You may end up with a problem bigger than the one you originally perceived. For example, when you take out a wall, this affects the natural sunlight in the room, the room's sound resonance and the air flow. All of these changes will affect the rest of your living space.

Using intention with feng shui

If you want to use feng shui to change your life, it's important to work from the inside out. For example, just putting a bowl of nine goldfish in your home (a traditional feng shui wealth cure) will not make you wealthy if you have a deep subconscious belief that rich people are unhappy. Because of a subconscious fear of being prosperous, you will continue to sabotage your efforts to increase your finances. However, if you begin by releasing your inner blockages, then you can use feng shui to reinforce your new direction and create magic in your life.

Also, combining your intention with a feng shui cure magnifies its effect. The human psyche responds to symbolic acts. If you put one goldfish in your home with the absolutely clear intention that your abundance level will expand because of this action, your chances of being successful are dramatically higher than someone who puts fifty goldfish in their home without much thought and who only hopes they may become more prosperous.

'Recruiting' a cure

There are times when a problem in feng shui cannot be cured. When this is the case, you will need to 'recruit' a cure. An example of how this process works can be seen in the case of the Davis family. They were living in a rented home with a big tree growing directly in front of their entrance. Although the tree was beautiful, the principles of feng shui indicated that it was blocking the flow of beneficial energy into their home, and they agreed that this felt true for them. Because the landlord would not agree to their removing the tree, and because they loved everything else about the house, they called me and asked if there was anything they could do. I offered several feng shui cures including the suggestion that they 'recruit' the tree. I explained that this meant asking the tree for its help in solving the problem. I told them to look at the tree as a home guardian, so that every time they entered or left their home they would know that their 'Guardian Tree' was providing a wonderful protective energy for them. As soon as they did this, everyone in the home noticed an improvement.

Another man called because his window looked directly out on to a brick wall. He told me he felt as though he was always running into insurmountable obstacles in his life and he wondered if this was a feng shui problem related to the location of the wall. I made a number of suggestions, but he wasn't enthusiastic about any of them. Finally I asked him, 'What do bricks represent to you?' He stopped for a moment before saying, 'They represent stability and strength to me.' I then suggested that he recruit the brick wall to support him, to be a source of stability and strength in his life. I encouraged him to offer thanks to the wall for bringing these qualities to his life. He later told me that almost immediately from the time he began to do this, his fortunes turned around. He had recruited the wall as an ally to help him reach his dreams.

It doesn't have to make sense to work

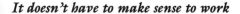

I usually like to explain the reasons behind my actions when I am helping clients balance energy in their home. I think it is helpful to understand the basis for the changes that are taking place. This is similar to a doctor explaining procedures to a patient, so that he or she can be a part of the healing process.

Many feng shui cures are plainly logical and easy to understand. It makes sense that if every time you open your door it makes an irritating sound, then people entering the home will feel irritable. However, not all feng shui cures are based on logic and it would be a mistake to reject the ones you don't understand solely on that basis. Often illogical cures stem from the experience of countless generations, and sometimes they are the most effective.

When you let go of your need fully to understand a process and you open yourself to possibility, this is the point where mysterious forces of the universe can pour into your life. If you go on an imaginary journey through your home, to discover what changes you need to make, and you intuitively sense something that seems silly or totally illogical to your conscious mind, you might want to try it anyway. Sometimes an idea such as this comes from the deep reservoir of knowledge within us, a repository of more wisdom than we know.

When you change your life, change your home

Feng shui is partially based on the notion that when you change your home it can change your life. Even small changes in your home can have a big effect on your life. However, many people don't realise that if you make a positive change in your behaviour, but don't make changes in your environment, *you will have a tendency to revert back to your old habits.* If you release a negative habit, addiction or pattern, it is *essential* to change your environment; otherwise, it is easy to fall back into older, more established behaviour patterns. For example, if you stop smoking, it is important to rearrange your home. Move the chair you usually sat in when you smoked to another area. Clear out your clutter. Paint the walls a new colour. Making definite and even dramatic changes in your environment will act as an affirmation of your new path.

Many adults notice how an environment affects their perception of themselves when they revisit their childhood home. Often as soon as they cross the threshold, they revert to childhood patterns and feelings. Sometimes this phenomenon can be explained by family dynamics, but it is also supported by the energy imprints that linger there. Seeing the same arrangements of furniture and other familiar objects in a childhood home can ignite memories and associations that may be buried, but which will affect behaviour.

Feng shui detective

Every home contains hundreds of clues to the secret lives of its occupants. These are easy to miss in our own homes because they are so familiar to us. But when you look through the eyes of a detective, new evidence appears everywhere. When you are using feng shui in your home, I suggest that you don the persona of Sherlock Holmes. Imagine that you are observing your home through the eyes of this famous sleuth.

One clue doesn't make a case, but when you have amassed a number that all point in the same direction, then you can usually come to conclusions about the forces at play in the life of the occupants of a dwelling, even if one of those occupants is yourself. For example, a friend had a cactus plant on her doorstep. A cactus outside the front door can be a subconscious way of saying 'Stay away'. However, this first clue is not particularly significant in itself. A second clue at the front door was the wreath made of barbed wire. Again, this is not significant in itself, but barbed wire could be another message that says 'Stay away'. A third clue appeared as soon as I stepped over the threshold.

Massive, almost threatening, elk horns pointed directly at me and were the first thing that I saw in the house. Animals use horns in defence, so this could be a third clue with a subliminal message that says 'Stay away'. A fourth clue emerged when my friend told me that a family of skunks lived under their home. This, again, was a clue, because most people when they see a skunk will 'stay away'. Again and again, we found clues with the same message. My friend realised that she had been closed off from people but was now ready to be open to relationships, so she decided to change her home so that the subliminal messages were of a more inviting nature.

When doing feng shui in your home, your intuition is your greatest ally in creating wonderful, expansive, vital energy in your home. No matter how much you learn, you will always need to tune into this amazing source of wisdom to see if a particular solution is the right one for your life. When you do, you immediately gain access to a limitless reservoir of magic and power.

Part Two

AWAKENING
NATURAL
FORCES

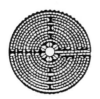

7

Awakening Natural Forces in Your Home

W<small>E LIVE</small> in a rhythmic universe. Every part of nature has a unique language and its own rhythm – every flower, bird and tree has its own rhythmic language; and rhythm is the underlying context that weaves all life together. We are constantly surrounded by rhythms of energy. If you take a moment to become very still, you can feel these rhythms of the natural world inside you.

The rhythm that begins softly and quietly in the morning hours, as darkness slips away, increases to an amazing concert of sound and light as the day unfolds. And then energy ebbs away again as night approaches. When you are still, you can feel this rhythm ebbing and flowing within you, because you are a part of the cycles of nature. The best way to awaken natural forces within your home is first to activate and become aware of them within yourself. When nature is alive inside you, the forces of nature will begin to sing around you, wherever you are.

I once spent the night in the outback with some Pitjantjajara aboriginal people in Australia, sleeping in a dry river-bed. When I awoke, I opened my eyes just in time to see the last star dissolve into the grey sky of early morning. It was so quiet, almost as if the earth held her breath for a moment. Then, as the earth exhaled, the first ray of light rolled across the land like a great wave. A hum began to rise as one kind of insect and then another joined together in a song of awakening. When birds joined in, it was like a grand orchestra where one by one the instruments join in, building to a crescendo. The rhythm of nature in that ancient land was palpable. I could feel the rhythm of the earth in my bones; I could inhale her rhythm into my body. It was like an immense heartbeat surging inside me, around me. And along with this rhythm I could feel a yearning growing inside me. It was like a deep longing for something I couldn't quite remember, but knew that I had lost.

The inner landscape of the soul

As nature is disappearing around us, we are losing vast tracts of the wilderness inside ourselves as well. It's as if the fertile soil of the soul is being gradually depleted. Every day as we lose part of our natural outer heritage, our inner heritage diminishes as well. Ancestral memories of life in the deep forest are being replaced by images of afternoon traffic and the sounds of pneumatic drills. The songs of the birds are drowned out by sirens. Something within us is dying as the chasm between humans and the natural world widens.

The ecological disintegration that is occurring in the environments around us is echoed in the inner landscape of the soul. In this time many of us sense that our inner life has become impoverished. We hunger to once again feel connected to the forces of nature and the sacredness of life. We yearn for a viable connection to the mountains, the trees and the sky.

In the deepest crevice of our being, the soul is searching for this connection, listening for it and sending out tentative tendrils of energy to find it. However, in spite of our apparent disconnection, there still exists a link intimately connecting the soul to the natural world. But this umbilical cord connecting us to the life-blood of the earth is stretched so thin that it is in danger of severing. It is now urgent to strengthen this life-cord so that vital energy can once again surge through it from the earth to us and back again.

One of the most powerful ways to activate the forces of nature within ourselves, our homes and our workplaces is to strengthen our connection to the natural world. The more our living spaces look and function like nature, the more likely we are to survive and thrive on the earth.

Gaia – the living earth

From a scientific point of view, nature and everything around you is composed of atoms, which are the basic building blocks of the universe.

Yet when an atom is examined, you discover that it is nearly all empty space. Most of it is a vast emptiness dotted with small amounts of matter, not unlike the void of outer space that is dotted with planets and stars. However, this emptiness is not barren and cold and lifeless. It is a potential of energy waiting to be born. It is an invisible force that holds the world together.

Native people intuitively knew about this vast space of the universe, but what scientists call emptiness they called spirit. Throughout history, earth-based people have always understood the earth to be a living being. The Sioux Indian holy man Smohalla, at the end of the nineteenth century, as white people were devastating the natural resources of North America, speaking about modern agriculture practices, said, 'You ask me to dig in the earth? Am I to take a knife and plunge it into the breast of my mother? But then if I die, she will not gather me again into her bosom.' Native people respected mother earth and gave thanks to her on a daily basis for her bounty.

This view of the earth being alive was not unique to native people. In the fifteenth century, the alchemist Basilius Valentinus said, 'The earth is not a dead body, but is inhabited by a spirit that is its life and soul. All created things, minerals included, draw their strength from the earth spirit. This spirit is life, it is nourished by the stars, and it gives nourishment to all the living things it shelters in its womb.' Today more and more people, including scientists, are coming to this same realisation . . . that we are a small part of a greater living whole.

In 1979, British biochemist James Lovelock set out his holistic theory of the earth as a living planet that he called Gaia, after the Greek earth goddess. Lovelock's journey began in the early 1960s when he was working with National Aeronautics and Space Administration (NASA) to determine if there was life on Mars. Considering the possibility of life on Mars initiated thoughts about his own planet. He marvelled at how the highly unstable gases that compose our atmosphere apparently stayed so stable. He wondered if air, rather than being just an environment for life, was actually an integral part of life itself. From this seed of thought he developed his theory that in fact the planet was an immense self-regulating and self-sustaining organism *that was conscious and alive*. Lovelock compared all the living and inert matter of the earth to the various glands and organs of the human body – separate yet working together to make one living organism.

The idea that something as big as our planet might be alive is very difficult for some people to comprehend. However, it is fascinating to notice that the earth regulates her environment in much the same way that the human body self-regulates in order to maintain constant

conditions within itself. For example, a human body in good health maintains a temperature of approximately 98.6 degrees Fahrenheit. During the summer and winter, despite the fluctuations of outer temperature, the body maintains a temperature very close to this norm. When body temperature drops below this, you begin to shiver and your skin contracts, raising body temperature. When body temperature rises above 98.6 degrees, your pores will open and release perspiration, thus bringing body temperature back down through the cooling process of evaporation.

Similarly, the temperature of the earth has remained at about an average of 55.4 degrees Fahrenheit for 3,800 million years, *even though the sun became 25 per cent hotter and brighter during this period of time.* As the sun became hotter, the plants on earth drew in more carbon dioxide from the atmosphere, thus reducing the greenhouse effect warming the planet. In other words, Gaia devised a way to maintain her constant temperature.[1]

Another example of the remarkable ability of the planet to self-regulate is the saline level of the sea. The level of salt in the ocean has remained at 3.4 per cent for thousands of years even though rivers are continually washing salt from the earth into the sea. Similarly, the oxygen content of our atmosphere stays at 21 per cent, which is the necessary level for life to exist on the planet.[2]

When you begin to think about the planet as a living conscious organism, it can shift the way you perceive your relationship to the earth. This in turn can affect the way you organise your home, so that it will reflect the nature of this relationship. If you want to honour and activate the hidden forces within your home, one of the most powerful ways to do this is to imagine yourself as the earth. This exercise can awaken the forces of nature within you and your home. Becoming one with the earth is an ancient and time-honored shamanistic tradition. Here is an exercise which comes out of that tradition.

Become the Earth

Enter into a meditative space. Imagine that your body is beginning to expand . . . becoming bigger and bigger . . . so big, in fact, that you can feel yourself as the earth. Feel the deep heat in your core. Let the coolness of your oceans refresh you. Sense the warmth and light of the sun on half of you, while the other side reposes in darkness. Feel yourself revolving around the powerful force of the sun. Day turns to night and night to day again. Half of you is in daylight and half in darkness. You are always in a balance. When the warmth of summer is on one side of you, the coolness of winter encompasses the other side of you. You are spinning in a vast and infinite cosmos.

> ### *Finding the Mountain in the Stone*
> Choose an object from nature, such as a stone, to hold in your hand. Focus your awareness on it and imagine yourself merging with the energy of the stone. Let your awareness expand, so that you share the consciousness of all stones . . . then expand further to enter into the awareness of all rocks, boulders, cliffs, mountains. By opening your consciousness to this one stone, you are expanding your connection to the natural world from which it came and thus inviting more of its energy into your home.

Morphic resonance

Another theory presenting the idea of a living earth was proposed by the English scientist Rupert Sheldrake. According to Sheldrake everything on earth – from the way that a snowflake forms to the way that whales migrate south in the summer – is influenced by a 'morphic field'. This term comes from the Greek word *morphe*, meaning 'form'. Morphic fields are the unique energy signatures of everything on earth – and every group of things, this concept proposes, has its own collective consciousness, or energy field, which connects all of like kind. For example, the consciousness of one hummingbird is connected to all hummingbirds. Therefore, Sheldrake believes, once an animal learns a skill, others of the same species will subsequently be able to learn that skill more easily.

Some scientific research supports this theory. In the 1920s a Harvard University professor, William McDougall, noticed that successive generations of rats learned skills faster *even when all possibility of genetic transference was ruled out*. Later tests carried out by separate researchers in Scotland and Australia duplicated these results.[3] Although some conventional scientists criticised Sheldrake's findings, his theories echo the native American belief that we are all connected. The Morphic Theory has relevance for each of us in our living spaces, because, for example, if it is true that every fern has a connection to all ferns, then when we include a fern in our home, on some deep, subtle and mysterious level, we are activating the energy of all ferns in our living environment.

Within every drop of water is the sea

Within every grain of sand is the beach; within every apple seed is the apple tree; and within every drop of rain is the sea. By putting just one grain of sand, or one seed or drop of rain into your home, on a subtle level you are inviting the forces of nature into your living environment. By placing a basket of red and yellow maple leaves by your front door, you are bringing the spirit of all maple trees into your home. When you place a vase of daisies on your kitchen table, you invite the spirit of all daisies, from the mountains of Spain to the prairies of the United States, into your home.

Ecopsychology

Research reveals that on average most humans spend 95 per cent of their time indoors. In fact, many people go for months without ever actually touching the soil. They are either inside temperature-controlled buildings, or in their cars, or walking on flooring or concrete. Even when they *are* out of doors and in the countryside, there is still a layer of rubber or leather separating them from the earth. Numerous psychologists believe that prolonged separation from nature can result in psychological problems such as depression, alienation and dysfunctional behaviour.[4]

These researchers feel that de-natured environments create de-natured people. A new field of study, called 'ecopsychology', has been created to address this problem. It studies how our psychological health is tied to our relationship with the natural environment. Theodore Roszak, founder of the Ecopsychology Institute of California State University, said, 'We have detached ourselves so [completely] from the natural environment that it is wounding our mental health.'[5] Research done at the ecopsychology division of the Harvard Medical School suggests that there may be a subconscious connection between a person's inner pain and what he or she perceives as the earth's pain.[6]

The renowned naturalist John Muir said that when you tug at a single thing in nature you will find it attached to the rest of the world. In the many Vision Quests I have led over the years, time and again I have found that when people spend three days alone in nature, one of the most common experiences that comes up is a deep sadness for the suffering of the earth. Even if we are not consciously aware of it, we are deeply connected to 'the rest of the world'. The field of ecopsychology is expanding rapidly as more and more research confirms what native people have always known – that it is essential for humans to stay in touch with nature.

The genetic need to connect with nature

Since nature provides us with deep psychological and aesthetic satisfaction, I believe that our bodies have a genetically programmed need to spend time in nature. For thousands of years human beings have lived in nature. Our bodies have adapted to nature, just as every animal and plant has done. Every aspect of nature is constantly changing in response to interaction with the environment around it – even when the environment is human. For example, beavers were once diurnal creatures. But now, having been hunted almost to extinction, they have adapted to their environment and have become nocturnal creatures in order to increase their survival rate. Dandelions are another case in point. Growing in the wild, they will reach about twelve to sixteen inches before they bloom. In a garden, where they are continually cut short by a lawnmower, they will often bloom when less than an inch in height – just a little lower than the threatening blades.

The beaver and the dandelion don't make conscious choices to adapt. There is something in their genetic make-up, which is also in the genetic make-up of human beings, that is constantly interacting with, and adapting to, the environment. Every species on this planet has evolved, not in isolation, but out of a deep and profound connection with the other aspects of the environment. There has always been an organic codependency in nature. For example, research has shown that the songs of birds and the air vibrations caused by the flapping of their wings helps the flowering and fruiting of plants. The birds need the fruit for food, and the fruit and flowers need the birds to spread their seeds and to assist their growth.

You and your body are a part of nature. Your body is the result of an evolutionary process of nature over millions of years. If human history for the last 40,000 years were represented by just one hour, then the amount of time that we have been living in such extreme isolation from nature would be represented by only a few seconds. Hence the bodies of generations of our ancestors had time to adjust to the changing rhythms of nature. Our present bodies haven't had time to adjust to the massive changes in our environment. *Our salvation lies in bringing nature back into our environments.*

When an animal is removed from its natural habitat, its energy usually wanes. It is genetically programmed to interact with its particular environment. Our bodies have been taken out of our natural ancestral environments, and most certainly this is causing great difficulties for us. If we do not include the forces of nature in our environments, not only do we rob ourselves of a rich source of aesthetic and spiritual satisfaction, we also place our health at risk.

ACTIVATING THE FORCES OF NATURE INTO OUR LIVES

There are three ways that we can activate natural forces into our lives. One way, of course, is to spend time in a wild region. This isn't always possible for every person, but even a few moments spent in a natural environment can allow the cells in the body to absorb natural energies. Here is an exercise that can help you absorb healing energy when you are in nature.

Absorbing the Energy of Nature

Find a grassy place outdoors. Tall, uncut grass in its natural state is best, but this exercise can also be done in your garden, or even in a park if you are able to find a place which offers some privacy. Spread your body face down on the ground. (You can use a blanket if your prefer.) Hold the image that your body is lying on the body of the mother earth. This is not unlike the way a child lies on its mother's breast. Feel yourself sinking into the spirit of the land. With every inward breath, feel vital life-affirming energy filling you from the earth. Lie still for about half an hour, and you should find yourself entering into a state of renewal.

Visualising yourself in nature

The second way to connect more deeply to nature is to visualise yourself in a natural environment. This works because there is a place in the brain that believes what you visualise is real and *responds physiologically*. For example, research done at Manchester Metropolitan University has proved that muscle strength can be improved by 16 per cent just by *visualising* exercising a muscle. In a study conducted by sports psychologist David Smith, the muscle strength in the small finger was first measured in a test group. The group was then divided into three groups. One group performed strengthening exercises; the second group only *imagined* exercising the little finger; and the third group did nothing at all. The exercisers increased their muscle strength by 33 per cent. There was no improvement in the group that neither exercised nor visualised, but the group that only visualised exercising the finger showed an improvement of 16 per cent in muscle strength!

Visualising yourself in nature has a similar effect on your body as *actually being in nature*. For example, when people are in nature, their blood pressure and pulse decrease. Similarly, when people *visualise* being in nature, their pulse and blood pressure are reduced. The brain often responds physically to the things we visualise, as if they were actually occurring. Even just a few moments of visualising yourself in a relaxing natural environment can help deepen your connection to nature.

Bringing the rhythm of nature into your home

The third way to activate the forces of nature is to bring the rhythms of nature into your home. Simulating the natural cadences, cycles, patterns, shapes and forms of nature in your home can activate dramatic shifts in the energies there and, consequently within your life.

Nature can be found in the four elements – Air, Water, Fire and Earth – that comprise the natural world around us. Each element has a unique rhythm that is essential to the balance of life, from the rhythm of the swirling winds and the undulation of sound as it travels through the air, to the rhythm of a stream as it plunges down a mountainside on its way to the sea; from the rhythm of the sun as the electromagnetic force fields flare and reside, to the deep rhythms of the earth as her currents of energy pulse at a constant 7.8 megahertz.

Through simulating the natural cycles of each element you can bring a wonderful healing energy to your home. For example, when you open your windows to allow the phases of the sun to flood in, you are connecting to the cycle of the sun and the element of Fire. If you have a fountain, the natural sound of the water on the stones can connect you to the movement and rhythm of the element of Water. Playing a recording of morning songbirds in your home, even if you live in a city flat, invites the element of Air and the bird kingdom in. When you bring the rhythms of these elements into your space, you will find that your life will be in harmony with the natural rhythm of all life on earth. (See Chapters 8 to 12 for specific ways to do this.)

BIOMIMICRY

The more our living spaces are a reflection of nature, the more likely we will be able to flourish on the earth. After 3.8 billion years of adaptation and natural selection, mother earth has discovered what works best on this planet. She carries the secret keys to our survival. Some scientists are beginning to examine these secrets in search of ways to live more in harmony with the earth. This new field of discovery, called 'biomimicry', looks at nature to find ways to utilise her wisdom. It seeks to consciously emulate nature for human benefit. The scientific findings within the biomimicry field are revolutionising how we view ourselves and our environment.

Goethe wrote, 'If nature is your teacher, your soul will awaken.' Biomimicry is based not on what we can extract from nature but what we can learn from her. For example, many of our modern inventions can be found in nature in a more refined and ecologically balanced form. Our most sophisticated temperature control systems cannot compare with that of the termite, who keeps his abode at exactly 86 degrees Fahrenheit all year round. Our radar is archaic when compared with the bat's complicated version. Dragonflies are far more precise than modern helicopters, and far less clumsy.[7]

By beginning to follow nature's example within our homes and environments we can live more in harmony with the cycles of nature. For example, in areas of drought the native plants are drought-resistant. But often people import into their gardens in these areas plants that are not adapted to dry environments. And then to compensate, they over-water (which depletes natural water reserves) and over-fertilise (which damages ground water), and then they continually struggle to keep their gardens green. It would be so much easier to follow nature's way and plant drought-resistant plants.

Another example of the wisdom of nature can be found in how we light our homes. Natural sunlight has a full spectrum of life-promoting colours within it. All life on earth is in one way or another dependent upon this full spectrum of light. Yet in our homes we use incandescent lighting, which contains only the yellow bands of the spectrum. Even worse, we use fluorescent lights, which deplete the calcium in our bones and promote tooth decay in children. If we want to mimic nature, we should use natural light as much as possible in our homes. Ideally, windows should be oriented towards the sun, skylights can be included to let in more natural lighting, and full spectrum lights can be installed to simulate natural sunlight in homes.

When you have instilled the rhythms of nature into your home, your life will become more in rhythm with all the cycles of life. (Chapters 8 to 12 give you specific ways to can implement the forces of nature in your living spaces.)

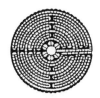

8

Shapes and Patterns of the Universe

WHENEVER you spend time in nature you find yourself surrounded by the patterns of the natural world. The way a tree branches, the veins of leaves, the lines of a seashell spiralling outwards from the centre, the crystal perfection of a snowflake – all of these patterns conform to the natural laws of an organic geometry. Just as you need sunlight, water, air and nutrients for your body, in the deepest sense you also need the shapes and patterns of nature to feed your soul.

Our ancestors, living in nature for thousands of years, were always surrounded by natural geometric shapes and patterns. Over hundreds of generations, the human body was conditioned and shaped by these natural geometric forms. Even though the artificial man-made environments we live in are, for the most part, devoid of a natural symmetry, I believe that the human body still carries a cellular remembrance of, *and yearning for*, the natural geometric shapes that underlie all universal order. This yearning can be so intense that sometimes the body may even spontaneously generate these patterns.

From early childhood, whenever I closed my eyes I could see constantly changing, vividly coloured geometric designs. They seemed to emerge from a point and then fold back on themselves, much like a kaleidoscope. As I grew older, I decided that there must be some defective wiring in my brain that was creating this anomaly, so I stopped paying much attention to it. However, when I later began studying feng shui and earth energies, I became curious about this phenomenon and wondered if anyone else shared a similar experience. I was surprised to discover that many other people did as well.

In Finland, I met an Irish woman named Jeannie who told me that since childhood she had seen brilliantly coloured geometric patterns whenever she closed her eyes. She said, 'It's like watching a kaleidoscope . . . like a matrix or a complete whole pattern that keeps changing. The size of the image remains the same, but the shapes metamorphose one into another. A rectangle might change into four arms like a cross, or into a round shape with ruffled edges.'[1] Jeannie still sees these images, although not as often as when she was a child. She says they are like 'a very nice slide show before I go to bed – so crystal clear and so perfectly formed – not at all like a dream, which can be vague and unclear'.

I now believe that this spontaneous firing of geometric images in the brain is not the result of 'defective wiring', but rather is the body's way of 'feeding' the soul with images of natural patterns, and that within these spontaneous productions of the brain are patterns that underlie the structure of the universe. I also think that there are secret codes in those forms that are essential to the very substance of our life. The body has an innate wisdom that is always striving to keep our health in balance. It produces dreams to keep us in emotional balance. I believe that the brain similarly generates these patterns, in some people, to keep them emotionally and spiritually healthy. These patterns fill a need generated in many instances by the absence of natural geometric forms in our environments.

If you are not surrounded by nature in your everyday life, it is essential to integrate the geometric forms of nature into your living environment. Using and understanding the principles of sacred geometry, fractals, labyrinths and mandalas brings a sense of harmony into everyday life.

SACRED GEOMETRY

Sacred geometry is a powerful healing force. It reaches inside us and touches that deep place in each of us that yearns for harmony and symmetry. Ancient people believed that the energies in nature were of a sacred origin, and that those energies could be revealed and activated through geometric forms.

The healing power of geometric forms was made very clear to me one summer afternoon. After my feelings had been hurt through a misunderstanding, I jumped in my car and took off for a ride. I didn't know where I was going, but I wanted to have some time to think. I drove aimlessly around until I found myself at a beach. I parked the car and walked along the shore. Emotions washed over me in great surges. When I reached the deserted end of the beach, I threw myself down on to the sand.

Feelings of anger, sadness and loneliness filled me. Tracing my finger in the sand, I began idly making designs as I replayed the hurtful incident in my mind again and again. However, with each replay of the scene, it became less and less hurtful, until finally I was filled with a sense of deep contentment. I didn't understand how my pain had subsided so quickly. Normally when I replayed a hurtful incident, it would build in power, as if in each replay I were accumulating evidence to justify my feelings to myself and the world. It didn't make sense why my feelings of pain were being so quickly replaced with feelings of peace. Then I looked in the sand. Without realising what I had been doing, I had drawn a beautiful geometric design. A realisation slowly emerged. My spontaneous creation of a mandala-like geometric form in the sand had shifted my consciousness!

Fascination exploded as I began to create different, intricate geometric shapes. Each pattern seemed to affect my emotions as well as my physical body in a different and unique way, as if they were striking musical mystical chords inside me. My body and soul were being finely tuned by these impromptu renderings.

A small crowd began to gather as I continued to make mandala-like designs. One person after another joined me in the sand and began to make their own geometric patterns. A vast elaborate patchwork of shapes, stretching to the edge of the sea, spontaneously occurred through the power of geometry . . . sacred geometry. We all left laughing and shaking hands, intuitively knowing somehow that we had co-created a moment of magic and power by the sea.

For ancient architects and philosophers, geometry reflected beliefs in an integrated holistic world. It represented the unity of spirit and matter through the unity of pattern and form. The circle or sphere symbolised the eternal perfection of the Creator and the heavens. The central point of a circle characterised focus, which brought a sense of orientation. The square represented strength, unity and the earth. It was a sign of stability and gave the psychological impression of foundation, firmness, stability. It represented the four directions, four elements, four seasons and the four sacred winds. The triangle was the Holy Trinity; mind/body/spirit; mother/father/child; past/present/future. It was a symbol of wholeness and represented protection.

These elemental shapes, circle, square and triangle, comprise the underlying structure or patterns of all life. Sound creates geometric shapes, colour is recognised because of geometric patterns. Animate life adheres to the laws of geometry: witness the sunflower, whose seeds grow in a spiralling geometric form. Inanimate objects in nature also abide by these patterns, as in the way ice crystals form on a window on a cold winter's day.

Plato declared that the world was governed by a divine being that manifested itself according to the laws of symmetry and geometric forms. He associated proportion with the natural order of the cosmos. In *Timaeus*, Plato stated that the universe was 'a single visible living being . . . a whole of complete parts . . . a single complete whole, consisting of parts that are wholes'. With this, he declared that the universe and spirit and all natural and human life were bound together by a matrix of proportions, shapes and patterns.

LABYRINTHS

A number of years ago, I was in San Francisco on a book tour. It is a wonderful city that piques my senses and makes me glad to be alive. As I had time between appointments, I decided to take a walk and enjoy the afternoon. After a strenuous hike I found myself on top of Nob Hill, which overlooks the downtown Union Square area. Perched like an eyrie on this stately hill sits the magnificent Grace Cathedral. Its tall regal towers seemed to pierce the heavens. The instant I saw the cathedral, a strong compulsion drew me towards it. When I reached the door, I stopped for a moment. It was as if I could sense a remarkable shift of energy at the threshold, like at the place where a river meets the sea. Holding my breath, I slowly opened the door and entered near the baptismal font.

Beneath soaring arches, radiant light streamed through the stained glass windows, illuminating a large labyrinth design on a plush tapestry on the floor. In sombre silence, people were slowly and meditatively walking the patterned pathway towards the centre of the labyrinth. Those who had reached the center were standing or sitting quietly, as if tuned into some internal whisperings from their souls. Drawn by some mysterious and ancient power, I slipped off my shoes and stepped on to the labyrinth.

Tears welled in my eyes. Some part of me seemed to know that I was participating in a sacred and holy act. With every step I felt inextricably drawn to the centre of the labyrinth, as if the centre of my being waited patiently for me there. I left the cathedral feeling washed clean, filled with a deep peace.

Determined to bring the energy of the labyrinth into my home, I purchased a postcard of it to use as a focus for meditation. Having a visual form of the labyrinth in my home seemed to quench a type of spiritual thirst. Through subsequent research I discovered that I was not alone in my yearning for these geometric designs. In ancient cultures throughout the world labyrinth designs were found etched on ceramic vessels, on clay tablets, engraved in stone and created with mosaic tiles. Perhaps my yearning for a pictorial form of the labyrinth was an echo of ancestral wisdom – lost knowledge that is once again resurfacing.

The dictionary defines a labyrinth as an intricate structure of interconnecting passages through which it is difficult to find one's way. But in a deeper sense a labyrinth is a sacred geometric pattern that serves as a centrepoint for integrating the forces of the earth and the forces of heaven. It creates a union between inward intention and outward form. A labyrinth can take the form of a pathway created with hedges, mounded earth, stones or mosaic tiles, or even a fixed pattern traced by dancers. The way to the centre through a complex network of paths has been compared to a journey to the womb. To enter the centre and re-emerge symbolises rebirth. Many experts believe that early Christians and ancient Greeks held that the labyrinth's pathway to the centre represented the arduous road to salvation or liberation.

Labyrinths have been found throughout the world. Even though very early civilisations were isolated from one another, there is a remarkable similarity in their labyrinth designs. For thousands of years the same designs appeared again and again, apparently filling an archetypal need. It is thought that these designs were based on spiral patterns found in nature. Some researchers believe that in medieval times parishioners and pilgrims walked on labyrinths without shoes to absorb sacred energy through the soles of their feet.

Although not everyone can create a labyrinth to walk on in their home or garden, having even a small representation of one can provide a powerful symbol that reaches straight into the psyche. The labyrinth is an archetype, a divine imprint which conveys ancient power regardless of the form or size of the representation. It is a subliminal message which activates subconscious memories of ancient times, a symbol of the winding pathway to the Creator.

Labyrinth designs can be incorporated into wall hangings, decorative table tops, necklace designs, or as a small finger pathway carved into wood or stone for use as a spiritual tool. Labyrinths displayed in the home allow an ancient mystical tradition to be imprinted into your

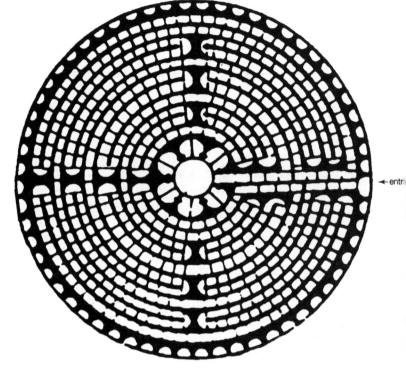

← entr

Take a chopstick or wooden skewer and trace this labyrinth. You can also make an enlarged photocopy of this page to colour and frame for display in your home. A copy can also be placed on a desk or coffee table for tracing the sacred path with your finger.

CHARTRES/GRACE CATHEDRAL LABYRINTH

subconscious. You can 'walk the sacred path' by tracing a tiny labyrinth with your finger. As you do this, think of the labyrinth as a metaphor for the journey in life back to the source. The turns in the path represent the various convolutions and changes in your life, yet the path always takes you to the centre.

As you 'walk the sacred path' with your finger, enter into a meditative state and observe the emotions, memories and insights that come up for you. Let go. Surrender to the path. Sometimes great insights can occur. But even if your journey seems uneventful, the tracing can be like a dream that you don't remember but which nevertheless allows for greater balance during your waking day. When you reach the centre of the labyrinth, take the time to be still and open. The journey back from the centre allows you to connect to that which is holy in your everyday life. Whether you walk or trace a labyrinth, or simply have a replica of one on the wall of your home or workplace, it is a powerful archetype providing you with a direct connection to the profound and the sacred in your life.

Divine Proportion

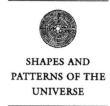
Ancient people recognised that there was a natural harmony and balance in the world around them. They used myth and religion to gain understanding of this natural order. Today we primarily turn to science and mathematics to explain the universe around us. This shift from an intuitive, instinctual approach to a rational, intellectual one occurred gradually. However, standing tall at the crossroads between these two forces was a remarkable man.

Pythagoras was an extraordinary Greek philosopher and mathematician who lived in the sixth century BC. He postulated mathematical theorems that are still taught today, but he also promoted understanding of the sacred significance of numbers and mathematics. To Pythagoras, every number had a sacred component that could be understood though meditation and contemplation. He felt that an understanding of the divine meaning of mathematics gave one a mystical understanding of the entire cosmos. One of Pythagoras' mathematical theories has great relevance for home design. He believed that in nature there is an organic harmony that can be expressed through numbers and proportions, *and that these proportions can be utilised for the design of a home or building.* Using the principles of his theory of Divine Proportion can instantly shift the energy in a home from a place which somehow just doesn't feel right to one where everything seems right in the world.

Proportions are created by ratios (the word *rational* originally meant the ability to comprehend 'ratios'). A ratio is a comparison between two different sizes or qualities. It measures differences between objects or ideas. Proportions create a basis for aesthetics, allowing for a balance in composition that elicits a feeling of wholeness and unity with all of life.

Pythagoras promoted a particular ratio that he felt was ideal for the welfare of human beings. He called it the Golden Mean (meaning the middle way), the Golden Section, or the Golden Rectangle. This magical proportion is also sometimes called the Divine Proportion because it can bring you closer to the sacred order of the universe. Although other ancient architects in cultures throughout the world had already discovered this magical ratio, it was Pythagoras who elevated it to a transcendental standard. This proportion is very pleasing to look at and occurs everywhere in nature. One example can be found in the nautilus shell, where each section is identical in shape to the one adjacent to it. While they differ in size, all sections have the same proportions, and all spiral out of the sacred centre. Each chamber generates the space for the next chamber, creating the mystic spiral. The Golden Section also relates to the proportions of the human body. Leonardo da Vinci's famous drawing (see illustration below) which correlated the human body with geometry dimensions is an example of this.

Ancient architects observed nature and discovered the Divine Proportion. They realised that it was a proportion that was pleasing to the human spirit. People generally like traditional building designs. This is partly because traditional architecture is often based on ancient building styles, which in turn were based on the Golden Mean. This proportion can be found in ancient buildings throughout the world. The Pyramid of Cheops corresponds to Golden Mean proportions. The floor of the King's Chamber in the Great Pyramid is an exact perfect Golden Mean. Greek temples such as the Parthenon on the Acropolis at Athens correspond to the Golden Mean. Divine Proportions are also found in the stunning Taj Mahal. Cathedrals and shrines in France from the tenth century onward were created using the Golden Mean in order to create an atmosphere that could provide worshippers with transcendental experiences.

The ratio of this classical proportion is 1:1.618, but you don't need to excel at maths to use the Golden Mean in your home. It is a tool accessible to anyone, because when an environment is in Divine Proportion it 'feels right'. (See the method for determining Divine Proportion on the next page.) You can use the Golden Mean for arranging the furniture in a room, when deciding where to hang a picture, or for designing your garden or landscaping.

Nautilus shell: it's outwardly spiralling shape illustrates the Golden Mean

Leonardo da Vinci's drawing of the human body that correlates the human body with Divine Proportion

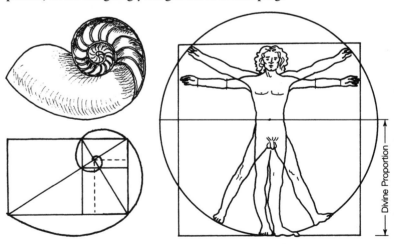

Divine Proportion

Changes in the placement of furnishings and plants create the feeling of a room with Divine Proportions.

It is easy to use this ratio in your own home. Carmen and her husband moved into a house with a long narrow living room. She said that every time she entered this room, she felt squeezed and constricted by its proportions. The sense of unease they felt in the room was so intense that she and her husband spent hardly any time there. Utilising the principles of the Golden Section, I showed them where the natural proportion in the room lay. I suggested moving furniture to emphasise this natural division, and also using colour, a moulding, or even a pillar, to divide the room. They decided to paint the Divine section of the

Discovering the Divine Proportion in Your Home

Measure the width of a room. Then multiply this width by 1.618 to find out the perfect length. For example, if a room has a 12 foot width, multiply 12 by 1.618 to obtain the perfect length of 19.416 feet (which is approximately 19½ feet). You do not need to have an exact measurement, down to the centimetre, for a room to be in divine proportion. You can have an approximate measurement, close to the Divine Proportion, and it will still feel good.

```
12.000 feet
x1.618
─────────
 19.42 feet
```

Multiply the width by 1.618 to find the perfect length.

12 feet

19.42 feet

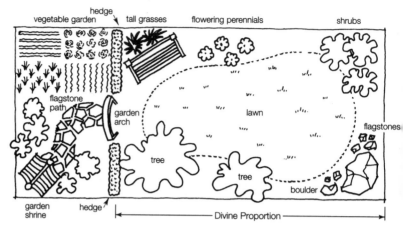

hedge
vegetable garden   tall grasses   flowering perennials   shrubs
flagstone path
garden arch
lawn
flagstones
tree
tree
boulder
garden shrine   hedge
Divine Proportion

This garden has been landscaped using the principles of Divine Proportion.

room a different colour, to add mouldings and to use furnishings to further emphasise the division. The end result was a room that 'felt great', one where they enjoyed spending time together.

When arranging a room it is not uncommon to find that, without having done any measurements or calculations, you have naturally placed objects in accordance with the Golden Mean. This is because these proportions *feel* right. However, as with all design concerns in your home or workplace, remember the bottom line is always: 'does it feel good?'

Proportions in your garden

You can also use the Golden Mean to determine the layout of a garden. For example, if you have a long narrow area, you can determine the Golden Mean ratios and then plant hedges or flower beds to create the feeling of harmonious proportions. You can even have a series of Golden Rectangles in your garden. Archways, paths, fences and gates can all be employed with the principles of the Golden Mean, thus creating a deeper opportunity for transformative experiences within your garden.

The Golden Mean and the pentagram

The Golden Mean has an intimate connection to the mathematical configurations of the spiral and the five-pointed star (or pentagram) which is considered to be a symbol for life. In nature, plants bearing food edible for humans usually have five-petalled flowers.[2] Although any kind of fresh flower in a home will instantly uplift the energy, if you desire to implement the power of the Divine Proportion, you might consider putting five-petalled flowers such as the rose – which has concentric layers of five petals – in your home occasionally.

When you have symbolic representations of the Divine Proportion in your home, or when the ratios in your home conform to this ancient principle, you will begin to notice a deep harmony extending into all aspects of your life. The Golden Section can powerfully, even mystically, deepen your connection and alignment with the natural forces of the world. Thus you will feel stronger and more balanced.

Activating the Divine Proportion

- Position furnishings in your home and garden to conform to this proportion.
- Place a chambered nautilus on display in your home.
- Buy or make a frame for a mirror or painting that is in Divine Proportion.
- Put five-petalled flowers (either real or artificial) in your home or office, e.g., roses, or flowers of edible fruit, such as apple blossoms.

Both feng shui and architecture are based on rules and guidelines, but these rules were established by human beings following their instincts about what felt best to them. The use of the Golden Mean will almost always greatly improve an environment. However, it is important to remember to continue to use your intuition. In other words, even if you have used the Golden Mean, if it doesn't feel good, it's not good feng shui.

MANDALAS

One of the most extraordinary experiences that I have ever had in my life involved a mandala. When I was twenty years old, I lived in a Zen Buddhist monastery. It was a wonderful time in my life. The creases in my soul, caused by a traumatic and violent childhood, smoothed out as I sat facing a wall and meditating for up to sixteen hours a day. I experienced such deep peace just sitting quietly in the lotus position, watching the shadow of a leaf slowly slip across the wall. I loved the simplicity of Zen Buddhism and the serene starkness of the zendo (monastery). My life was simple but very fulfilling.

One sunny afternoon I was in my quarters when I heard a small crackling sound. I turned around and saw what looked like a three-dimensional frame floating in the air about five feet in front of me. It was a square approximately two feet square, and four inches deep. Geometric patterns shifted and moved inside it, while red flames danced on its surface. Though rather frightened by this appearance, I stepped forward for a closer look, and it instantly disappeared. I was incredulous. It was not my imagination: I was wide awake in the middle of a sunny day. I went to the Zen master to ask him about what I had seen. He said, 'It is just *makyo*. Ignore it.' (*Makyo* refers to the visions which appear to some Zen students.)

I couldn't forget what I had seen, so I went to talk to a therapist about it. This therapist, who had trained as a Jungian analyst, said quite simply, 'Oh, what you saw was a mandala.' I hadn't heard of mandalas before, so the therapist explained that I wasn't crazy, that other people had similar experiences, and that the mandala appearing before me was a portent of integration and wholeness. He explained that a mandala (which means 'circle' in Sanskrit) is usually created in the form of a circle or square and contains geometric forms surrounding a central point. Sometimes sacred paintings surround the mandala or are contained within it.

The therapist said that mandalas represent the whole self and the entire universe, and were often used as a visual aid in meditations and religious ceremonies. He told me that Carl Jung had considered the spontaneous appearance of a mandala to be a symbol of healing and transformation. I have come to believe that not only is the mandala the symbol of healing, it is, in fact, a *catalyst* for healing, and that having a

The mandala has long been thought to be a sacred circle of transformation, healing and unity with the creator. Meditation upon the mandala activates these qualities in one's life.

Native American mandala

Tibetan mandala

Sri Yantra mandala

mandala in your home brings an energy of wholeness and integration into your life.

To understand the potential power of mandalas in your home or workplace, it is valuable to learn some of the history of this remarkable tool. Carl Jung wasn't the first person to discover the virtues of the mandala. People have been creating mandalas for 20,000 years. The most widely known mandalas are from Tibet. Tibetan Buddhists have always used mandalas as part of their spiritual practice. The patterns within the Tibetan mandala are thought to portray subtle frequencies that, when meditated upon, allow for supreme realisation and enlightenment. Like the labyrinth, they can represent the spiritual pathway from the material world to the spiritual realm. There are usually four gates into the mandala, which represent the four cardinal directions. (See Chapter 12). Each gate leads into the centre, which represents the Infinite Centre.

In Eastern tradition the most sacred sound is Aum (Om). This Sanskrit word has a vibration intonation that is said to be the sound of all creation, a sound that can carry one to ultimate transformation. The Sri Yantra mandala is a focus for meditation in Tantric Buddhism. Believed to be the visible vibrational equivalent of Aum, it is a very powerful mandala to have on display in a home. It is a constant visual activation of the primal sound of the universe. Having this most holy symbol in your living space radiates a sacred energy into your home.

The Native American form of the mandala is called the Medicine Wheel. The Medicine Wheel is a visual representation of all the cycles of the natural world – birth, death and rebirth, the seasons, day and night, the waxing moon and waning moon. The centre of the Medicine Wheel represents the Creator and the creative forces of the universe. Earth-based cultures throughout the world have employed the mandala in their spiritual practices.

Creating a mandala

The creation of a mandala for your home can tap directly into the inner-most workings of your psyche and can help you activate the wisdom that dwells within you. Creating a mandala can also bring forgotten or repressed memories to the surface so that healing can occur. There are a number of ways you can make a home mandala. You might choose to make a sand-tray mandala which is constantly in a state of change and transformation. This mandala can be kept on a coffee table, shelf or corner table. It can be one that is used by other household members or it can be the private mandala of one person only. Guests also usually love the opportunity to create their own mandalas in the sand.

Drawing a Mandala

Materials

- Compass

  If you haven't got a compass, obtain various sizes of circular objects around which to draw circles of varying sizes.

- Protractor

  You only need this if you are going to make precise geometrical lines within your mandala.

- Pencil and eraser

  It is often helpful first to draw your design in pencil before colouring it in.

- Colouring tools of your choice.

  Crayons, pastels, oil or acrylic paints can be used.

- Meditative or inspirational music

Line-drawing mandala process

- Start by drawing a large circle.

- Make a dot in the centre of your circle. This dot is the symbol of the Creator and the life-force energies of the universe. It also represents your sacred centre.

- Close your eyes and focus on your home. Notice what colours, images and feelings come up for you as you do this.

- As you draw, stay in a meditative state. Doing this while you are creating your mandala imbues it with energy that will continue to radiate out from it into your home.

- Before you display your mandala in your home, bless it to activate its energy.

Hand-drawn mandala, representing the healing
force of Interior Alignment™ feng shui

Making a Sand-Tray Mandala

Materials

- Tray

  Obtain a round or square tray with a lip around the edge of at least 1–2 inches in height. You may want to decorate the tray or leave it plain. It should be at least 12 inches across, but preferably larger. (A large shallow bowl such as a pasta platter can be used.)

- Sand

  Place sand about halfway up the lip of the tray. (Sand can be purchased at a garden centre or builders' merchants or collected from a beach.)

- Optional

  Stones, crystals, beans, etc., to place around the mandala.

Sand-tray mandala process

- Place yourself in a meditative posture and still your thoughts.
- Slowly allow your fingers to move through the sand, creating swirls or symmetrical designs.
- Watch your emotions and feelings. When you feel a synthesis or the mandala just 'feels right', you know that you are complete.
- Optional: when your sand mandala is complete, place around it the objects you have chosen.

The sand-tray mandala is an expressive way of calling the mandala energy into your home.

You can create a home mandala for a specific purpose. For example, you can create a healing mandala, or make one dedicated to abundance, prosperity and flow in the home. Using mandalas in the home is one of the fastest and most potent ways to activate life-force vitality and energy into a living environment.

FRACTALS

One aspect of geometry that can impart vitality into our home environments are fractals, organic patterns created by the movements – the 'chaos' – within nature. Fractals signify a type of geometry that focuses on dynamic interactive movements within nature. They define the rough, raw vital life force of the world. The way a tree branches and roots, the way a river twists and turns, the pattern of veins on a leaf, the way a boulder tumbles down a hill, even the way the blood vessels in your body branch and branch again: these are all examples of fractal movement.

Although so much in nature seems totally random, there is an underlying order in the chaos of nature. The weather is a good example of this mysterious, yet ordered, phenomenon of fractals. It is unpredictable, yet it adheres to subtle and numerous shifting energy fields. The interrelationship between these kinds of systems is so subtle that the movement of an electron at one end of the universe will have an actual effect on the other end of the cosmos.[3]

The science of fractals creates a context for understanding the dynamic gyrations of nature. Within the seeming tangle of systems emerging and disintegrating within nature, there is a kind of untamed predictability of wildly divergent natural systems. Each system interfaces and fluctuates with all the other systems. The leaves of the maple tree flutter in a random pattern of reds, oranges and yellows to the earth, where the wind whirls and tumbles them into the stream that twists and turns and eddies in tiny swirls to the sea. All systems from the smallest stone to the tallest redwood to a frothing river are constantly interacting in a great drama of holistic interconnection.

There are two kinds of fractals: regular and random. *Regular fractals*, also called 'geometric fractals', consist of large structures that are made up of smaller, yet identical, structures. For example, a fern has a small section that is a duplicate of a larger, and then larger, section. (See opposite.) This quality is called *self-similarity,* meaning that if you peer deeply into the structure of something you will see self-repeating patterns – images of 'self' on a smaller and smaller scale. In *random fractals*, large-scale and small-scale structures are mathematically related, but differ in detail. Examples of this might be a lightning bolt as it flashes across the night sky, or a river and its rivulets and streams.

If you spend time in nature you are constantly surrounded by fractals. They are the signature of the dynamic interplay in nature that renews and regenerates the world. Surrounded by the natural world, your body and soul are constantly being renewed by the liberating chaos in nature. However, if you are isolated from these natural forces, the soul begins to dwindle. I believe it is essential to surround ourselves with fractals, either in symbolic representations or with actual objects from nature.

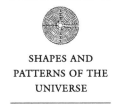

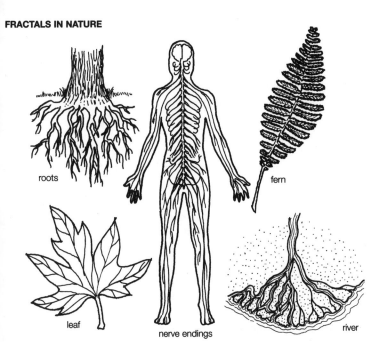

roots

fern

leaf

nerve endings

river

Living plants, or photos of plants and trees, are an easy way to activate the power of fractals into your home. Plants exemplify the fractal process through the way the leaves grow around the stem and the veining of their leaves. Having natural objects around you that contain fractal geometry helps activate your life force, subliminally yet powerfully.

Another way to bring these forms into your environment is through art. Some modern art contains unintentional fractal geometry. Psychiatrist Lewis Wolberg, noting the way that many artists subconsciously create fractal patterns in their work, said that artists 'may be responding to the same interacting processes that operate in all of creation. As Emerson expressed it in his essay *Nature*: "Compound it how she will, star, sand, fire, water. tree, man, it is still one stuff, and betrays the same properties." '[4] You can even create your own fractal art by obtaining a fractal program for your computer.

SPIRALS

The swirling movement of rotating down to a centre point and then spiralling back again has fascinated humanity from the most primitive times. In every ancient culture the spiral, which is the natural form of

growth and movement, has been man's symbol of the journey to eternal life. The spiral shape was used as a mystic symbol of the soul's quest for liberation. It represented the path winding down into the centre of the Divine.

The spiral is the most ancient and sacred symbol for humankind. In sites around the world spirals have attracted the attention of anthropologists. Drawings of double spirals were carved with care into caves by Stone Age peoples who must have understood the inherent power of the spiral. Although no one is exactly sure of their exact historical meaning, they are thought to be associated with the Great Mother Goddess, the source of all life. Spirals as sacred symbols have been discovered in cultures throughout the world – from ancient stone swirls in Europe, to Islamic arabesque designs, to the interlocking spirals of the Chinese yin yang symbol. They have appeared in sacred art on rock carvings, earth drawings, in various forms in temples and cathedrals, and on pottery, coins, seals, and mosaics.

The spiral has also been associated with the Great Wheel of Life, symbolic of the ever-changing cycles within nature – all of which are represented by and contained in the mystical energy of the spiral. In Cabbalistic tradition the soul spiralled down the Tree of Life to assume a physical presence at the time of birth. It was thought that at death the action was reversed as the soul spiralled upwards again.

The spiral symbol appears in science and nature as well as in sacred art. It describes the spinning of the universe, the revolving movements of the stars and the cosmos. The movement of water, whirlwinds and tornadoes, and even the tiniest spirals of DNA within the nucleus of the cell, all conform to the vortical laws of the spiral.

**SPIRALS IN
NATURE
AND ART**

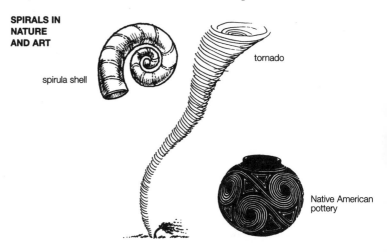

spirula shell

tornado

Native American
pottery

The spiralling vortex not only rules life from the galactic level to the subatomic, it also reflects *and even dictates* consciousness. The spiral can stimulate spiritual attunement. For these reasons it is very valuable to place drawings, paintings or photos of this remarkable symbol in auspicious places in your home or workplace.

It is interesting to note that in every doctor's office hangs a medical diploma that includes a spiral created by the caduceus with its two intertwined serpents. This ancient symbol of healing continually radiates the spiral energy throughout the doctor's office, and on a subtle level may contribute to healings. There are many forms of spirals that you can put in the home. Placing a picture or painting of the Chinese yin/yang symbol, which is a flat spiral, can help invoke the spiralling energy. Any type of spiral in the home echoes and invokes the cosmic rhythms of creation.

Activating the Patterns of Nature

Geometry
- Place in the home objects from nature that display geometric forms, such as shells, crystals, ferns, plants, leaves, etc.
- Bring photos or paintings of scenes from nature (all nature contains geometric forms).

Labyrinths
- Place paintings, pictures, photos of labyrinths on the wall, shelf, floor or home altar.

Mandalas
- Create a mandala for display in your home.
- Put paintings, pictures, photos of traditional mandalas on the wall, shelf, floor or altar.
- Make a coffee table sand-tray for geometric designs.

Divine Proportion
- Landscape your garden using Divine Proportion.
- Have a framed mirror or photo that conforms to Divine Proportion.
- Organise the furnishing in your home according to Divine Proportion.

Fractals
- Get a kaleidoscope – either one that reflects nature or one that tosses and turns coloured bits – and use periodically.
- Place fractal art or living plants in the home.
- Place pictures or photos of fractals in nature.

Spirals
- Have pictures of spiralling objects on display.
- Feature plants with a spiralling leaf formation.

SHAPES AND
PATTERNS OF THE
UNIVERSE

What is fascinating about the patterned nature of the universe is that you can find these formations in every aspect of life, and in the four elements that comprise the substance of our world: Air, Water, Fire and Earth. For the Native American, the elements not only represent the *real* air, water, fire and earth, but they are also four conditions of matter. Air refers to all gases, Water to all fluids, Fire to all radiant and electrical phenomena, and Earth to all solids. They also represent principles of life: Air represents *movement*, Water represents *fluidity*, Fire represents *transmutation*, and Earth represents *stability*. The next four chapters contain information about these four dynamic natural forces that comprise our world and how you can active their energy into your home.

9

The Spirit of Air

IT WAS a cold, dreary December. One grey day followed another, each filled with the kind of chill that seeps through your skin and into your bones. My husband, daughter and I were all sick with a particularly virulent flu virus. Every night on the news there were reports of the numbers of people who had been hospitalised in what had become a flu epidemic. Because we were too ill to go shopping for groceries, neighbours left food for us at the far end of our porch. They were afraid to come any closer because of the highly contagious nature of the flu strain. One night I heard the sound of Christmas carollers. I pulled open the blinds and watched as the group strolled, singing, down the pavement.

It was so dark outside they were barely visible. Although their voices weren't unusually loud, their singing seemed to rise and swell through the air, vibrating into the walls and windows of our home. At first, the subtle vibrations seemed tenuous, and then I felt a harmonious wave of energy flow through our home and everything within it. Wave after wave followed, each stronger than the one before.

It seemed that the sound of the voices had entered the unhealthy rhythms of our home and harmonised them. I knew something magical and wondrous had occurred. When I walked around our home, it felt different. The singing had changed the energy. That night we all slept soundly, and when we woke in the morning we felt refreshed and on the road to recovery.

AIR: A UNIFYING FORCE IN THE WORLD

Air is sound. Air is oxygen. Air is life. With every breath you take, you are inhaling air that has been in every nook and cranny of our world, from the dry region of the Sahara, to the peaks of the Himalayas, to the lush and humid Amazon rainforests. According to Harvard astronomer Harlow Shapely, our atmosphere contains argon atoms which disperse so rapidly around the world that a breath you take now will contain at least fifteen of the *exact same argon atoms* you breathed one year ago.[1]

The breath that you just took contained at least 400,000 of the same argon atoms that Ghandi breathed throughout his life. Shakespeare inhaled some of same atoms that you just breathed, as did Plato, Eric the Red and Geronimo. The air that you are breathing now has been in me, and the breath that I am taking now has been in you. Thus aligning to the Spirit of Air is a powerful way to connect deeply with the world.

AERIAL VORTICES: SPIRIT OF AIR

Imagine a spring breeze flowing through the forest. As it blows over every leaf, every blade of grass and every pine needle it creates small delicate vortex trailers. The pine needle separates the air momentarily and when it reunites behind the needle it swirls and eddies in tiny vortices. Since this remarkable phenomenon occurs behind every bird, butterfly and flying insect, the entire forest is filled with invisible spirals of energy. Even the most delicate feelers on the tiniest insect are creating swirling, spiralling circles of energy.[2] In addition, temperature variation in the forest causes the air to spiral up or down. This, combined with the wavelike vibrations of sound from the birds and animals, creates an immense ebbing and flowing harmonic energy field that swirls and dances in geometric patterns throughout the forest. Infused in this great dance is the life force Spirit of Air.

There are many ways to activate the Spirit of Air in your home. Open a window, breathe deeply and say (silently or aloud), 'Welcome, Air Spirits, into my home.' This simple act will expand your awareness of this element and invite it into your life. Wind chimes, mobiles, flags and banners all acknowledge and call the Air Spirits. You can also improve the quality of the air in your home by changing the air filters on your heating system. You might want to use an air-purification system if you live in an area with air pollution.[3]

One of the most direct and powerful ways to connect with the

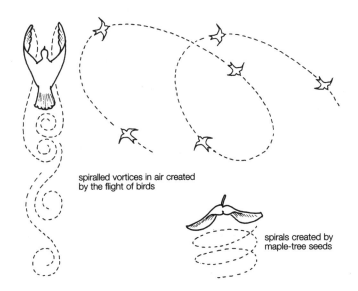

spiralled vortices in air created
by the flight of birds

spirals created by
maple-tree seeds

Spirit of Air is through the winds which are continually blowing across our planet. When you go out of doors, notice the movement of air across your skin. Whether it is the subtlest breeze or the powerful wind of a storm, currents of air always bring freshness and a sense of vitality with them. The Cherokee people and many other Native American tribes believed that the winds were messengers sent by the powers of the four directions, and that they carried information from the sacred realms. Listen to the wind when you leave your house in the morning. See what messages it might have for you. Smell the air and sense where it has been. Open your windows and let the wind blow through your home. It will quickly clear out any stagnant energy and leave the air cleansed and full of the energy of nature.

Creating a 'Wind-Catcher'

A wind-catcher is a symbolic tool you can use to activate the Spirit of Air into your home. To make one, simply take some feathers and wrap their quills with twine, cotton thread or strips of leather. (The feathers symbolise the energy of air.) Attach these so that they hang freely from a piece of driftwood or circle of twigs. You can include beads, moss, ribbons, or whatever evokes the Spirit of Air for you. Once you have completed your wind-catcher, attach a cord to suspend it from and then hang it in a protected area outdoors or inside your home.

wind-catcher

SOUND: ACOUSTIC FENG SHUI

Another highly effective way to activate the Spirit of Air in your home is through the use of sound, which has also been called 'acoustic feng shui'. Frequencies on the sonic spectrum can pass through water and solid matter as well as air, but we usually think of sound as a phenomenon primarily associated with the air element.

Feng shui is the study of the physical structures we occupy and how they relate to the greater forces of the universe. However, the sounds in our environment affect us just as deeply as the physical structures of our dwellings. Even sounds that occur in your home *when you are not there* will profoundly affect its environment.

We are constantly surrounded by sound. Some sounds are disruptive, such as road works or low-flying aeroplanes. Other environmental noises are pleasant and soothing, like the peel of distant church bells or the songs of birds in your garden. And there are sounds that we create in our environments, as when we walk, talk, cry or laugh. We are also influenced by the 'sound quality' within our homes, which is the way that noise reverberates there. And all of these sound fields interact in a way that will either enhance or diminish your personal energy.

You can transform the energy in your home by learning about sound and also learning how to draw empowering sounds into your environment. Sound travels in waves, similar to the way that water travels in waves when a pebble is dropped into a still pool. The human ear can only perceive sounds that occur within a very narrow range of frequencies. Other species have a much wider range of hearing than we do, and the sound spectrum continues far beyond their capabilities as well. But *whether or not the sound around us is audible or inaudible, it none the less exerts an influence on us.* In addition to perceiving sound with our ears, we also physically conduct it through our bones. Sound reverberates throughout the entire body. It has been suggested that we 'hear' vibrations from the earth through our body, which acts as a conductor.

The sounds and music in your house can have a dramatic effect on its overall feng shui. Some sounds produce a fractaloid melodic structure whose impact on us is like that of sacred geometry. Some sounds function as a stimulus that penetrates into rigid objects in your home or workplace so an amazing reorganisation of their energy fields can occur. Other tones have the effect of harmonising and unifying discordant energy. Carefully considering the sounds you have in your home can make a dramatic impact on the energy fields that surround you. *Sound can change the vibrational frequency of your home.*

Pythagoras and sound

One of the first known evaluations of sound was made by Pythagoras in ancient Greece. He postulated that the universe was created by an intelligent life force that expressed itself through a mathematically perfect system. He believed that these numbers could be expressed through sound, and that there was a musical harmony to the world and the planets, which he called the music of the spheres: a symphony of the universe.

Cymatics: the sacred patterns of sound

The ancient theories of Pythagoras are echoed in present-day sound research. One exciting area that has great significance for the energy of homes is the field of cymatics, research into which was spearheaded by the Swiss physician Dr Hans Jenny, who was inspired by the renowned visionary Rudolph Steiner. Dr Jenny's work reveals that static powders, on a drum-like membrane, form amazing geometric configurations when they are exposed to a variety of sounds. The shapes that the powder takes are determined by the sound it is exposed to. They are similar to geometric forms found in nature. Many of them are very beautiful and remind me of ancient mandalas.

Some sounds produce flowing shapes, such as a circulating figure-of-eight pattern. Some tones cause clockwise movement, while others result in anticlockwise flow. By changing the frequency and amplitude of the tones, Dr Jenny was able to cause material to transform from one symmetrical shape into chaos and then again into another geometric structure. This fluctuation between chaos and structure is an echo of the physical dynamics governing the universe.

This research is very important because it reveals the power of sound on our homes and lives. Different sounds produce different effects on the structures which surround us. Some sounds in your home can strengthen you and some can weaken you, *even long past the time that the sound has been heard.* This is because sound creates geometric patterns in matter that last long after the sound has died.

HEALING WITH SOUND

Sound waves travel through physical form. The sounds in your home pass through the walls and objects within it. Whenever sound enters the objects in your home, it subtly rearranges their energy fields. Usually we don't notice the differences caused because they are so

subtle. However, there are many times when the energy imprint left by music or other sounds will last long after the sound has faded into silence.

One example of the way that sound actually changes the structure of physical objects can be seen with old violins. Over time the musical vibrations created by playing a violin will alter the molecules in the wood of the instrument itself. When a violin is played by a virtuoso, it becomes ingrained with the beauty of the inspired playing. This is why old violins that have been owned and played by masters are so valuable. Their worth lies not only in the quality of the instruments, but also in the energy imprint left by the exquisite music that has been played upon them. Accomplished violinists do not usually like their instruments to be played by less skilled players, because the structure of the violin becomes aligned with discordant tones. The wood in your home is equally susceptible to sound imprinting. Sounds that occur in your home can be embedded as physical imprints in the molecules of the wooden walls and furniture within it, so if you have a wooden house you should be especiallly conscious of the sounds.

Another example of the effects of sound on the environment can be seen in research on the effects of music on plants. In the 1960s, a woman named Dorothy Retallack performed experiments in which various plants were exposed to different types of music. Plants that were continually exposed to acid rock music were stunted and sparse when compared with control plants. On the other hand, plants thrived when exposed to Bach choral preludes, Indian ragas and the music of Duke Ellington and Louis Armstrong.[4]

Retallack's experiments were based on the earlier work of two botanists, T. C. Singh, head of the botanical department at Annamalai University in India, and George E. Smith, a botanist in Illinois. When Singh exposed plants to violin music and Indian ragas, he found that these harmonic sounds increased both their rate of growth and their productivity. When he applied his findings to rice paddies in India, he found that playing ragas over the fields increased their yield from 25 to 67 per cent as compared with that of silent fields. George Smith planted crops of soya beans and corn in a greenhouse where he played Gershwin's *Rhapsody in Blue* continually. These crops sprouted faster and developed better than those grown under identical conditions without the music.[5]

These studies all confirm that the sound environment in your home is a very important factor affecting your health and wellbeing. It is essential to balance and heal the sound energy in your home so that it will nurture and sustain you.

Singing bowls

One magical method you can use to do this is to create 'sound mandalas' with singing bowls. Singing bowls are bowl-shaped instruments which are played by running a mallet around their inner or outer rim. This creates a ringing tone that builds in density and volume. These instruments are usually made of metal and come from Tibet or Nepal. The methods used to combine the metals and fashion these bowls remain secret, but the deep resonance and sound mandalas created by playing them are astounding. As you circle the bowl with your mallet, you will be generating incredible geometric sound-shapes that will imprint on the walls, ceiling and floor of your space long after the sound has faded away. Sometimes this energy imprint will last for months and even years, depending on the intensity of the focus of the individual who was playing the bowl.

Some singing bowls are made by spinning silicon into crystal-glass bowls. Silicon is the base component of quartz crystal. Generating sound through quartz crystal creates radiant sound mandalas of pristine clarity. These sound forms penetrate an environment with the intensity of a laser beam. Vivid waves of energy in precise geometric shapes fill a space when using these remarkable tools. The crystal of the bowl transmits and magnifies the sound waves produced. The sound seems to waver and resonate in the air for a long time after it has been played.

THE POWER OF BIRD SONG

The songs of birds can have a very special effect on your home environment. Some remarkable properties of these sounds were discovered by a young man named Dan Carlson after he witnessed a terrible event that changed the course of his life.

In 1960 Dan was a young army recruit in the demilitarised zone between North and South Korea. Nothing that he had experienced had prepared him for the tragedies of war. Every day images of a war-torn country were seared into his soul. One freezing winter day, Dan watched in horror as a Korean mother threw her four-year-old son under the wheel of a moving lorry, crushing the child's legs. It happened so quickly that there was nothing the young man could do. When the doctor arrived, the grief-stricken young woman explained that her family was starving. She had felt forced to cripple her son so that he could beg for food to support him and her two other children.[6]

Dan was devastated. Out of the horror of this event, there arose

within him a conviction to devote the rest of his life to eliminating starvation in the world. He determined to find a way to grow food inexpensively on even the poorest soil.

After returning home, Dan enrolled in an agricultural programme at the University of Minnesota, where he did research on plants. He theorised that a plant could survive in poor soil by taking in additional nourishment through small openings in the leaves called 'stomata'. Plants normally open these stomata to absorb moisture and exchange gases, and the success of Dan's plan depended on finding a way to get them to open their stomata when the fertiliser was applied.[7]

After trying out a number of approaches, Dan finally discovered that the stomata would open in response to certain frequencies and harmonics of sound. Curiously, these sounds turned out to be very similar to the chirping sounds of birds. This discovery was profoundly significant because it revealed that birds' songs were not only related to establishing their territorial boundaries, as had been thought, but were also *intimately linked to the mysteries of plant growth and seed germination*. In other words, bird songs increase the health and vibrancy of plants![8]

Dan Carlson's methods are being used today in farms around the world, with remarkable results. In one orange grove in Florida, trees were sprayed with liquid nutrients at the same time that birdlike sonic tones were played throughout the grove. The oranges from these trees were not only sweeter, but also had 121 per cent more vitamin C that the surrounding orange trees. In Pennsylvania a dairyman reported that when his cows were fed with sonically grown alfalfa, their milk production increased by 7 per cent *even though the cows were eating 25 per cent less food*. A farming association in Pakistan reported that after using Carlson's methods the yields of their potato and corn crops increased by 150 per cent and 85 per cent respectively.[9]

Research into the effects of bird song on plants is also relevant for our species, because from the earliest periods of our history humans have usually lived where they could hear the sound of birds. Since bird song is beneficial for plant health, it is probably so for the wellbeing of humans too. Listening to birds can have a soothing and centring effect in your life. It will link you to the world of nature that surrounds you.

If you do not have bird songs outside your window, there are wonderful recordings of bird songs on tape and compact discs. I believe that playing these by themselves or in combination with music can create a wonderful healing energy in your home. When I put on a tape of bird songs in one of my seminars, everyone can feel a difference in the room almost instantly. People relax and breathe more deeply. When deciding what kind of bird songs to play in your environment, whenever possible choose ones that are indigenous to your area or to your ancestral lands.

Bringing in nature sounds

Playing nature sounds in your home will powerfully activate the spirit of nature there. Doing this is especially helpful if you don't live in an area surrounded by nature. *Simply hearing these natural sounds can have an immediate and positive effect on you and your home energy.* There are so many recordings of nature to choose from on tape or compact discs. These sounds immerse you in a realm, for example, where the sea pounds against the shore and sea gulls cry plaintively. A recording of a mountain stream against the backdrop of bird song and droning insects can instantly create the feeling of a spring morning in the mountains where the air is fresh and clean, and life seems full of possibility.

Research has shown that when people listen to nature sounds their blood pressure goes down and their heart rate slows. Many find that they have more energy and are more creative when they listen to all kinds of sounds from nature. These sounds create great organic 'sound shapes' that can imprint the healing forces of nature on your home or workplace. When using recorded nature sounds, it is important to make sure the recording was made using actual sounds from nature, because synthetic sounds will not produce the same magical effects on the energy of your environment.

SING A SONG

The human voice is a powerful tool for balancing energy. The resonant qualities of singing and chanting can penetrate the most stagnant energy and instantly cleanse and uplift the atmosphere of a home. So when you are thinking about how to create a positive sound environment, be sure to consider the option of using your voice.

Children often sing to themselves. Sometimes they sing songs they have learned; other times they sing little songs they make up themselves. This spontaneous and natural activity combines the power of vibration with the power of self-expression. It is a very effective way of attuning both your own body and the space around you. The sound waves of your voice will resound between your walls to immediately create vibrational harmonies in the objects around you as well as the spaces within you.

In France there is a beautiful Benedictine monastery which has been famous for the chanting of its monks for hundreds of years. During the 1960s it was decided that the practice of chanting should be replaced with more productive, practical activities. However, this change in routine resulted in a remarkable decrease in the overall health of the monks. While previously they had felt well with only three or four hours of sleep per night, without their regular chanting they complained of feeling tired and they became sick easily. These symptoms did not decrease even when their sleep was increased and their diet was adjusted. It was not until after the daily practice of chanting was reinstated that the good health of the monks returned. The famous French physician Alfred Tomatis concluded that the resonant frequencies of the chanting stimulated the electrical potential of the monks' brains. Therefore this was an important source of energy for them, and without it they became ill.[10]

The practice of chanting has been used by shamans around the world to shift and transform energy. In a similar way you can use your voice, combined with visualisation of a symbol, to implant energy into your home. For example, while singing or chanting, you might visualise a rose (a symbol of love) to bring more love into your home. This process is very powerful and can be done with any combination of sounds and symbols. For example, if you chant the Sanskrit Om (aum), visualise the Om symbol at the same time as you focus your attention on a particular wall or object in the room, then the sound will implant the sacred symbol in the area of your focus. The energy from this 'planting' will continue to resonate for a very long time.

Sanskrit symbol 'om' which is the sacred sound of life.

MUSIC: LIFE FORCE FOR THE HOME

Music is the harmonious voice of creation; an echo of the invisible world; one note of a divine concord which the entire universe is destined one day to sound. Mazzini

Very few things can evoke an emotion or feeling more immediately or more powerfully than music. One piece of music can ignite your passion, while another may give you a deep sense of peace. Psychologists call this 'codability' – the ability to *encode* a concept or experience into our memory through music. Musical preferences are very personal. Often we choose to play a particular piece of music in order to evoke a particular state of mind or emotion, or to recreate the memory of an earlier time when we listened to a piece of music. Most people are aware of the power that music has on the emotions. However, there is research suggesting that *music also affects the physical space around you* as well as your inner feelings. There are sounds, rhythms and tones that can directly and positively influence your physical body *and shift the energy in your home.*

Studies have shown that it is the higher frequencies of music that generate the most sonic healing energy. To increase the higher frequencies when you play music, turn down the bass and turn up the treble on your sound system. If you have a graphic equaliser you can also turn down the midrange. Even a few minutes of playing music in this way can have a beneficial effect on you and on the objects in your home. Some individuals find that the music from vinyl records gives a richer, fuller energy than the music created by compact discs because it is not digitised. On a turntable there is an actual vibration creating the music, rather than small units of sound.

Classical and baroque

The music that you play in your home can have a powerful effect on you and the objects, animate and inanimate, in your environment. Classical music is a good choice for any home or office. When J. S. Bach's violin sonatas were broadcast over a field of wheat, the yield increased by 66 per cent and the seeds were larger and heavier.[11] A Japanese sake factory in Ohara plays Mozart to aid the fermentation process: the yeast increases in density by a factor of ten.[12] When monks at a monastery in Brittany played Mozart for their cows they received much more milk in return. It follows that playing classical music in your home or office will have a positive effect on the plants, animals and humans that reside there.

Classical and baroque music is an excellent choice for your office. It has been shown to improve memory retention for some people, particularly when they were learning unfamiliar material, such as foreign languages. It is theorised that the even and orderly rhythms of this music help to create a mental state that is open to learning. The violin concertos of Scarlatti, Bach and Vivaldi, symphonies by Brahms and Beethoven, Handel's *Water Music* and Mozart's *Jupiter Symphony* were all found to be excellent.[13] In the United States, officials at the Department of Immigration play selections of baroque music and Mozart during English classes for immigrants from Cambodia, Laos and other Asian countries because learning dramatically improves.[14]

Mozart is a particularly good choice for your office. Researchers at the University of California documented a positive correlation between listening to Mozart and improved IQ. After they listened to Mozart for ten minutes, students' scores of spatial intelligence went up by eight to nine points. One of the researchers postulated that the complexities of the music stimulated complex neural patterns in the brain.

Gregorian chants

Many generations of monks have used Gregorian chants to deepen their connection to the spiritual aspects of life. The sonorous quality of this type of chanting can feed the soul in a deeply satisfying way. True Gregorian chants are monophonic and without the repetitive rhythms that accompany most music. They have an organic sound that is restful and can synchronise the energy of your home to the deep rhythms of the earth.

Hildegard of Bingen

Hildegard of Bingen was a twelfth-century Benedictine nun. She was also a mystic, composer and artist who was renowned for her extraordinary celestial visions. Hildegard's musical compositions were based on the music she heard during her visions.[15] She discovered geometric forms and light shapes in the music she heard, which she communicated through her music. She wrote, 'Every element has a sound, an original sound from the order of God.' There are currently a number of recordings of her compositions that can bring the mystical power of Hildegard's visions and the splendid *geometric forms* in the music into your home.

Jazz, rap, Latin American

Dr Dee Coulter is the Director of Cognitive Studies at Naropa Institute in Boulder, Colorado. Her specialty is the relationship between musical patterning and neurological development. Dee has found some unique qualities of jazz that put listeners into *theta* brain consciousness, which is the brain wave associated with creativity. She has found this to be particularly true of the music of Miles Davis, John Coltrane, Wynton Marsalis and John Cage.[16]

Dee's research has uncovered some interesting information about other forms of music as well. She believes that rap music is a valuable aid to survival in the inner city, where it evolved, because it sharpens focus on the environment, which in this case can be very chaotic and dangerous. She explains that New Age music often appeals to those who live a structured life with an emphasis on mental activities because it allows them to relax and let go.[17]

> *Observing How Sound Influences Your Home*
>
> Put a piece of music on. Close your eyes and take a few deep breaths. Feel the sound vibrating though you, connecting you to the essence of the music. Now imagine that you can see the colour and energy of the music as it flows throughout your environment. Notice what is occurring in the walls, the objects in the room, the floor and ceiling, and notice how you are being affected by the music. Be aware if the shifts in the room enhance or diminish its energy.

SOUND LEVELS

We are constantly surrounded by sound. I have used a stethoscope to listen to the walls of a home that seemed quiet, only to find a host of sound vibrations moving through the walls. Most people don't think much about the ordinary sounds in their homes. Nevertheless this is a very important factor affecting the way we feel about our environments. Some living spaces are under constant bombardment by sound and, although we get so used to this we don't consciously hear it, it is a constant drain on our energy. According to the American Academy of Otolaryngology ('ear, nose and throat'), over twenty million Americans are regularly exposed to levels of sound that are unsafe. In a study done in New York's public school system, it was discovered that students who lived in areas where they were exposed on a daily basis to the noise of passing trains *were eleven months behind* students not directly exposed to the high noise levels.[18]

> *Reducing Noise Levels in Your Environment*
>
> - Add rugs – hard surfaces magnify sound.
> - Weatherstrip the windows. Thick, foamed-back stripping has the best acoustical qualities – metal or hard plastic stripping keeps out the weather, but not the noise.
> - Hang curtains at the windows instead of, or in addition to, blinds.
> - Move your furniture further away from the source of noise.
> - In an office you can erect sound enclosures to mute unwanted sounds.
> - Invest in an inexpensive sound meter to measure and monitor sound levels. (See Resources at the end of this book.)
> - Use rubber mats under washing machines, blenders and other noisy appliances to lessen the sound produced.
> - Plant trees and leafy shrubs around your house to insulate it from environmental noise.
> - Create a special room or area in your house devoted to quiet.
> - Install soundproof windows.

Playing music on a continual basis is another way to cope with high levels of unwanted noise in your home. This is an effective strategy for creating a positive sound environment, because one of the unique properties of sound is that some sound waves can actually cancel out others. This phenomenon is called 'wave cancellation'. Additionally some sounds will mask other sounds because their frequencies dominate other frequencies to the point where you can hardly hear them. It isn't that the offending sound isn't there (as in wave cancellation), but its qualities are enveloped by the more dominant sound. You can use an understanding of these principles to deal with unpleasant sound in your environment. You will know that you have been successful in your attempts to heal the sound energy of your space when you feel a sense of relaxation and peace surrounding you.

SOUND QUALITY

Every room in your home has a different sound quality. One room might have a subtle echo, while in another room sounds seem muted or muffled. Take the time to go from room to room in your house. Either ring a bell or speak in each room to sense the sound quality there. If you find a place where the sound quality doesn't feel right, then you might try rearranging the objects there to shift the sound quality. Sometimes a simple adjustment, such as putting up a wall hanging or curtain, can greatly improve the sound quality in a room.

AIR FLOW

An essential aspect of the air in your home is your air ventilation. In nature, the air is constantly moving and being regenerated and it is important to recreate this refreshing aspect of nature within our homes. However, many houses today are built without enough ventilation. They may be well insulated to cut down the cost of heating, but what has been lost is adequate air flow through the home. Many people experience a decrease in their overall health as a result. In some cases, to increase the flow of oxygen into these homes mechanical ventilators have been installed, but these don't fully alleviate the problem.

It is valuable to have an adequate movement of fresh air through your home or workplace. This not only helps avoid stuffiness and assists breathing, it has been shown to stimulate the skin. It can also affect the thermal comfort of your home, the ratio of negative to positive ions, electromagnetic radiation, and the flow of air pollutants. *Ideally the air movement in your home should simulate nature, where the flow of air shifts and flows in a variable way.*

Complicated systems that help with air flow in a home are available, but a simple solution is to leave a window slightly open. If this creates too much cold or draughty air, then choose a window away from your major living areas. This will allow fresh air to circulate throughout your home in a natural way. (If you live in a region with high pollution, then this method is not recommended for days when the pollution index is high.)

One way you can ascertain how the air is flowing through your home is to light incense and watch the flow of the smoke. Gentle undulating swirls of smoke usually indicate good air flow. A horizontal, fast-moving flow of air might indicate too much air flow, while a perfectly vertical plume of smoke would probably suggest you need additional air flow.

Calling the spirit of nature with scent

A quick and easy way to immediately activate the forces of nature in your home is with scent. The smell of juniper can transport you to a mountain forest, the scent of lemons can carry you to a Mediterranean citrus grove, and lavender can make you think of an English garden. Smells can also instantly evoke memories of a past experience. The smell of baking bread might remind you of your grandmother's home and the smell of tomatoes may take you to your grandfather's greenhouse. Research has shown that certain essential oils can create mood changes through their effect on brain-wave activity. This would seem to explain why many of the smells in nature are so relaxing. Surrounding yourself

Activating the Forces of Nature through Scent

- Use only natural essential oils or incense.
- Use a diffuser, or put a few drops of scent into a spray bottle to mist your home.
- If possible, choose scents that are indigenous to your area, because these will connect you to your land. For example, if you are from Australia, a wonderful Australian lemon essential oil will potentially have a more potent effect on you than a lemon essence from Spain.
- Try scents from the natural environment of your ancestors. For example, cedar was used by the Cherokee Indians, so this scent would have a special significance for someone with this heritage. There may be genetic memories associated with the smell that will increase its potency in the home.

with your favourite natural smells is a wonderful way to connect deeply with the spirit of nature.

When you are using scents in your home remember to vary their intensity and to alternate between one and others from time to time. Doing this will provide a sense of freshness and vitality which might diminish over time otherwise. In nature smells fluctuate from season to season, from day to day, and even during the hours of a day. To seem natural, a fragrance should come in waves. So open your window occasionally, turn off your diffuser and allow the scents to ride the currents of air as they do in nature.

Air is always present. It is so much a part of our experience that we are rarely aware of it. Usually, only in those times when we have been in a stuffy, shut-up room, or when we have had trouble breathing, are we mindful of the qualities of fresh air. Air is life. Every day take a walk outside. Fill your lungs with the marvellous, bounteous, invigorating gift of air. Let the Spirit of Air expand your body/mind/soul.

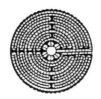

10

The Vitality of Water

W E DON'T KNOW when we will die and, because of this, we tend to think that life will continue in an ever-flowing stream before us. Yet, the truth is that everything that occurs in our life will happen only a limited number of times. How many more times will you see shooting stars? Ten times? Twenty times . . . or less? How many double rainbows will you see in your lifetime? Some experiences will happen only once – the poignant moment when you hugged your child on her first day of school, the joy you felt when your first sunflower blossomed, the afternoon when you danced with abandon in the spring rain. Sometimes events that at the time seem ordinary are, in retrospect, special and even sacred, because of their finite nature. One of my most cherished experiences, which seemed unexceptional at the time, allowed me a deeper understanding of the Spirit of Water.

I have a special swimming hole in the mountains, a place where icy glacial waters tumble down into a deep pool. I love to plunge into the crystal-clear water and feel its silky texture on my skin. One summer day, as I swam in my secret pool, I heard a splash and turned to see a river otter swimming next to me. As I looked into his eyes, he seemed to wink at me, then dived under the water and popped up again not far away. For about an hour we swam together.

Normally the water is so cold that I can stay in for only a few

minutes, but something magical occurred that day. It was as if I became a part of the water. The currents and eddies of the stream swirled around me, but also seemed to swirl within me. The water seemed alive and conscious. I felt an intimate kinship with water unlike anything I had ever experienced, and yet it seemed so very natural.

OUR PRIMAL CONNECTION TO WATER

Our connection to water is primal, and the longing to yield ourselves to the comfort of her fluid form goes back to the beginnings of our individual lives and the beginning of life on earth. From immersion into a baptismal font, to relaxing in a warm scented bath, to swimming naked on a balmy moonlit night in an alpine lake – the pleasure and deep meaning attached to our experiences of water are profound. There is something very powerful, almost orgasmic, about waiting with outstretched arms to welcome a summer thunderstorm. We begin life in water and we are universally drawn to its soothing, cleansing, healing, joy-giving qualities.

This deep attraction is not hard to understand, given the fact that our bodies are made up mostly of water. Its life force flows through our veins every moment of our lives. The water that flows within you didn't start its journey with your birth and will continue to flow after your death. That very same water has gently flowed down the golden Nile, it has been a gentle mist high in the Sierra Mountains and a cloud over the Brazilian rainforest. Beyond the obvious need we have to hydrate our bodies with water, there is perhaps also an etheric memory stored within our genetic imprinting that connects us to all waters and reinforces our yearning to meld with it.

One time I was travelling with some friends in Western Australia during an unusually hot and dry season in which fires had ravaged the land. The charred remains of eucalyptus trees and brush were everywhere in the still smouldering bush. Smoke tinted the air with a yellow, acrid-smelling haze. We wound our way, mile after desolate mile, in grim silence. Suddenly one turn of the road brought us to an area of abundantly lush green vegetation. We got out of our four-wheel-drive vehicle and pushed our way through the bush to discover a glorious golden river. With an almost desperate urgency, we threw off shirts and shorts and dived in. Even though these were dangerous waters known for poisonous snakes and other perils, the urge to be completely immersed in the water was greater than any fear. I felt like a great membrane welcoming the fluid life force of the water through my skin and into my entire being.

Water is continually giving birth to itself through the grand scheme of evaporation, precipitation, flow and return. It never ends. It forms a kind of backdrop against which we live out the course of our lives. It is a metaphor for the eternal journey of the soul. Although the form of water continually changes – into ice, mist, freshwater streams, brackish bogs, snow, hail, summer rains, billowing clouds, sea water or mighty rivers – nevertheless there is never a drop more or less of this precious substance in our world.

WATERS OF LIFE

In ancient times water was considered to be a treasure itself. Communities grew up around rivers and the river was their lifeblood. Wells and fountains formed the central axis for towns and villages. It was here that women would gather to do their washing and to draw water for families and animals. And it was here that people would gather to discuss the weather, their crops and the business of the town. Stories were shared along with strategies for meeting the challenges of life. The source of the water created a web of cohesion bonding the community together. In some unseen yet potent way the water was the catalyst for the building of community and the bridging of cultures. From hamlets high in the mountains to nomadic communities in the desert, water holes were gathering places where information was disseminated and wisdom was gained.

Some societies worshipped the spirits of the water, and certain waters were believed to contain healing properties. The Egyptians, Persians, Indians and Greeks all had deities associated with wells, fountains and streams. On the Continent and in Britain, pagans worshipped at sacred springs. In France, the cathedrals of Chartres and Nîmes were built over springs which had been centres of worship before Christian times. Pilgrims are still making journeys to Lourdes in France to receive the healing water there. In England, York Minster, Carlisle Cathedral and Glastonbury were built over sacred pagan springs, and in Ireland St Patrick chose sacred well sites for his churches.[1]

WATER FOR PURIFICATION

Throughout history, water has represented purification and cleansing. One well-known example of this is India's holy river, the Ganges, which is revered by millions of Hindu pilgrims who bathe in its waters every day to cleanse and purify themselves spiritually. Some Buddhist temples

also have places for ceremonial ablution. In Islamic tradition, ritual acts of ablution are performed using water outside the mosque.

Legends about great purifying floods are found in many cultures of the world. The biblical story of Noah and his ark is perhaps the best known of these, but the ancient Sumerians and Greeks told similar stories, as did the Native Americans. The kind of momentous cleansing and subsequent rebirth of the earth that is represented by these flood stories is reflected on an individual level through the sacrament of baptism. Although baptism is often considered to be a Christian ritual, many other religions and cultures have also used water for rites of purification.

THE IMPORTANCE OF THE WATER IN YOUR HOME

Our modern-day associations with water are chiefly utilitarian, but none the less, within the subconscious there persist ancestral and genetic memories, accumulated through thousands of generations of human history. At a deep level we know that water is a source of nurturing, healing and spiritual purification. Within each of us lives a genetic memory of water as a source of life, and *the water in our home, workplace, or garden can subliminally awaken these genetic memories.* It is therefore very important to pay attention to the different forms of water in your living spaces, and even to create an emulation of water flowing as in nature. One way to do this is with a home fountain. The cascading waters are a powerful means to connect us genetically with the purifying, rejuvenating energy of natural waters.

Home fountains

The sound of flowing water can immediately shift the energies in your environment. Including a fountain in your home or workplace is an easy way to generate an abundance of life-force energy there. Even the smallest fountain can make a difference. In addition to creating a subliminal link to ancestral memories of shared times around a sacred well or river, the fountain will also give off negative ions. Negative ions, which are created by the action of the water splashing against the stones of the fountain, will neutralise pollutants in your air and will also make everyone feel more alert and revitalised.

There are many types of ready-made fountains to choose from, or you could simply obtain an inexpensive small pump at a garden centre or pet store and instead build your own fountain. Place the pump in a waterproof container of your choice. Add stones, glass pieces or any waterproof ornaments that you like. Pour in water, switch the pump on, and *voilà*, you have created a home fountain![2]

Perhaps more important that the way a fountain looks is the way it sounds. This sound can have a deep impact on your personal space and can even be a powerful source of healing. I have a friend who has travelled the world to record the sound of flowing waters. Using very sensitive sound equipment, she records tiny tinkling streams that are little more than a trickle, slow meandering streams, and roaring waterfalls cascading down the side of a mountain. She says that she develops an intimate relationship with each of them through the *sound* they make. Some waters create bright cheerful sounds, some are very tranquil, some are exciting, while others sound dark and melancholic. The distinctive sound of each stream reflects its energy and the energy of the surrounding area.

Once you have created your fountain, try moving around the objects in it to see what kinds of sounds are produced. Different materials in a fountain will alter the sounds it makes, as will the height and pressure of the water flow. Smooth pebbles will create a sound different from that of jagged objects. Try out different alternatives to see which ones sound best to you. Allow yourself to enter into an almost meditative state in which the sound seems to sink inside you. You will reach a point at which you can *feel* that the sound is right. A fountain that has been 'tuned' in this way will bring a constant source of inspiration to your living spaces.

SPIRALLED WATER

One of the most remarkable men of our time was born over a hundred years ago in Austria and named Viktor Schauberger. His father, grandfather and ancestors were *wild Meisters*, which are a kind of park warden. Viktor followed the steps of his forebears and eventually became a *wild Meister* of a large Austrian forest himself. During the course of his work he spent many hours observing water in nature. He believed that water was alive, that it had cycles of birth and death and transformation. He watched the infinite spiralling patterns, formed by naturally flowing streams, and came to the conclusion that spiralling movement was the way that water renewed itself.

After observing schools of lake fish creating vortices in the water as they swam to the surface, he theorised that the fish functioned as natural 'vortex machines' because their movements always created

spirals in the water in their wake. He extended his hypothesis to include not only streams and lakes, but also the sea, reasoning that there was something about the looping, spiralling motion taking place in all these waters that rejuvenated them.

These observations in nature led Viktor to develop systems for purifying and transporting water. The results of his research and development were remarkable. Many of Viktor's observations are now being verified by scientific research. For example, experiments have shown that when water spirals as it does in nature, it develops an electrical potential that is naturally resistant to bacterial growth. When water travels in a straight path, such as through the supply pipes into our homes, it is devoid of this electrical charge.

The German naturalist Theodor Schwenk conducted studies comparing water from natural sources with water from home taps. By photographing complex patterns of flow in water drops, he was able to demonstrate that natural flowing water is more 'alive', because it contains innate spiralling patterns. Polluted water and tap water did not carry those patterns and didn't have the electromagnetic current of natural flowing water.

Recently researchers from Schwenk's Institute for Flow Research and the University of Freiberg conducted experiments using natural spring water from the Black Forest. They discovered that at the point where the spring emerged from the earth, the flow patterns in the water were clear and distinct. However, samples taken further downstream, where the stream had become polluted and sluggish, showed no flow patterns. Still further down the stream the water again flowed freely and the pollution was diluted. Samples from these sites revealed re-emergence of the flow patterns. Researchers concluded that the spiralling movements in the water assisted its oxygenation and revitalisation.[3]

Past generations of farmers in Europe knew about the power of spiralling water because they used it to increase their crop yields. They would stir water in barrels, first one way and and then the other. This practice was called 'clay singing', because they sang and tossed small amounts of clay into the water as they worked. The spiralling 'potentised' the water, which was then flicked with twigs or brooms on to the land. Water charged in this way made the soil more productive and resulting crops were more abundant.

Creating spiralled water

This information about making spirals in water can be applied to energise the water in your home. Spiralling the water that you use reinstates some of its natural life force. There are a number of ways to do this. For example, before you step into your bath water, swirl it in a figure-of-eight pattern. In this way, you will be bathing in revitalised water rather than water that is lifeless. Spiralling the water you give to your plants and animals has been shown to have a beneficial effect. Seedlings grown in spiralled water are more vigorous and have stronger cell walls than those grown in regular tap water. When you spiral the water that you drink, the water you bathe in and the water you give your animals and plants, you are emulating the natural flowing movements of water in nature.

UNDERGROUND WATER

Although it is a theory at odds with modern hydrology, there is historical and anecdotal evidence suggesting that flows of underground water have an important effect on our health and wellbeing, in both positive and negative ways. From a positive perspective, an underground stream beneath your home can have an energising effect on you, especially if you spend only short periods of time directly above it. This is because of the subtle, stimulating electromagnetic fields that it generates. This energising effect of underground water is thought to be the reason that many of the sacred sites around the world are placed over underground streams.

Underground water and sacred sites

Although scientists cannot explain it, their equipment confirms that there is often a magnetic field around sacred standing stones which does not occur around other stones of similar stature. One theory explaining why this is so is that the electromagnetic currents are caused by water flowing beneath the earth at these sites.

Water flowing underground creates a static electric field as a result of the friction produced by the water flowing over rocks and through clay. This current builds up and radiates to the surface of the earth, where it has an effect on living things. The crossing of two streams underground intensifies this effect, even if one is lower than the other and their waters never mix. Many researchers believe that ancient people placed rocks or standing stones on these places to act as amplifiers for the energy generated by the underground water.

Until his death in 1941, Reginald Allender Smith was one of the most distinguished archaeologists in Britain. He declared that there was a correlation between underground water and megalithic stone circles, which he called prehistoric temples. He believed that these sacred sites were purposely erected precisely over areas of underground water flow.[4] His belief continues to be held by geomancers today.

Renowned Welsh water diviner and electrical engineer Bill Lewis believes that ancient people intuitively sensed the strong earth energy areas where there was a crossing of underground streams and marked them with standing stones. Bill also believes that the electromagnetic field generated by the underground flowing water rises up *in a spiralling pattern* through the stone. He notes that the strength of the field fluctuates in accordance with solar, lunar, polar and planetary influences.

The hazards of underground water

Even though standing over a water flow for a few minutes can energise you, remaining there for long periods can deplete your energy reserves. Sleeping above an underground water flow is considered to be particularly unhealthy. Geomancers believe that spending a lot time over underground water flows can make us ill, because the external electrical field interferes with the balance in our bodies. We are sensitive to such fields because our bodies are primarily constituted of water, and the electrical fields around us shift *the patterns* in our internal water. This can interfere with brain rhythms and cellular renewal, and also affects the body's electrical and nervous systems.

The fact that a building is located above underground water will not necessarily result in negative effects for its occupants. Lines of geopathic stress and water flow usually have clearly defined edges, and ill effects are only experienced if you spend large amounts of time over the area of flow. It is possible to sleep or sit for long periods within a few inches of a line and feel no ill effects at all. Because most underground streams are no wider than a few feet across, it is usually easy to relocate beds, and other furniture used for many hours at a time, out of the line of flow.

Our ancestors understood the effect of underground water on humans. Medieval roads that at first seem random and meandering have been shown, through the use of infrared technology, to follow lines of subterranean water. One theory suggests that this plan ensured that homes would not be built over these potentially harmful sites.[5] An alternative explanation might be that the movement of the underground water aided movement of traffic in the roads above it.

Discovering influences of underground waterways

There are a number of ways that you can discover if there are any underground water flows beneath your home:

1 **Dowse** One of the best, time-proven methods for detecting underground water is dowsing. Information on how to do this is contained in Chapter 5. You can also go on an inner journey through meditation to discover underground water.

2 **Hire a dowser** There are professionals who specialise in finding underground water flows. A list of dowser associations is provided in the Resources section at the end of this book.

3 **Empirical evidence** If you are particularly tired and listless much of the time, there may be an orthodox reason. However, it could be that your bed is located over an underground stream. Move your bed – even a few feet can make a difference – to another location and see if you notice a gain in energy.

Plants respond to the energy associated with underground water flows in different ways. Roses, azaleas and celery grow poorly in areas of subterranean water flows, whereas asparagus, mushrooms, oak trees, elms, ashes and willows all do well. Elderberry and many medicinal herbs will also thrive above lines of geopathic stress and underground water. Sometimes the path of an underground stream through your home will be revealed outdoors by a line of unhealthy plants in an otherwise lush area. Also, animals will sometimes avoid areas of your home or garden that lie above underground water. Dogs, horses, pigs, chickens and cattle usually avoid these lines, especially for sleeping. Cats, on the other hand, are very attracted to geopathic stress areas of all kinds. Honey bees also seem to be attracted to these areas. They will produce more honey if their hive is over a line of geopathic stress or subterranean water flow. Ants and termites will sometimes build their nests along underground water lines.[6]

Neutralising the influence of underground water

Authorities on earth energies, believe it is best not to try to manipulate or alleviate negative earth energies. In their opinion, any manipulation will be effective only for a short while. It is better to accept the presence of underground water and move your bed (or desk, etc.) However, if it is not possible for you to move your furniture, here are some common remedies:

Copper pipe

- Drive a two to three foot length of copper pipe (about half an inch in diameter) straight into the ground at the *upstream* end of the flow. It needs to be only a few inches into the earth to be effective. The electromagnetic energy of the stream is attracted to the pole and is discharged before it enters your home; this is why the pole needs to be upstream. (Dowse to discover the directional flow of the stream.)
- If it is not possible to drive a pipe into the ground (perhaps you live in a block of flats, for instance), then place a copper pipe across the *upstream* path of flow as close to ground level as possible. Periodically discharge the metal pipe by putting it in salt water. This means if you discover a flow that crosses your bed, to discharge some of the energy you should lay a copper pipe on the floor next to the wall where the energy of the stream comes into the room.

Crystals

- Place crushed marble or quartz around your home. It is believed that the pizo-electric qualities of quartz crystal dispel some of the static charge generated by underground water.
- Cleanse crystals used in this way by regularly washing them in fresh, running water.

WATER ELIXIRS

Water has the ability to hold, carry and absorb energy. This makes it particularly useful for instilling desired energy in your home. It is easy to do this. Water that has been infused with energy (see below) can be dispersed throughout your home or workplace either by using a plant mister or flicking with your fingers. Doing this can dramatically shift the feeling and energy of a room. The growing accumulation of anecdotal evidence about the effectiveness of water elixirs gives credence to this ancient alchemy.

Precious dew

Paracelsus was a remarkable sixteenth-century Swiss physician and a pioneer in the application of chemistry to medicine. He held that the cycles of all living things were interconnected, postulating that plants revealed their connection to humans through their 'structure, form, colour and aroma'. He recommended that a physician relax in nature and notice, 'how the blossoms follow the motion of the planets, opening their petals according to the phases of the moon, by the cycle of the sun, or in response to distant stars'.[7] He urged physicians to look

> ### Capturing the Dew
>
> If you want to bring an absolutely magical energy into your home, get up early, just after sunrise, and collect dew from the plants near your home. Use a clean glass jar (not lead crystal) and gently shake the dew off the plants and into the container. Use your intuition to discover the best plants to use, and choose dew that is shimmering with *sunlight*. Don't use metal to shake the dew. Use your hand, or something made of wood or glass.
>
> When you have finished collecting the dew, add filtered water or spring water to fill the jar. (Even a few drops of dew can imbue all the water in the jar with energy.) You now have a wonderful elixir that can be sprayed or tossed in your home to bring a magical purifying and uplifting energy. To bring vitality to your home, collect dew at the time of the full moon. To bring peace and serenity, capture dew during the new moon. It is best to use it up within a few days of collecting it, because this is when the dew is most potent.

within themselves for spiritual insights that would lead them to understand the healing influences of plants.

Paracelsus used to gather dew during various phases of the heavenly bodies, for he felt that planetary influences were captured within each dewdrop. He believed that dew contained the essence of a plant within it; in a more mysterious way, it also had the power to connect people with the greater cycles of the universe, and in turn to bring balance to the inner cycles of their lives.

Flower essences

The English physician Edward Bach was a twentieth-century adherent of Paracelsus who gave up a lucrative Harley Street practice in the 1930s to search for more natural methods of healing. Bach believed that there were subtle energies in plants, especially during the flowering stage, that could facilitate physical and emotional healing. He would first observe a flower's form, habitat and growth patterns, and then use his intuition to discover the meanings of the plants.

Like Paracelsus, Bach believed in the spiritual essence of dew. He ascertained that the energy of flowers had a rarefied yet potent healing effect which could be captured in a dewdrop. Bach believed that the light and warmth of the sun activated those very special properties until each drop was full of healing power and life force.[8] He had amazing success with his patients using dew remedies. A particular flower would have a similar healing effect even when used on different people, he discovered.

Creating Flower Essences

- **Type of water**   Use spring water only – either from a local spring, or bottled at the source.
- **Kind of flowers**   You may want to obtain a book about the various qualities of individual flowers (see Resources section), or you can use your intuition to choose the flower that feels best for you.
- **Picking the flowers**   Plants should have grown without any artificial chemicals and must be picked at their peak of vibrancy. Wild flowers are best. Collect your flowers in the early morning when there is still dew on the plant. Some dew results from condensation, but some of the fluid actually comes out of the plant and contains an energy imprint of it.
- **Floating the flowers**   At sunrise, gently float the flowers on the surface of the water in your bowl (glass or ceramic, not metal). Do not submerge them. The floating flowers act as filters for the sunlight in the water.
- **Timing**   You will know the moment that the energy of the plant has been given into the water. This can take an hour, or even two. Rarely, it will occur in as little as half an hour.
- **Mother tincture**   Once the flower energy has entered into the water, filter the water with a very clean cloth. Then take a very clean bottle and fill it with a mixture of 50 per cent brandy and 50 per cent flower-infused spring water. The brandy should be French or any high-quality brandy. This creates what is called the 'mother tincture'. It is your concentrated stock from which you can make bottles of your flower essence.
- **Give the plants back to the earth**   Give thanks for the giveaway of the flower and carefully return it to the earth.
- **Your stock bottle**   Put two drops of the 'mother tincture' into a clean 30-ml bottle (or five drops in a 50-ml bottle) which contains a mixture of 50 per cent brandy and 50 per cent spring water. This creates your stock bottle.
- **Misting your home**   Transfer three drops of liquid from your stock bottle into a spray bottle that contains 10 per cent grain alcohol or brandy and 90 per cent spring water. This is the mixture you use to mist your home. You can omit the alcohol from your spray bottle if you will be using the contents up within one week.
- **Spiralling the water**   To increase the potency of your flower essences, you can first spiral the spring water that you use. Stir it first one way and then the other. Alternatively you can swirl it in a figure-of-eight motion. The spiralling movement increases the energy and potency of the water.

Because it was difficult to gather enough dew to make his remedies, Bach devised a second method for obtaining the same potent energy from flowers. He would pick a flower in full bloom on a cloudless summer day and then float it in fresh water, allowing sunlight to illumine the water. He would then lift the flower out of the water with two blades of grass, so as not to touch the water with his fingers. The clear fluid was then transferred to bottles which were filled with a mixture of half water and half brandy as a preservative. Bach found that the energy of the sun infused the water with the healing properties of the flowers, so that the water gained the same healing energy as the dew. He eventually discovered thirty-eight flower remedies, which are used by patients all over the world today.[9]

Using flower essences can subtly and powerfully shift the energy fields in your home. These essences can weave a delicate gossamer web of energy throughout your environment. A space that has been misted with flower essence feels different. It feels lighter and brighter, the way you would feel if you were in a meadow filled with wild flowers on a sunny day.

It is my experience that the best flower essences are those that are created by people who have devoted their lives to this work. They usually have a highly atuned ability to sense the energy of plants and are able to assist the infusion of the flower's energy into the water. However, there are times when you might want to create your own flower essences for your home. It can be exhilarating to participate in this process. Ruth Toledo, a Brazilian flower-essence practitioner and international teacher, kindly assisted me in compiling information on how to do this.

Star essences

If you want to bring a rarefied celestial energy into your home, then you might consider creating star or moon essences. The practice of infusing water with energy from the stars goes back before written history. The phases of the moon and the stars produce physical effects on the waters of the world, as well as on the water which composes most of your body.

The Italian scientist Giorgio Piccardi discovered that the rate of chemical reactions taking place in water solutions was affected by cosmic influences. Lunar and solar sunspots, solar eruptions and even meteor showers all had a measurable effect on the reactions taking place in the water. This is because water is highly sensitive to even the subtlest of influences.[10]

To activate a celestial imprint on water, follow all of the instruc-

tions for creating flower essences (see page 160). However, place your bowl of water outdoors on a beautiful starry or moonlit night. You can also hold your hands approximately ten inches above the bowl and visualise energy from the heavens cascading down into the spring water. Then you will have water infused with starlight, as well as the astrological influences of the stars and planet overhead on that night. Your star elixir makes a wonderful housewarming gift, to bring starlight and joy into a new home.

WATER TO STIMULATE ABUNDANCE

In traditional feng shui water is associated with abundance and prosperity. If you want to activate more prosperity in your life you might try adding the element of water, especially flowing water, into your home. When you do this, focus on your intention of becoming more prosperous. Below are some traditional feng shui cures that many have found helpful for focusing their intention on creating abundance.

WATER TO INVOKE THE DIVINE FEMININE

Many myths tell a story of creation taking place in the Great Waters, which usually represent the Great Mother. The scientific view that life

---

Introducing Water for Abundance

- Place an aquarium or fountain in the prosperity area of your home. This is located in what is the furthest left-hand corner when you are facing the front of your home.
- Keep either nine goldfish (eight red and one black) or a hundred guppies in an aquarium to stimulate abundance. One (or five) arowana fish will also have this effect.
- Place a fountain or cascade of water outside your front door, preferably on the right-hand side of the door as you enter. This allows good fortune and abundance to flow into your front door.
- Place a model of a sailing ship (with the sails up) facing towards your work area (desk, cash register, computer). This will symbolise the boat sailing on smooth waters, carrying abundance to you.
- Make sure all drains are clear to stimulate flow of finances. Do not let water stagnate in drains.
- A meandering stream in front of your home bodes good fortune and abundance.

---

on earth began from a primordial soup in the seas corresponds to this perspective. Throughout history goddess shrines have been associated with sacred springs and wells. These sacred sites often symbolised birth-canal entrances to the underground womb. We carry in our genetic encoding the innate association with water and the feminine forces. Whether you are a man or a woman, if you desire more of the qualities associated with the Divine Feminine in your life, then including water in your home can call the power of the goddess into your dwelling and into your heart.

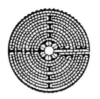

11

The Power of Fire

L ION ROCK is a special place high in the Cascade Mountains where I
collect sage for my space clearing ceremonies and where I feel close
to heaven. From there I can see mountain ranges in all directions. It is
one of my favorite places on the planet.

Late one autumn afternoon, my husband and I drove up to Lion
Rock and made camp in a beautiful meadow. As evening turned to
night, we lit a small campfire. David pulled out his drum and, as he
began to drum, we chanted together. Under the stars, we sang late into
the night until we both fell asleep. When I awoke in the early morning
the fire was out and it was cold. I could see my breath. David was curled
up next to me with our new puppy snuggled in his sleeping bag. He
looked so serene, I decided not to wake him.

I pulled a sweater over my head, slipped into my jeans and walked
across the meadow to an elevated point where I wanted to wait for the
sunrise. In the distance I could see Mount Rainier. She looked like a
slumbering giant, snow-capped and majestic. I have always felt a special
affection for this sacred mountain and in that moment I felt we were
deeply connected, like two old friends sitting and waiting together for
some momentous event. Everything was so quiet.

Suddenly, like a flaming spear thrown across the heavens, the first
shaft of morning light hurtled across the sky and touched the earth. I
could feel the sun's fiery light expand within me as a wonderful warmth
flowed through me.

Fire enthrals us with its primal essence. In ancient times it was thought to be a gift from the gods that carried the spark of life and the power of renewal. We honour the power of fire because it can maintain life and it can destroy it. It is the warmth of the hearth, but it is also the lightning bolt striking from the sky. Fire can purify and transform and it can annihilate. It is the etheric light of the aurora borealis and it is the erupting volcano. It is the mediator between the visible and the invisible; between energy and form. It is also all radiant and electrical phenomena. The ultimate symbol of fire is the sun.

To many ancient people the sun was not only a sacred source of light and warmth, it was honoured as a god. The Egyptians called the sun Ra. In Greek mythology, Apollo was the sun god who would fly across the heavens each day in his fiery chariot. Kings throughout the world declared that they were direct descendants of the sun. They recognised it as a source of life. What we know today in scientific terms about the sun is fascinating and reinforces what the ancients knew to be true – that without the sun there would be no life on the planet.

Our sun is an immense, raging nuclear furnace, over 300,000 times as big as the earth, with temperatures of 15 million degrees Celsius. Not only does it provide heat and light, it also is the source of a wide spectrum of electromagnetic fields, from gamma rays and X-rays, to ultraviolet rays, visible light, infrared radiation, microwaves and radio waves, many of which would be potentially deadly without our protective atmosphere.

SUNLIGHT

The sun synchronises the rhythms of growth and dormancy, rest and activity, and even of life and death. We are affected by the cycle of day and night, as well as the monthly and yearly cycles of the seasons, which are all governed by the sun. All life is dependent on this fiery star. No aspect of our lives or our homes is not affected by its mighty influence.

The cycles of day and night and the constant interplay of light and shadow continually affect the energy within your home. *The Pattern Language*, a book which has been called the architect's bible, states that a building's position in relation to the sun is the single most important factor to consider when deciding where to site it on a plot of land. If the building is placed so that the surrounding land is full of sunlight, it will be pleasant, 'full of activity and laughter'. If it is not, then the most beautiful building design in the world 'will not prevent it from being a silent gloomy place'.[1]

It is important to become aware of the effects of this daily drama of light and darkness within your home, and to find ways to utilise it to your best advantage. Rooms that are devoted to social activity are best situated in the south (if you live in the northern hemisphere). When this is so, then the energy in your home will be joyous and cheerful. If these rooms are situated to the north, then the energy can seem dark and dreary. On the other hand, rooms whose purpose is rest and retreat are best in the north. Research has shown that rooms with an abundance of natural sunlight tend to be the most used, while those without this lighting are often avoided.

Ideal Places for Sunlight

- a breakfast nook that faces east to catch the morning sun
- a bathroom that gets full morning sunshine
- a workshop with southern exposure for sunlight throughout the day.
- a bedroom with morning sun, if you are an early riser
- a living room with midday sun
- a kitchen with either morning or midday sun
- a porch facing west for afternoon sun

CHRONOBIOLOGY

In order to function optimally, many of our biological rhythms require sunlight. All living things, even the smallest single-celled organisms, have some sort of internal time-keeping system. Within our bodies are numerous biological clocks. The scientific studies of these body rhythms is called chronobiology. The internal rhythms of humans are highly complex with deeply ingrained repetitive cycles. Our body temperature and seratonin levels change with remarkable precision every day. A woman's moontime cycle follows a monthly rhythm. The level of the hormone regulating human growth is higher during the summer than the winter. In fact, every single biological function of the body follows precise cycles that are dictated by the sun. These rhythms evolved at a time when humans lived more closely aligned with nature. For example, the body's metabolism would slow down in the autumn, probably as a way of conserving body fat for the long cold winter when food was scarce.[2]

Although some of our natural cycles have evolved to the point where they can be maintained without natural sunlight, our health and wellbeing decreases without exposure to this basic supply. To promote health and vitality to your home, bring in as much natural sunlight as possible. Open your curtains wide in the daytime. When the weather permits, open your windows and let natural light pour in. If you are building a new home, install skylights. Bringing the energy of the sun into your home will have enormous benefits for both your physical and mental health.

The natural cycles of the sun

The modern inventions of electricity and light bulbs have brought us more freedom and increased productivity. However, these advantages have also disconnected us from the natural cycle of day and night. One of the ways you can re-establish your connection to the rhythms of the sun is to emulate natural cycles of light in your home. For example, if it is still dark outside when you wake up on a winter morning, instead of immediately turning on bright lights begin your day by lighting a candle or using a very dim light. Gradually progress to full-intensity lighting. This modulation reflects the way that the morning sunlight starts with pale light which slowly increases in brightness and intensity.

In the evening, instead of keeping your home brightly lit until you go to bed, gradually lower the lights (dimmer switches are great for this), light candles or light a fire. Decreasing the light in your environment bit by bit will help to prepare you for a night of deep rest. Having our homes regularly lit up at eleven o'clock at night creates an artificial day that moves us away from our natural alignment with the cycles of the sun.

ALIGNING ACTIVITIES
WITH THE SEASONS

Our ancestors lived in harmony with the cycles of the sun. In most places in the world, summer days were long and the sun was bright. In the winter the dark prevailed. For thousands of years the lives of our forebears were dictated by this wheel of the seasons. The yearly cycle has not been altered, but our perception and alignment with it has changed considerably. Because we spend so much time indoors, we have lost our sense of connection to the seasons. In our diurnal cycle, the day is the time of activity and the night is the time for rest and rejuvenation. Similarly, the cycle of the year contains times that are better suited for busy activities and other times that are good for withdrawing into yourself. Here are some examples of how you can utilise the energy of the seasons in your home:

- **Spring** If you want to start a new project or break free of an old limiting pattern, the energy of springtime will give an added boost to your efforts. To activate this energy in your home, bring in spring flowers, do a spring cleaning, wash the windows and clear out clutter. Your subconscious mind will recognise the signs of spring that have been associated with new beginnings since the beginnings of our history.

- **Autumn** If there is a project you want to finish, this is the time to do it, because the psyche recognises autumn as the period of completion and endings. Fix the broken window, repair the table leg that wobbles. To honour the energy of endings, collect and make arrangements of autumn leaves. In ancient times, autumn was also the time for gathering food supplies for the winter. This season is an excellent time to organise your store cupboard. Throw away foodstuffs that are old and replace them with new ones.

STARS: FIRE IN THE SKY

One way to connect to the element of fire is through the stars. Every star is a sun, and most of them are bigger than our sun. To bring the energy of the night sky into your home, you might consider painting stars on the ceiling. This has been done in temples throughout the world, perhaps to create a feeling of being close to the heavens. You can also use adhesive fluorescent stars that glow at night. Or if you want to create an astronomically accurate reproduction of the heavens, you can rent a machine that will reproduce the constellations from your region with fluorescent dots right on your ceiling. (See Resources section at the end of the book.)

HOME HEARTH: SACRED FIRE

When I was in Africa several years ago, I was privileged to spend some time with the Zulus. Among the memories of that time I cherish is one of us sitting on the earth around the ceremonial fire at night, where we gathered to share stories. The fire formed a sacred centre-point for our time together.

Since earliest times humans have gathered around fires. The fire created a circle of light and warmth that fostered a sense of community. The word *focus* comes from the Latin for hearth. The hearth was originally in the centre of the home and served as a focal point for family life. It literally brought people together to warm themselves and to eat the food that was prepared there.

Describing a home he built, Carl Jung once said, 'At first I did not plan a proper house but merely a kind of primitive one-storey dwelling. It was to be a round structure with a hearth in the centre and bunks along the walls. I more or less had in mind an African hut where the fire, ringed within stone, burns in the middle and the whole life of the family revolves around this centre. Primitive huts concretise an idea of wholeness, a familial wholeness . . .'[3]

In ancient Greece the goddess Hestia presided over the family hearth. The matriarch of the family would make offerings to her via the flames. In Roman times, the Vestal Virgins presided over a public hearth believed to be the centre of the universe.[4] I believe that every human being has an innate primal memory of sitting around the fire in the dark. Because of these ancestral memories, all fires connect us to past fires, to a time when the hearth was a sacred centre-point of the home. This ancient connection to the Spirit of Fire is activated by even the smallest use of fire in the home.

A fireplace forms a natural spiritual centre in your home. If you have a hearth, you might want to use it as an entrance point for Spirit. To do this, dedicate it as a sacred place. Make it as beautiful as possible and place comfortable furniture nearby. Include cosy blankets and soft pillows so that you can curl up in front of the fire to sleep and to dream. Make a bed for your dog or cat in front of the fire, too. A contented pet in front of the fire adds a special feeling of warmth to a room. It also echoes early times when man first domesticated wild animals around the home fire. Dedicating a hearth to the Spirit of Fire is a very ancient practice which can ignite healing energy throughout your entire home.[5]

Even if you haven't got a hearth, the simple act of lighting candles in the evening can bring the revitalising power of fire into your home. The soft and glimmering lights of candles can turn the most ordinary evening into a time of magic.

If you can choose the type of cooker you have in your kitchen, I highly recommend a gas stove rather than an electric one. Preparing meals over an open flame is a very different experience from using a heating element, because it aligns your energy with the ancient and sacred practice of cooking food over a fire. Often we may feel irritated by the repetitive chore of cooking. However, realising on a deep level that preparing food is a sacred act, a way of caring for yourself and those you love, can transform the experience from a prosaic one to a rite of deep meaning.

The open flame of a gas stove provides more immediate access to this awareness. However, even if you are using an electric cooker, focus your thoughts on the service that you are providing. Know that you are receiving the bounty of the earth and transforming it through fire into nourishment for body and soul. Doing this will fill the food you are cooking with vitality and love.

DECOR COLOURS

Colour is an aspect of the element of fire because it is a part of the electromagnetic spectrum of the sun. The colours in your home have an immediate effect on your emotions and your physical body. For example, being in a red environment increases your blood pressure, while cool colours decreases it. We not only perceive colour with our eyes; we also absorb it with our entire body.

There is even a kind of sensory perception, called 'skin vision', whereby colours are perceived through the sense of touch. Research at the Soviet Academy of Science in Moscow substantiated that certain people have the ability to distinguish colours with their fingers. The researchers discovered that one in every six people could learn to differentiate between two different colours solely by touch. The test subjects all agreed that they were able to distinguish colours by their textures. For example, yellow felt slippery, while orange felt hard and rough. Some of the subjects could sense a colour *without actually touching it*. Researchers concluded that skin vision was the result of an interaction between electromagnetic fields emanating from both the subjects' fingers and the colours they were touching.[6]

This research has important implications for everyone, because it shows that the colours surrounding us are continually influencing us even when we are asleep. There is an enormous amount of information available about the use of colour in the home (see Resources section); however, a very simple way to select the best colours is to use your intuition. Below is an exercise that will help you with this.

Choosing Your Decor Colours

Close your eyes. Imagine that you are walking about your home. In every room stop and imagine that room in different colour schemes. (If you are having trouble coming up with ideas, look at magazines and books about colour and decorating. These can really get your own colour imagination going.) Keep shifting the colours in the room until you find one that makes you feel really good – strong and happy. This is the best colour for this area.

ELECTRICITY AND ELECTROMAGNETIC FORCES

The sun is a spiralling ball of fire, fiercely radiating particles of energy out into space. These particles are drawn to the poles of the earth. Magnetism enters and exits the interior of the planet through the North and South Poles, thus creating the natural electromagnetic field of our earth. Because we evolved within this environment, every function of the human body is designed to be in harmony with the earth's electromagnetic field. For example, the rhythm of the earth is 7.8 hertz and the rhythm of the human biocircuitry is also 7.8 hertz. Hertz is the unit used to measure the frequency (rate of occurrence) of waves and vibrations of an energy field.

We are constantly influenced by electromagnetic fields around us. Shamans around the world perceived these mysterious forces. They sensed that in some places the earth's energies felt stronger than in others. Such places were deemed sacred. The ancient ones intuitively sensed the pull of the earth's axis and knew that this affected all of life. The did not need scientists to tell them that beneath their feet flowed a subterranean stream of energy which formed patterns, electrostatic fields and negative ion concentrations. Nor did they know that waterfalls, mountains tops and electrical storms had beneficial electrical effects. They simply experienced these influences and knew that they were a sacred part of the living universe.

In modern times, these natural flows of the earth's electromagnetic forces have been disturbed by an enormous increase in man-made electrical fields. The electricity in our homes and workplaces has a devastating effect on our health, which is often ignored because electricity is not something we can see or smell. Nevertheless, it is essential that you think about the electricity in your environment and minimise the amount of time you spend in artificial electromagnetic fields (EMFs). Research has shown that exposure to EMFs can cause a decreased number of immune cells, decreased hormone production, and changes in genetic RNA. Some studies suggest that such exposure may also contribute to the growth of cancer cells. Children appear to be at greater risk than adults, perhaps because their immune systems are less developed.[7]

EMFs are a fact of life. However, there are ways to diminish their negative effects on you. The best way to do this is to maintain some distance between yourself and them. Even keeping a few feet away from a field can make a big difference, because EMFs dissipate rapidly with distance. Create a grid map and plot where the EMF's are in your home

171

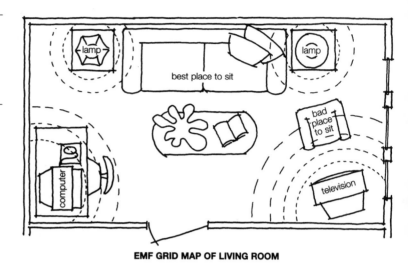

EMF GRID MAP OF LIVING ROOM

and workplace. (See example above.) Obtain a gauss meter[8] and measure which fields are strongest. Approach the EMF areas from several directions and note the readings you receive. Then record the information on your grid map to create a picture of the strongest EMFs in your home. This will enable you to see where you want to avoid spending much time.

If you are concerned about the EMFs, you might also consider hiring a professional to do an assessment of your environment. There is new technology available that can shield entire walls of your home. (See Resources section.)

Electromagnetic Hazards

- **Television**   The amount of EMFs emitted by a television varies widely from one set to another. Some studies have shown a pronounced increase in leukaemia in children who were exposed to high EMFs, while other studies have shown only a slight increase. In any case, do not sit directly in front of your television or allow young children to do so. Even when a television is turned off, it still emits a strong EMF.
- **Stereo**   Stereo equipment tends to emit a low EMF. However, to be safe, do not allow your children to keep a CD- or cassette-player right next to their bed. Encourage them to keep some distance from it during play as well.
- **Lights**   Lighting generally has a low EMF. However, as a precaution do not sit for long periods of time with a reading light directly over

your head, or read in bed with a light close to your body. It is better to use a more powerful light that has a beam directed at your reading than a weaker one right next to your head.

- **Computer** As the use of computers is on the rise, health problems associated with them are also increasing. However, computers are a fact of modern life. To decrease the negative effects from EMFs when you are not actually using your computer push your chair away from it. Most emission-blocking screens available block only the electrical field and glare. They don't block the magnetic field, which is the most damaging. There are some firms that will install magnetic shielding equipment in your computer, but doing this usually voids the warranty of your computer and can cause problems with its functioning. Some shielding devices encase your computer. These are a bit bulky and expensive, but they will shield you from the harmful EMFs.
- **Electric analog or digital clock** Keep at least three feet (preferably more) away from your body while you are sleeping.
- **Microwave oven** Although microwave ovens are very convenient, they also have very high levels of EMFs. Stay completely away from it while it is in use. Some older models leak microwave radiation, which can cause chromosomal damage. I suggest using your microwave only for emergencies; at other times keep it unplugged.
- **Electric cooker** Minimise your time in front of an electric hob or cooker. Be particularly careful about using the extractor fan while cooking. Avoid it unless absolutely necessary. If possible, select a gas stove, which doesn't emit magnetic fields. In addition, if you are designing your kitchen, plan worktops away from the stove and refrigerator if possible.
- **Refrigerator** Do not stand for long periods of time in front of this appliance, as it emits a strong electrical field.
- **Dishwasher** ` Run your dishwasher when people are out of the kitchen. It can be tempting to lean up against the warmth of an operating dishwasher on a cold day, but don't do it, as it emits a strong field with accompanying potential for health problems.
- **Small appliances** All small electrical appliances produce EMFs. Limit your use of them, and stand back if possible when you're operating them.

Fire is a volatile force that from the beginnings of time has carried both the potential for life and for destruction. Using the energy of this force in your home requires discretion. Deciding how best to use it, as well as how to decrease its potential for negative impact, will allow you to create an environment that is exciting, invigorating and full of abundance.

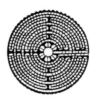

12

The Wisdom of the Earth

WHEN I WAS five years old, we lived in a rural town in central California. Our house was small, with two storeys, and was located on a hill. Although we lived there for only about a year, and I haven't been back since, the memories from this home are still vivid in my mind. The land and trees surrounding it continue to feed my soul nearly half a century later. Behind the house was a wood of massive oak trees. I used to seek comfort there when the stress of living in a fragmented family became too great. Next to an old gnarled oak tree was my 'dirt hole', which I thought was the most wonderful thing in the world. About two and a half feet across and a foot deep, it took me a long time to dig, using only a spoon that I had pilfered from the kitchen.

I loved the earth in that place. I remember reaching my hands deep into the soil and holding it as if my life depended on it. I loved the feel of its rich texture. I would bring it up to my nose and inhale the fertile scent of composted leaves. A large boulder nearby was superbly smooth and strong – the perfect place to rest my back while admiring my creation. I used to eat some of the soil there. It tasted so good. I was sure there was no other soil like it in the whole world. I would allow only my closest friends to visit my special place. They too said it was the best-tasting earth they had ever tried.

When I was sad, I would run into the wood to curl up in my hole.

There I felt comforted. It was almost as if I could feel Mother Earth's loving energy embrace me. It was true magic, the deep, healing wisdom of the earth. I would return from my special spot feeling nurtured, strong and whole.

BORN OF THE EARTH

Our connection to the earth goes back to the beginnings of our history. Folklore abounds with stories of human beings emerging from the earth, and in some languages the word 'man' meant 'earth born'. The Romanian historian Mircea Eliade wrote that, 'Even among Europeans today there lingers an obscure feeling of mystical unity with the native earth; and this is not just a sentiment of love for one's country or for the ancestors buried for generations around the village churches.' He believed that this sense of connection to the earth was a primary part of man's psyche, transcending time and culture. He called this inner instinctual belief a 'cosmo-biological experience', which gave people a sense of belonging.[1]

CONNECTING TO THE EARTH

Since earliest times humans have had a dynamic relationship with the earth. Throughout ancient history, people saw the world as teeming with spirit life. Every rock, tree, mountain and river had a spirit. The context of human life was firmly rooted in a natural world infused with divinity.

We no longer interpret the natural world around us as peopled with spiritual identities with whom we can communicate. Although this shift in perspective has resulted in tremendous gains in scientific understanding, we have lost our sense that we have a place in the cosmos, and we no longer feel intimately connected to the land. However there are ways this can be restored. Go into your garden or, if you live in an area of the city where there is no bare earth, find the closest park. If possible, remove your shoes to let the energy of the earth enter through the bare soles of your feet. Imagine the earth's energy rising up through you.

Beneath your feet lies a vast and shifting array of energies influenced by gravity, electromagnetic fields, soil composition, wind, weather, sun angles, sun flares, seasons, positions of the stars, phases of the moon, heat and cold, underground water flows, and vacillations of human activity, plant, insect and animal life. Supporting all these ever-changing energy fields is *a living conscious planet*. As you stand on the earth, imagine that you are dissolving into the spirit of the land.

THE TREE OF LIFE

My first spiritual teacher was a Hawaiian shaman. She told me that you could always recognise a shaman's home because it would have an invisible spiritual tree superimposed over it. She said that shamans and mystics used these ethereal trees to form protective shields around their homes, and to travel into other realms along the roots and branches. She once showed me a building, saying, 'Denise, can't you see the tree surrounding it? It is there because a kahuna [shaman] works in that building.' To be honest, I couldn't see it, but I did sense a special feeling there.

A tree represents cosmic integration. It sends its roots down into the underworld and reaches its branches to the sky. In many ancient traditions the sacred Tree of Life channelled the energy of the universe into the world, thus connecting heaven, earth and the underworld. Some cultures revered the tree as the source of life. In many cultures the Tree of Life was an 'axil' point, meaning that it was considered the centre point around which the world revolved. Black Elk, the famed Sioux Indian mystic, spoke of a sacred tree in one of his visions. He said, 'Behold the circle of the nation's hoop, for it is holy, being endless, and thus all powers shall be one power in the people without end,' and in the centre of this sacred circle stands a 'holy tree'.[2]

The Tree of Life and your home

To bring a grounding, strengthening energy into your home, I suggest that you superimpose over it the Tree of Life. Doing this connects your home to the earth. In addition, the boughs that will stretch, umbrella-like over the top of your home will act as a form of protection for all of its inhabitants. Here is an exercise to help you do this.

Superimposing the Tree of Life

Allow yourself to become very relaxed. (If you have any recordings of soft drumming music, or if you can get a friend to drum while you do this, it can deepen your experience.) Begin by clearly imagining your actual home. Then imagine that a huge spiritual tree is slowly enveloping your home. Its roots go deep into the earth, connecting you, and everyone who lives in your home, to the nurturing energy of the earth. The trunk of this tree completely encompasses your house. The branches reach high over your roof, creating a protective canopy. Renew this visualisation four times a year, at each solstice and equinox, to reaffirm this potent force in your home.

EARTH INFLUENCES

The earth influences your home in many ways. These influences are called earth energies, and it is helpful to understand what they are and how they are affecting you.

Geomagnetic energy

I recently visited Brazil. It was fascinating to spend time with a Brazilian Indian shaman and compare South American Indian traditions with

North American Indian ones. However, while I was there I felt an unusual kind of exhaustion that I had never experienced before. At the time I attributed it to the high pollution levels of Sao Paulo. However, less than a month later I was in Mexico City, where the pollution was worse than in Sao Paulo, and I felt great.

I was puzzled about the source of this fatigue until I learned that the geomagnetic force is twice as strong over North America than over Brazil. This phenomenon is called the 'Brazilian low' by geophysicists, and every time the Hubble telescope passes over Brazil, researchers must put their instruments into a 'sleep mode' to keep them from malfunctioning as a result of the anomaly's effects.[3] (Perhaps the magnetic fluctuations over Brazil are due to the fact that this diverse country is sitting on a huge bed of quartz crystal.)

Scientists do not fully comprehend the effects of the geomagnetic field on humans, but they do know that they are strong. Upon returning to earth after a year in space, Russian cosmonauts had lost 80 per cent of their bone density, a condition attributed to the absence of the earth's magnetic field. As soon as they installed artificial magnetic fields on spacecraft the problem was corrected.[4] This is but one example of how important the magnetic field is to our wellbeing. *Every person on the planet is influenced by this magnetic field.*

The observed reactions of animals prior to an earthquake may reflect their awareness of changes in the earth's geomagnetic field that occur shortly before. Research suggests that many animals, including humans, have sensors in their bodies that register magnetic fields. Honey bees, homing pigeons, many fish and whales have magnetite (also known as lodestone) in their brains. Magnetite in human brow ridges and vertebrae has been linked to our magnetic sensitivities.[5]

To understand how these forces affect your home, it is necessary to understand a little about the earth's magnetic flow. It is believed that the earth's geomagnetic field is generated by the movement of molten magma within its core. This energy field flows around and through the earth and extends far beyond its atmosphere. It is stronger on the side of the earth which is turned away from the sun (the night side), because the sun's radiation compresses the magnetic field on the side facing it (the day side of the earth). This means that the earth's magnetic fields affect you more strongly while you sleep than when you are awake. It is believed that a stronger magnetic field is more conducive to good health that a weak one.[6]

Research has shown that increasing numbers of humans ailments can be attributed to 'magnetic deficiency syndrome'. This syndrome is on the rise because the widespread use of metal in our environments interferes with the beneficial geomagnetic field generated by the earth. Metal buildings, metal desks, metal beds and bedsprings all decrease geomagnetic energy. Also, the magnetic field of the earth has declined by about 80 to 90 per cent over the last 4,000 years (from 4.9 gauss to 0.4 gauss).[7] What this means is that our bodies are genetically adapted to a higher level of geomagnetism than is now present in our environment, and so we are suffering from a deficiency. This is why magnet therapy can be so helpful for a variety of ailments.

All cells have a magnetic field. Your body draws upon the earth's magnetic field to enhance chemical reactions and improve cell repair. Most cell repair occurs at night during the first two hours of sleep. In a natural magnetic field, healthy vital cells are created. In an artificial, erratic magnetic field (which is common in most modern homes) the natural cell repair and division is altered. This can contribute to health problems. Research at Baylor College of Medicine in Houston found that 76 per cent of patients treated for pain with magnet therapy reported improvements, whereas only 19 per cent of the control group (who were treated with dummy magnets) reported relief. This research reinforces the importance of magnetic forces to human health.[8]

Magnets have been used for healing for thousands of years. The first written account of magnets was in the Yellow Emperor's Book of Internal Medicine, dated approximately 2000 BC. Ancient Egyptian, Hindu and Tibetan practices included the therapeutic use of lodestones, and it is claimed that Cleopatra wore a lodestone in the centre of her forehead to prevent ageing.

You spend more time in your bed than anywhere else in your home. Sleeping on a magnetic bed pad can shield you from erratic magnetic fields. These pads simulate the earth's geomagnetic field and contribute to rest and healing. They will also ground you. 'It brings you down to earth every night,' says Dr Dean Bonlie of Alberta, Canada, the chairman of the Scientific Research Committee of the North American Academy of Magnetic Therapy.[9]

Earth disturbances

I have been in areas where I couldn't feel much life force in the land. When I have investigated the history of these areas, I have usually discovered a recent disturbance to the earth. For example, a new quarry may have been dug, or perhaps explosives were used for industrial purposes. Another event that can cause this dampening of earth energy is the creation of a dam on a river.

When these disturbances occur, the balance of the earth goes into

shock for a period of time. This phenomenon can be compared to a human body going into shock after an injury. Polygraph tests of plants have recorded a similar response when they are damaged. Immediately following the injury, the plant goes into shock. Then it slowly begins to emanate a wobbly and erratic energy, something like the jagged breathing of someone who is in a great deal of pain. Likewise, the earth will begin slowly to recover following a large-scale injury, but her energy too will at first be erratic and weak.

The earth will heal from trauma, although it may retain a subtle energy imprint of the event, rather like a scar. Usually after a number of months, healing and rebalancing occurs. However, in an area where the trauma reoccurs regularly, as when explosives are used again and again in a mine, it is difficult for the energy of the earth to heal and return to normal. This is like a wound that is continually reopened. Healing will be much slower or will even stop altogether because of the repeated injury. Our connection to Mother Earth is so close that we often respond to these variations in her energy without knowing it.

If you live within ten miles of a quarry or an area with underground mining (or, to a lesser degree, in an area where there are underground trains vibrating through the earth), then I suggest that once every twenty-eight days (every moon cycle) you radiate love into the earth around your home. If possible, place your hands on the earth to do this. This is like a mother holding the injured area of a child to help it heal. If you can't actually put your hands on the earth, position them palms downwards and imagine radiant, loving energy passing out of your hands and into the earth. You may want to visualise the colour green as you do so. This exercise will help soothe the earth energy. It will also bring a more harmonised energy to your home.

INVITING THE EARTH SPIRIT

There are numerous ways to invite the Spirit of Earth into your home. The easiest is to bring natural stones indoors or have healthy vibrant plants there. However, here are three ways that I have found helpful to invite the Spirit of the Earth into your environment.

1 Spirit houses

In many countries offerings are made outdoors to the spirits of the land and the 'landcestors'. Landcestor is a word I have coined to describe the ancient spirits of the land. It encompasses the ancestral guardians of the

a converted birdhouse

a handmade spirit house

earth and the spiritual guardians of the land, animals and plants. In Thailand, a traditional shrine dedicated to these spirits is called a spirit house. These beautiful little shrines, made of teak, are adorned with flowers, fruit, incense and grain as a way of saying thank you to the earth for her bounty. Every day fresh offerings are placed in and around these small ornately carved houses.

You can make your own spirit house to honour the land around your home. (If you don't have a garden, you can place it near a window.) Any type of wood that will stand up to the weather can be used. If you are handy with tools, a small, four-sided house with a pitched roof is not too difficult. You can leave the wood plain or decorate it with symbols that are meaningful for you. If the prospect of building your own spirit house seems too daunting, you can purchase a birdhouse and enlarge the entrance to make a wonderful little shrine.

2 *Elementals*

I was once invited to give a consultation to someone who lived in an urban, gated community. I always like to assess the surrounding neighbourhood before a consultation, so I arrived early and walked around for a few minutes. Although all the houses were maintained perfectly, something seemed to be amiss.

It felt as though a grey pall hung over everything. I was curious about how the plants could look so perfect without seeming to have any real life force. Also, there were no elementals anywhere . . . not one

fairy, elf, or gnome. When I diplomatically shared my observations with my client, she told me that all the residents in the community had signed an agreement to have their garden *sprayed with pesticides four times a year.* Since there were several hundred homes in the community, this meant that the spraying was continual. I then understood why there was no life force. The constant barrage of chemical pesticides had unbalanced the force of nature. Although everything looked good, the gardens might as well have been plastic because they were not emitting a health-sustaining life force.

A garden needs to have its own life cycle of birth, blooming, dying, and some disorder. Organic gardening methods also contribute to increased life-force energy. A true garden not only looks nice, it creates a sustaining habitat for plants, insects and small wild animals. To bring the elementals into your garden, leave one section a bit wild and dedicate it to the wee folk. They will come!

3 *Bounty of the earth*

In the coolness of early morning I like to make myself some green tea and with my cup nestled between my hands, enjoy the warmth that permeates my fingers. The delicate fragrance of the tea carries me to a sunny hillside in China, lush with tea bushes. As I cut thin slices of fresh ginger to slip into my tea, I visualise a tropical forest in Hawaii, heavy with the smell of ginger flowers and frangipani. My morning cup of tea connects me to these distant places. And as the steam from my cup rises in lazy spirals, the energy of these lands fills my home.

Honouring the food you bring into your home is one of the most powerful ways to activate the forces of the earth in your environment. Physical matter and life force become one in the food we eat. When we remember this, every meal becomes a sacred rite.

Food is a gift from a living planet, which is made up of many interdependent systems. Beneath the smooth purple skin of a plum are subtle energy imprints retained from its origins. When you eat a plum, you are ingesting not only its flesh, but the sun, blue sky, clouds and the rain. If you were to pick a plum from a tree, these connections would be obvious. When you purchase one in a supermarket, it is easy to forget about these things.

Most of our food comes to us prepackaged, after it has travelled hundreds or thousands of miles from its source. It may have been placed in cold storage, dehydrated, transported in lorries, then been boxed and shrink-wrapped before it arrives in your grocery store. By then it has become an inanimate object *and, more importantly, it has lost its ability to connect us to the natural world.* To activate this connection, take a moment to think about where your food came from. For example, your pasta was once part of a vast field of wheat swaying in the wind. Taking the time to imagine the source of your food will result in much more nourishing meals and will link you more deeply to nature.

DESIGNING ENERGY FIELDS THROUGH FOOD

Just as you combine textures, shapes and colours in the design of a room, so too can you design energy fields, through the use of food. For example, if you live in a cool rainy climate, place brightly coloured bowls of oranges, grapefruit, lemons and limes in your home. These citrus fruits contribute a signature energy of hot days and warm nights. The colour, smell and taste of these warm-climate fruits bring the energy of the sun into your home, to balance the cool energy of the natural climate there.

To activate the earth's energy in your home with food, it's best displayed in baskets or bowls. However, even the food kept in your refrigerator will emanate some life force into your home. For example, if you decide that you need more grounding in your home, you might want to buy carrots, potatoes and other root vegetables, because they are full of grounding earth energy. If you place them in transparent drawers or containers in your refrigerator, you will see them and be able to connect with this energy every time you open the fridge door.

All natural and healthy food will generate earth energy in your home, but different foods contribute different kinds of energy. Apples, for instance, carry a wholesome life force that speaks of health. To activate this energy in your home, place bowls of apples where they will be seen and admired. The bright colour of oranges stimulates optimism, expansiveness and self-esteem. Peaches bring an uplifting energy that says life is good. Although fresh fruit is best, even a bowl of artificial fruit can help bring the qualities associated with it into a home.

Corn, rice and grains signify harvest and abundance. Since ancient times grains have represented prosperity. In Egypt, grain was used as a form of money, and in every culture around the world it has represented the lifeblood of people. It is traditional to place grain on altars to signify abundance. Storing your grains and pasta in clear containers, so you can see them, will subliminally deepen your connection to the abundance of the earth.

Connecting to the individual source of your food

If you are not a vegetarian, then another powerful way to connect to the natural world is through the meat and fish that you bring into your home. Native people, living close to the land, understand this. When they take the life of an animal and eat it, they know that they are also ingesting a bit of its spirit. Embracing this ancient tradition can revolutionise the way we relate to the meat in our homes and can also call forth the energy of nature into our space. For example, if you eat beef, take a second to connect with the *particular* cow that the meat was from and give thanks for the gift of its life.

Every animal has a unique personality. You might imagine travelling on a cord of light, back in time, to the particular animal that provided you with that steak, as it grazed on green grasses, revelled in the warmth of the day and slept under the stars. In ancient times there was an profound relationship, often a mystical connection, between hunter and prey. The hunter was acutely aware of the specific animal that provided meat for the winter. Eating the animal brought its spirit into one's life. We have lost this connection. Most people who use animals as a source of protein would never consider killing one and might even judge those who do. They have lost the power of the connection between them and the food that they ingest. When you reinstate this connection, you bring the natural forces into your home.

Organic produce and meat have more life-force energy from nature than chemically processed foods. I believe that it is important to consume meat, eggs and dairy products from animals which have been humanely treated. In this way, you do not support inhumane treatment of animals and you *do not bring the energy of pain and fear into your home.*

A kitchen garden

One of the most powerful ways to invite the energy of the earth into your environment is to grow food. This taps into a subliminal ancestral memory within us, of living close to the land and growing our own food. Even the tiniest kitchen can usually support a small pot of herbs or a glass jar of living alfalfa sprouts on a windowsill. These bring vitality into your home. Remembering to care for the plant and harvesting it can activate earth energy in your home like no single other action.

Putting prayers into your food

The emotions and thoughts that you have as you prepare food will emanate from it when it is consumed. An angry chef creates meals that emit anger; a joyous chef creates dishes that generate joy. Food preparation can be a kind of alchemy. To infuse your food with life force, wash your hands ceremoniously before you begin. With each item of food, visualise its origin. As you proceed, place prayers in the food. This can be as simple as, for instance, stirring the batter and chanting in rhythm with the circling spoon. Or as you knead dough, repeat the name of the Divine with each fold. Visualise vital life force energy surging through you into the food. When the meal is complete, bless it. Not surprisingly, food tastes better when prepared in this way. And it creates an energy that fills your entire home.

Part Three

MEDICINE WHEEL FENG SHUI

13

Introduction to Medicine Wheel Feng Shui

THE PREVIOUS chapters in this book have shown you how you can activate the forces of nature in your home and use your home as a template for balance and harmony. The next six chapters will show you how to integrate this information into a viable and powerful system that I call Medicine Wheel Feng Shui. It is a system that calls forth ancestral wisdom into present time to bring a remarkable vitality into your living environments.

Medicine Wheel Feng Shui is based on the innate understanding that ancient people had about the natural forces that shaped their world. These wise predecessors instinctively understood that the rhythms of the elements and the magnetic flow of the four cardinal directions were powerful forces which profoundly affected all life on earth. They knew that within each element were patterns of energy that permeated the universe. They used this understanding to develop cosmological models to orient themselves on earth and create a sense of balance in their homes.

Native Americans called their model for living the Medicine Wheel. In the Native American way, 'medicine' does not refer to

Western allopathic medicine. Rather, it is anything that helps you to achieve a greater connection to Spirit and the natural world around you. The Medicine Wheel is a symbolic sacred circle that provided a context for life. It is represented by a circle of stones laid on the earth, a physical outer form for invisible inner forces. The Medicine Wheel signifies the meeting place between heaven and earth – a place where the four directions and four elements come into a fusion of power. It is a mandala of the universe in which everything created finds its appropriate place. And it is a powerful tool for bringing balance to our homes.

MEDICINE WHEEL FENG SHUI

For many years I explored the ways of my Cherokee Indian ancestors. I led vision quests, taught Native American spirituality and was a drummaker. At the same time, I also explored the spiritual traditions of other cultures, because I believe that modern life has much to gain from the ancient ways. Seventeen years ago, these explorations led me to the Chinese art of feng shui. I was delighted to find a system that confirmed so many things I had learned from my Native American heritage, as well as from shamanistic practices of other cultures. I became fascinated by the many areas of overlap between the wisdom of feng shui and that of my own Native American ancestors. The possibility of combining the two traditions into one workable whole became my dream. It was out of this desire that the concepts of Medicine Wheel Feng Shui were born.

There were times when the concepts of one tradition seemed to be at odds with the other. Over time I realised that, beneath the obvious differences, the two systems were different faces of the same reality. Both spoke of the unity of all things. Both eloquently presented a model of living in harmony with nature. Once this became clear to me, I no longer worried about not being able to synchronise them perfectly. I gleaned from the richness of both to weave something new, a set of tools that could be used to create environments full of hope and joy and health. The longer I worked with these tools, the deeper was my certainty that I had found my life's calling.

Deepening your connection to the natural cycles of life

Everything an Indian does is in a circle, and that is because the Power of the World works in circles, and everything tries to be round . . . The sky is round and I have heard that the earth is round like a ball and so are all the stars. The wind, in its power,

whirls. Birds make their nests in circles, for theirs is the same
religion as ours. The sun comes forth and goes down again in a
circle. The moon does the same, and both are round. Even the
seasons form great circles in their changing, and always come
back again to where they were, The life of a man is a circle . . .
and so it is in everything where power moves.[1]   Black Elk

Using Medicine Wheel Feng Shui in your home can deepen your
connection to the cycles of nature and can bring a natural perspective
to your view of life. The Medicine Wheel honours all cycles in life: the
circle of birth, death and rebirth, the cycle of the seasons, of rising sun
and setting sun, full moon and new moon, dark and light, hot and cold.
When we embrace the understanding of the Medicine Wheel, it allows
us to take our part in the great cycle of life. We see our contribution in
relation to the greater whole. Each part matters; nothing is too small to
be significant.

Our homes can either separate us from nature or connect us
more deeply to this source of power. The Medicine Wheel deepens our
connection to the earth. In a profound way it helps us heal the earth.

STONE MEDICINE WHEELS

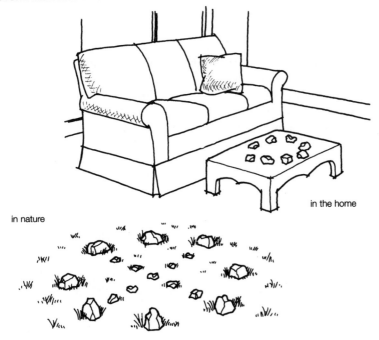

in the home

in nature

When we honour the forces of nature in our homes, our dwellings can become templates for harmonious union with the earth. Creating homes that honour and reflect nature helps to heal the betrayed trust between humans and the earth. Guardianship of the earth is one of the most sacred duties of our time, and when we fulfil this duty we heal not only the planet but ourselves as well. Living in harmony with nature helps us to discover our place in the great web of life. We can then begin to unfold the mystery of who we are, why we are here and how we can best live on the planet.

The wisdom of the elders

Understanding how our ancestors occupied space on the earth can help us transcend the stress of contemporary life. By learning about their ways, we can recreate wholeness in our lives today. The elders understood that there is a rhythm and pattern to all aspects of life. They knew that healing didn't mean only treating an individual's disease; the object was to bring the person back into harmony with himself, his family, his tribe and the earth. They understood the significance of a person's personal environment and used the energy there as a tool for healing and transformation. We need to call upon this wisdom now to transform our environments into homes for our souls. By using the Medicine Wheel, you can bring the wisdom of the elders into your space.

Medicine Wheel Feng Shui is a compilation of all I have learned in three decades of study. The traditions of many ancient cultures have been synthesised into tools which can help you diagnose the energy in your living areas, invoke nature's energy into your home or workplace and create a circle of protection for your dwelling. The next chapters of this book will show you how to use these methods to create an environment that will nurture and heal you.

14

The Cardinal Directions

THE FOUR FORCES OF THE UNIVERSE

Although you may not consciously be aware of it, at this very moment you are being affected by the four directions. They are encoded in your brain, and their energy flows through you as through a lightning rod. The magnitude of their effect on our lives cannot be overestimated.

In current times, when so many have lost their sense of orientation because of the increasing influx of technology and change, it is essential to activate the energy of the directions in your home. By harnessing the energy of East, South, West and North, and by calling upon the Guardians of the Directions, you can bring balance and peace into your home and your life.

The four directions orient our lives

Human beings have always interpreted the world around them in terms of their own experience. From the beginning of time, we have defined the space around us in terms of four body orientations – i.e., we see things as being either in front of us, behind us, to the right or to the left of us. This system of orientation corresponds to our experience of our planet: it rotates on an axis which defines north and south; the sun appears to arise out of the east and to set in the west. This division of the natural world into four parts has deep roots in the metaphysical traditions of many cultures.

Early people yearned to comprehend their place in the universe. They looked to the world around them to discover their own niche in the scheme of things. Every day they watched the sun's progress across the sky, catching the excitement of new possibilities in the morning as it rose in the east, experiencing the peace of completion as it set in the west every night. Over time, the emotions associated with the phenomena of the directions evolved into the patterns of philosophy, mathematics, religion and art.

In the northern hemisphere, people observed that the south was the direction of warmth and light, while the far north was the land of cold winds and darkness. Native cultures and civilisations all over the world oriented their dwellings and their lives according to nature's directions. In every tradition, the centre was the place from which all the directions emanated and was therefore considered sacred. It was the place of the Creator and the divine forces of life. At the centre the four directions became one.

In modern times, Carl Jung created a model of personal balance within the psyche based on the four directions. Aspects of the self were correlated with each direction, and the centre represented the place of balance between these attributes. He characterised the east as being linked with intuition, the south with feeling, the west with sensation and the north with thinking.[1]

Science and the directions

Research has shown that many animals, and perhaps even humans, have internal compasses, which are oriented to the earth's magnetic field and which provide a biological orientation to the directions. Many animals become agitated or seek shelter hours before an earthquake. It is believed that this occurs because they sense a change in the magnetic flow of the earth. It is this magnetic field, not the North Pole, that is the prime organiser of the earth's directions. Recognition of the properties and the powers of the directions may be related to an ability within each of us to sense the currents of the earth's magnetic fields.

Ancient cultures and the four directions

Ancient people assigned qualities of intelligence and personality to each direction. They believed that each direction had very specific and unique energy traits and, in addition, conscious life force. Some cultures worshipped the directions as gods. Others venerated the directions as angelic forces that brought harmony and balance to life. Ancient Christians prayed to the angels who were the overseers of each direction: Michael, Raphael, Gabriel and Uriel. Some cultures called the directions the Four Sacred Winds, and in many traditions there was a guardian of each direction who protected the world from harm.

The Aztecs used the directions to divide the world into four regions, with each region representing a transition in life: birth, growth, weakening and death. In India ancient diagrams have been found depicting the universe as expanding outwards from the centre of the cosmos in four directions, with each direction guarded by a deity. The Tibetan mandala shows four gateways corresponding to the cardinal directions and all leading to the centre, the place of enlightenment and self-realisation. Navajo sand paintings symbolise the four directions and are created during a sacred ceremony re-enacting the creation of the world.

Ancient architecture and magnetic directions

Sacred sites and buildings throughout the ancient world were aligned with the four directions. The great pyramids of Egypt were built on a north/south axis. Many of the Olemec temples in Mexico were also built in alignment with the magnetic directions, as was the entire sacred Mayan city of Teotihuacán. A number of the great cathedrals of Europe were constructed by the Freemasons, who based their work on a mystical understanding of the directions and used a lodestone to determine the directions. There is much historical research documenting the significance of the directions to ancient architecture and the layout of cities. At the same time, native people throughout the world were using the principles of the directions to determine their life and their dwellings.

Directions in Native American tradition

Native Americans lived in close alignment with nature and had an intimate knowledge of the four directions, which they honoured as Spirit Keepers. Early morning was the time to face east and send prayers to the Creator. Entrances into dwellings usually faced east to allow the energy of the rising sun and the Spirit of the East to empower life. Each direction of the Medicine Wheel represented a specific aspect of the great cycle of life. The great Sioux visionary Black Elk said:

*I fill this sacred pipe with the bark of the red willow; but before we smoke
it, you must see how it is made and what it means. These four ribbons
hanging here on the stem are the four quarters of the universe. The black
one is for the west where the thunder beings live to send us rain; the white
one for the north, whence comes the great white cleansing wind; the red
one for the east, whence springs the light and where the morning star lives
to give men wisdom; the yellow for the south, whence come the summer
and the power to grow.*[2]

The Guardians of the Directions

In ancient traditions around the world, shamans called upon the
Protectors of the Directions to act as guardians for a place. In Native
American tradition each direction had a Spirit Keeper that functioned as
a guardian. These guardians often took the form of a totem or spirit
animal, such as a bear or a buffalo. When someone wanted to call upon
the power of a direction, he appealed to the totem associated with it.
Although different tribes attributed different meanings to various totem
animals, there was consensus that these practices had great value.

In the Persian *Avesta*, directional guardians are known as the
Chieftains of the Four Sides. In both Jewish and Buddhist traditions,
there is a guardian associated with each direction. Medieval tombs were
engraved with images of four saints who were linked with an animal in
a manner reminiscent of Native American animal totems. St Mark was
symbolised by the lion, St Luke by the bull, St Matthew by an angel or
man, and St John by the eagle. Each was thought to be a guardian of
the dead.

The following exercise, based on ancient shamanistic practices, can
help bring protective, strengthening energy to your home or workplace.

Invoking the Four Guardians to Protect Your Home

Close your eyes and relax. Imagine that you are either inside or outside the
eastern part of your home. Call the Guardian of the East to create a ring
of protection around your entire home. This guardian spirit may appear to
you as an animal spirit helper, an angel, or as an unseen power. Some
guardians take the form of symbols. Let your mind be empty and ready to
receive the presence of your guardian in whatever form it chooses to take.
Repeat this meditation for each of the four directions. Call the Guardian of
the South, West and North to come and join together with the East, to
form a mighty ring of power and protection for your home. When you are
complete, ask the Creator to fill the centre-point of your home with peace.

The directions and feng shui

The ancient origins of feng shui can be traced back several thousand years, but its roots extend even further back in time, to the practices of the earliest shamans. These ancient visionaries understood the power of the directions and used their skill to activate this energy. They embarked on inner journeys to the far reaches of each direction, in search of wisdom and guidance for their people. These shamanistic traditions continued through time and branched into many forms. One form became the art of feng shui.

The directions play an important part in feng shui. Ancient Chinese masters understood the power of the hidden forces flowing from each direction, which are emphasised in the Compass School of Feng Shui. In this tradition the directions of a compass (called a *lo pan*) are used for many deliberations and decisions. Feng shui masters were called upon to locate the best site for a building to make sure that it would be in harmony with the directional powers. Like the Native Americans, feng shui masters assigned a mythical animal to each direction as a connector to the power of that direction. The dragon represented the beneficial, creative powers of the east, the phoenix symbolised the expansive, joyful energy of the south, the tiger signified the unpredictable, transforming power of the west, and the tortoise embodied the wise, enduring strength of the north.

SYMBOLISM OF THE DIRECTIONS

Each direction has a potent influence on the energy of your home and everyone who lives there. In order to activate the power of the directions in your life, it is helpful to understand some of the meanings attached to each of them. This is because *the meanings you assign to the directional powers will activate these qualities in your life*.

The meanings associated with each direction vary from one culture to another. The colours, elements, animals and qualities attributed to a direction vary according to the traditions of different peoples. Although there is little consensus about the particulars, none the less there is strong agreement about the cyclical and seasonal aspects of the directions.

In the northern hemisphere we associate north with winter, but south is the direction of this season in the southern hemisphere. The qualities I have listed here for north and south should therefore be reversed if you live in the southern hemisphere. However, because the sun always rises in the east and sets in the west, the qualities assigned to these directions will be relevant for both hemispheres.

Spirit of the East

The qualities associated with the power of the east are derived from the fact that this is the direction of the rising sun. For this reason new beginnings are commonly associated with this direction. The Spirit of the East is aligned with the power of springtime, the season of awakening after the darkness and dormancy of winter. East is the home of dawn and the waxing of the new moon. Freshly planted seeds, shoots pushing their way up through the soil, eggs waiting to hatch in a nest, newborn babies: these are all images linked with the east. It is a time of growth, renewal and vibrancy. The east is a place of hopes, dreams and new plans.

Image   To experience the energy of the Spirit of the East, imagine waking in early spring, throwing open the window and inhaling the fresh morning air. Birds are singing and the new day is just beginning. Your day and your life are filled with power, potential and vitality.

Key words   Activation, inspiration, optimism, striving, growth, vigour, enlightenment.

Spirit of the South

The power of the south lies in expansion and rapid growth. It is the home of summer, the midday sun and the full moon. Crops are tall. Days are warm. The south is associated with the rapid growth of childhood. The idea that is born in the east is now nurtured and strengthened in the south.

Image   Imagine a perfect summer day. The sun is high is the sky. There is an abundance of life all around you. Tall grasses sway in the breeze; flowers are in bloom; fruit is ripening.

Key words   Expansion, nurture, trust, abundance, energy, fruitfulness, activity, passion, exuberance, vitality.

Spirit of the West

In the cycle of life, the west is the realm of autumn, the setting sun and the waning moon. Crops are harvested. Leaves fall from the trees. The west is associated with the years of change, maturation, discovery, transformation, experimentation and completion. It is the time when childhood has been surrendered and adulthood has emerged. The idea or the project that was born in the east and nurtured in the south is now tried out and revised. Cycles of experimentation move towards completion.

Image Travel in your mind to the top of a plateau. As you arrive you see that the sun is just setting. The bright colours of the day are slowly turning to the deeper colours of the night, as the warmth around you ebbs into the coolness of evening. A profound sense of peace settles over the land.

Key words Completion, transformation, harvest, change, transition, surrender, release, purification, withdrawal.

Spirit of the North

As you complete the circle you arrive in the north, the realm of winter, the longest night and the dark of the moon. North is associated with introspection, the achievement of maturity, and the wisdom of the elders. It is also the realm of death and rebirth. In terms of creativity, the idea that was conceived in the east, nurtured in the south, and tried out in the west, now reaches the phase of consolidation and realisation in the north.

Image Imagine a night when the sky is filled with stars. A thick layer of snow blankets the land as far as you can see. Beneath the stark beauty and silence of the snow, a remarkable metamorphosis is occurring as life prepares itself to begin again.

Key words Consolidation, introspection, tranquillity, meditation, retreat, rest, renewal, dormancy, inner guidance, incubation, wisdom, reflection.

Spirit of the Centre

The centre is the place where the many become one, where the separate parts of the self come together to become whole. The centre is the heart of harmony and the home of Spirit. It is the place of healing where fragmentation is magically transformed into integration and unity.

Image Imagine a great spiral of light and sound. All life, all awareness, all consciousness, is spinning round and round. Allow yourself to merge with this spiral. Feel the swirling energy flowing upwards and downwards within you, merging and melding all aspects of you into oneness with Spirit.

Key words Focus, spirit, awareness, intuition, unity, oneness.

Aspects of the Four Cardinal Directions				
	EAST	SOUTH	WEST	NORTH
Season	spring	summer	autumn	winter
Sun cycle	dawn	noon	sunset	midnight
Moon cycle	waxing moon	full moon	waning moon	dark moon
Creativity cycle	activation	expansion	completion	consolidation
Key word	inspiration	intuition	transformation	introspection

THE POWER OF THE FOUR DIRECTIONS

Consciously connecting with the power of each of the directions will increase your ability to access their energy. There are many methods you can use to do this. One of my favourites is first to create a circle of stones large enough for you to sit in, then to face each direction and accept the gift of its energy into your life. Most people notice a very different feeling in each direction.

The meditation on page 201 is a powerful way to connect with the Spirits of the Directions. It is an exercise that I have done with many people with remarkable results.

THE DIRECTIONS AND YOUR HOME

Flowing from each direction is a powerful force that is constantly affecting the energy in your home. To discover the influences of the directions it is valuable first to draw the outline shape (a bird's-eye view) of your home. Then use a compass to determine the directions in relation to your home and add these to your drawing. This will give you a picture of how the directional energy is coming into your home. Next draw the outline shape again and add surrounding buildings, vegetation and land forms to show where your house sits in relation to them. Notice how any of these factors may be affecting the flow of directional energy into your home. For example, if there is an abandoned factory directly facing the eastern side of your home, it could be blocking the East's creative energy from entering your home. Are you having problems getting projects started? Do you yearn for a new beginning to no avail? This might be an indication that you need to activate the energy of the East, to help diminish the blocking effect of the factory.

If nothing seems to be expanding in your life, or if things feel somewhat stagnant, take a look at what lies to the south of your home.

Meeting the Spirits of the Directions

Imagine that you are walking along the moss-covered banks of a gently meandering stream. Early-morning light filters through the leaves of the tall trees. Turning to the east, you see a beautiful young Indian woman walking towards you. Her black hair hangs in two shining plaits and in her arms is a bunch of fresh herbs and spring flowers. She is the Spirit of the East. Take time to listen to the messages that she has for you. Before she returns, she gives you a gift that will connect you to the Sacred Realm of the East.

You travel on your way, following the path of the stream. From the south there comes a powerful Native American warrior, striding towards you out of a tall stand of aspen trees into the bright midday sun. You sense immense strength, passion and vitality radiating from him. Listen to his messages for you from the Spirit of the South. When he leaves, he gives you a special gift to connect you to the Sacred Realm of the South.

The stream gradually broadens until it has become a wide river. As you sit down to rest on a smooth riverside boulder, a medicine woman comes to you from the west. Her face is filled with wisdom and compassion, and she is dressed in leather and fur. She shakes her painted rattle and slowly begins to dance, weaving a spell of energy around you. You can hear her messages from the Spirit of the West, not so much in words but in silent images that imprint upon your soul. As the sun sets she returns to the west, leaving you a small medicine bundle which is a gift to you from the Sacred Realm of the West.

As daylight fades and the warmth of the earth ebbs into the coolness of night, a vast tapestry of stars appear, shimmering brightly overhead. From the silence of the north comes a wise Indian elder. He is surrounded by a silvery light that seems to emanate from within him as much as around him. In silence, he looks into your eyes with love, and then places his hand on the centre of your chest. You know – it is almost as if you can hear his words of wisdom in your soul – that something wondrous is occurring beneath the surface of your mind. With a wise nod he turns and disappears back into the north.

Listen to every adviser. Pay particular attention to any information they share with you about your home and your life.

Directly south of Jason's house (see illustration on page 202) there was an enormous apartment building which visually seemed to overpower his home. In our interview, Jason repeatedly told me that he felt constricted, that he just couldn't move forward in life. During our assessment, other clues in his environment also pointed to a blocked

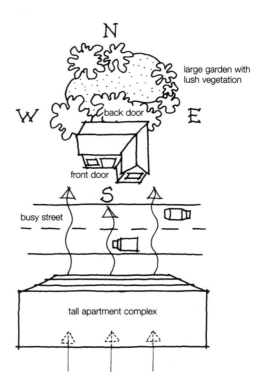

Tall apartment complex blocks southern energy.

flow of southern energy into his home. After he took steps to counter-act these influences he felt more expansive, because then the nurturing energy of the South began to support him.

The objects and land forms surrounding your home can also serve to enhance directional energy flow. Nancy experienced her life as always being in a state of change and transformation. No sooner would she complete one project than she would find herself immersed in another. She took up painting and eventually had a solo show of her work at a local gallery. Not long after she took up study of folk dancing, she found herself teaching dance. Her life was an exciting creative whirlwind and people called her a Renaissance woman. She enjoyed her life and excelled in all areas of it. On the western side of Nancy's house was a beautiful garden which supported a strong inflow of western transfor-mational energy into her home.

Activating directional energy

There are times when it is helpful to activate the energy of a particular direction in your home. Doing this can promote desirable qualities in your life and can also counteract a directional blockage. For example, if you are ready for a new beginning in your life, pay attention to the eastern part of your home. Clean this part, then beautify it by putting things that increase the life-force energy there, such as a house plant. If you want more stability, then activate the energy of the North. To do this, you might choose a symbolic object that represents stability, such as a painting of mountains, and hang this in the northern area of your home. Also decorating with dark, restful colours, solid furniture and even photos of winter scenes can invite the energy of the North.

Another way to stimulate the energy of a particular direction is to cultivate the part of your garden that lies on this side of your home. Planting flowers, bushes or trees, or creating a garden shrine, on the eastern side of your home can instantly enhance the East's energy of rebirth.

Whenever you honour and respect the influence of the four directions in your environment, the energy becomes much more balanced, which in turn creates more harmony for the occupants.

15

Finding the Centre of Your Home

AT THE CENTRE of my soul rests an ancient land. It is a holy place where sacred mountains carry memories of creation deep within their folds; a place where rolling hills undulate between the plains like great buttocks, breasts and pregnant mounds of life. It is where deep gorges are filled with forgotten dreams and sonorous flowing rivers carry the secret of life. In my dreams I follow hidden pathways to this timeless place, for when I am in the centre of this inner landscape I know that I am home.

A CENTRE IN YOUR LIFE

In life we yearn for a sacred centre, a nucleus around which our lives can unfold and evolve. Evidence of this yearning is embedded in our language. When we feel in balance with the world around us, we say, 'I am *centred.*' When we speak a truth from the core of our being, we say, ' I am coming from my *centre.*' Places where alternative healthcare is practised are often called healing *centres* rather than healing clinics because the word 'centre' is associated with ideas of balance, harmony and essence, which are so important for health.

As the pace of life has quickened, it is increasingly important to become more centred in life. Distractions pull us away from our sense of connection to the soul, so it is essential to create home sanctuaries where we can retreat and find spiritual solace. Such places anchor us to what we know is true; they bring us home to ourselves.

Axis mundi, *the centre of the world*

The idea of organising life around a central focal point is a very old one in human culture. Public buildings, monuments and homes in ancient times were almost always constructed in a way that honoured this theme. The centre-points of temples, cities and natural structures in the landscape lent definition and meaning to life. The centre-point was thought to be the *axis mundi* – a cosmic axis passing through heaven, humans and the underworld – a place in which to commune with the gods. It was a tangible symbol that joined sky and earth, a gathering place of power. Ancient Chinese geomancers identified the centre-point where buildings would best be located, which they believed was the place of the greatest concentration of 'cosmic breath'.

The centre also served as a focal point for social groups. My teacher, Dancing Feather, was a Tewa Pueblo Indian. The entire culture of his people revolved around the idea of a sacred centre. In Tom Bender's book *The Heart of Place* he quotes Rina Swenzell, an architect who speaks passionately about the differences between modern and traditional Tewa approaches to architecture:

> *When a community is founded, the center of the community is located first, before any action is taken on layout or construction. This process is gone through . . . to connect with the forces of nature – the mountains, the stars, the clouds, the animals and the birds. The water spider is asked where the center of the universe is, and there the community is built. If there is any question, the rainbow is asked also where the center of the universe is. A human place is only significant in how it connects us with the larger forces in the world . . . the center is marked with a mere stone . . . It is the point where the earth breathes, where its breath moves throughout the cosmos.*

When Roman legions wanted to establish a town, they would first divine the centre-point. They then performed a ceremony that included ploughing around the perimeter of the town three times. At each of the four directions the plough was lifted to avoid 'severing the breast of the Earth'. In the Middle Ages towns were surrounded by a perimeter wall, with gate towers for each of the four quarters. This allowed the Earth spirit to flow into and out of the town centre and provided rejuvenation for the entire town.[1]

In modern times, many towns are built around a centrally located square or park. The ambience of towns with these focal points is generally better than in those situated along a road. Centre-points help define the identity of the town and promote a sense of community there, which in turn makes these places more likely to have long-term residents and lower crime rates than towns without these features.

The omphalos

History is full of myths about the stone at the centre of the world. In ancient Greece, an *omphalos* was a kind of stone which symbolised the connection between the earth and the gods. The word 'omphalos' itself literally meant 'navel'. Since prehistoric times, cultures around the world have used stones to symbolise sacred centres of power. Many old European churches were built around a central point marked by an omphalos, and an omphalos sat in the very centre of the Forbidden City in China. The Ka'ba at Mecca holds a small black meteorite believed to have been kissed by Muhammad. For Muslims this omphalos represents both the centre of the earth and the gate to heaven.[2] In the traditions of the Celts and Saxons, ornate omphalos stones were used to mark the centre-points of sacred places from Ireland to Germany. They were also the preferred sites for the coronation of kings, because monarchs were symbolically joining with the umbilical cord of life when they were crowned next to an omphalos stone.

The omphalos was inextricably connected to the concept of creation and symbolised a link between the visible and invisible realms. Although the omphalos was usually a stone, sometimes it took the form of a pole, pillar, or mound of earth. Whatever the form, it always represented a connection to the sacred source of life. The omphalos was believed to anchor the energy of the earth. The interlacing designs carved on the surface of many omphalos stones were symbolic of binding this earth energy. In both ancient Greek and Chinese traditions, the energy of the earth was represented by a coiled snake, as with the Kundalini energy of the chakras; the omphalos captured this energy and held it in a sacred domain.

Perhaps the most famous sacred stone was the omphalos at Delphi. According to Greek legend, Zeus had chosen Delphi to be the centre of the world. The untamed turbulent energy of the earth was said to be contained and focused by the power of the omphalos and channelled outwards in all directions.[3]

The Centre of the Ancient Home

Ancient homes were usually built in a symmetrical design surrounding a central point. Whether the overall shape was round, square or rectangular, it was usually easy to identify the centre-point. Often the fire or hearth was located in the centre of ancient and native homes. It provided a focal point for the life of the family. Often, too, home altars were placed by the hearth, further increasing the energy there. The centre-point of the home provided an anchor for the family.

The centre-point was also the place where the energy of the four directions converged in the home. Because of the symmetrical design of ancient homes, the amount of energy entering from each direction was equal. Consequently, the qualities associated with these directions were balanced as well. The stable energy of the North was in balance with the vital energy of the South; the initiating energy of the East equalled the transformational energy of the West. Because these energies were in balance, there was harmony throughout the home.

Many modern homes and workplaces often lack a recognisable centre-point. In our desire to be innovative and distinctive, we have forced buildings into unnatural forms. What is sometimes lost is a natural balance of proportions. Living in a structure with no sense of centre can leave you feeling uncentred and out of balance.

Finding the Centre of Your Home

The importance of establishing your life around a centre cannot be overemphasised. A centre-point fills a deep need for connection and balance. Within us there is a subconscious conviction that this is the place where we can connect with divine forces and commune with the sacred aspects of life. Therefore, creating a sense of centre in your home is essential. As soon as you do this, you will feel more balanced, and your connection to the spiritual realms will also deepen.

Since most ancient and native homes were symmetrical in design, the centre-point was obvious. Where the centre of your home lies may not be so clear. To find it, it is helpful first to recognise there are two different forms of centre-point. One is the physical centre of the home and the other is what I call the Dynamic Centre. In ancient homes, these two kinds of centre usually coincided in one place. However, in modern homes it is more common for there to be a place that turns out to be the dynamic energy centre, which lies far from the geographic physical centre of the home.

FINDING THE
CENTRE OF YOUR
HOME

The physical centre

The physical centre of your home is in the middle of its physical structure. Given the complexities of modern home design, it is often not possible to pinpoint the exact physical centre, but you can come close enough for our purposes. It is necessary to identify where this area lies in order to analyse the balance of energy throughout your home. Here are two methods to help you find it.

Finding the Physical Centre of Your Home

Method One   Using cardboard and graph paper, create the outline shape of your home as seen from above. To do this, first measure the outside dimensions of your home. Then map out these measurements on the graph paper, using a scale of one square per foot (or any ratio you like). Next cut it out and trace around it on a piece of stiff cardboard. Cut this cardboard shape out and balance it on the flat end of a pencil. You will probably have to experiment a bit to find the exact point where it will balance, but when you do you usually will have identified the physical centre of your home. If your home has more than one floor, this centre will exist as an axis running through your home from bottom to top. (This method doesn't work for all houses but it is often a good indicator.)

Method Two   If your home has a fairly symmetrical design – that is, its shape is more or less a rectangle or square – you can calculate its approximate physical centre. First measure the length and width of your home. Then find the point at which half the measurement of the length intersects with the halfway point of the width measurement. (See diagram below.) This will be the physical centre of your home. As with the first method, if your home has more than one floor this centre point will exist as an axis running through your home from bottom to top.

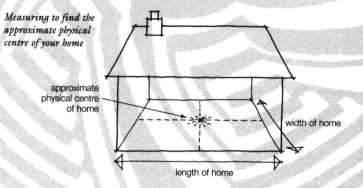

Measuring to find the approximate physical centre of your home

approximate physical centre of home

width of home

length of home

The Dynamic Centre

The Dynamic Centre is a place in your home that exerts an energy pull on the rest of the environment. You could call it the 'energetic centre' of your home. It might be the place where people gather together the most, or it could be a space which is not often used, but none the less all the *chi* (energy) of the home gravitates to this area. The Dynamic Centre draws the home's energy towards it, and therefore it exerts a tremendous influence on everything that happens in the home. It also dramatically determines the influences of the energy from each direction as they flow into your home.

The Dynamic Centre operates as a kind of vortex, drawing energy in and then radiating it outwards again in a spiral motion throughout the home. You can change the location of the Dynamic Centre but first you need to discover its location. Here are two methods.

Finding the Dynamic Centre of Your Home

Inner journey   Close your eyes and imagine that you have the ability to see energy. Walk around your home and look for the places where energy seems to flow. You will eventually notice that, while there will be small collections of energy throughout the house, they are all ultimately moving in the direction of one large energy draw. This is the Dynamic Centre of your home.

Dowsing   You can also dowse to locate the Dynamic Centre of your home. (See Chapter 5 for detailed information on dowsing.) Using either a dowsing rod or a pendulum, walk slowly around your home. Focus your mind on your intention, but don't try to control the process. Just go with the flow and see where you are led.

The best place for the Dynamic Centre

Ideally, the Dynamic Centre and the physical centre *should be in the same place*. However, if this is not the case in your home, then it's important to decide carefully the best place for the Dynamic Centre, for it determines the influence of the directional energy. For example, if the Dynamic Centre lies near the southern wall of your home, then you may find that there is too much northern energy. Sometimes people suffer from depression, or feel that they are stagnant, if there is too much northern energy. On the other hand, people in a home with a Dynamic Centre in the northern portion of a house, might feel the influence of too much southern energy. They might always be 'on the go', with no time for refuelling or reflection.

Homes with a Dynamic Centre in the west might be flooded with a predominance of eastern energy. Residents might rush to begin projects, but never manage to finish them. A Dynamic Centre in the east might result in an abundance of western energy. Here people may have an easy time adjusting to changes, but there might be a corresponding lack of stability and harmony.

The maxim 'If it's not broken, don't fix it' is very applicable here. If your life is great just the way it is, *do not change the Dynamic Centre.*

An abundance of southern energy

An abundance of eastern energy

Establishing the dynamic centre in the north/west increases energy flows from the south and the east, thus bringing vitality and new beginnings into the home.

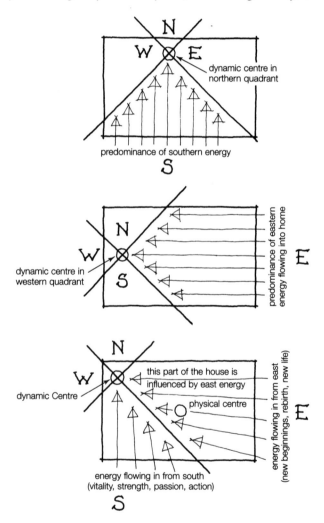

210

However, if you are feeling out of balance or uncentred, or need a new direction in your life, then you might consider shifting the location of the Dynamic Centre, (or alternatively you can strengthen the deficient directional energy).

This might sound confusing, but it is very easy. For example, if you discover that the Dynamic Centre is in the northernmost part of your home, and there always seems to be a surfeit of frenetic activity in your home, this might mean that there is too much southern energy surging through on its way to the Dynamic Centre. There are two things that you can do about this. You can either change the location of the Dynamic Centre, perhaps by designating it in the middle of the home. (See methods below.) This will neutralise the oversupply of southern energy. Or, alternatively, you can activate more northern energy by placing objects that symbolise qualities of the north – such as solidity, quiet and repose – in the northern quadrant of your home. A photo of a snow-covered mountain is an excellent choice because it can combine the tranquillity of the north with the winter qualities of the north. Also a statue of a tortoise is good, because a tortoise withdraws into the sanctuary of his shell, thus representing the peaceful inner qualities of the north. Whenever you place an object, you might say a small prayer such as: 'I dedicate this object to feelings of peace, quiet and stability in this home. With this object, I am calling these qualities into our lives. So be it.'

Usually it's best to have the Dynamic Centre in the middle of your home, in order to have an equal amount of the energy from each of the directions. However, there are times when you may shift the Dynamic Centre to invoke a particular kind of energy into your home. For example, if your Dynamic Centre is in the physical centre but you want more vitality in your life and you are ready for a new beginning, you might consider establishing it in the northwest quadrant of your home. Here, it pulls into your home a greater amount of the energy of new beginnings from the east and the vitality from the south. (See illustration at the bottom of page 210.)

When you are shifting the Dynamic Centre of the home to a new area, it's valuable to know that generally a true Dynamic Centre is deeply established and it will take some effort to realign it. However, you will eventually be successful and the results in terms of increased happiness and effectiveness will be more than worth it.

Anchoring the Dynamic Centre

There are a number of excellent ways to anchor the Dynamic Centre in your home. One of the easiest and most powerful ways is to create your

own omphalos stone to establish and designate the focal point for the energy flows in your environment.

Finding your own omphalos stone

Stones contain highly concentrated energy from the earth. By placing a specially designated stone at your Dynamic Centre you literally anchor the centre-point energy of your home. You can purchase a stone for this purpose, but it would be best to find your own special omphalos stone in nature by means of a 'trance walk' technique used by ancient shamans and mystics for finding power stones.

Often the best stones are large, heavy ones of oval shape. The river variety are excellent because the water has worn them to smoothness. However, whatever stone you are drawn to is the right one for you, even if it has none of these qualities. In ancient tradition, an omphalos was either carved or decorated with sacred designs. You may want to do this, but it is not necessary. Place your omphalos somewhere in the Dynamic Centre and dedicate it to the balance and protection of your home.

Lingham stones are also excellent for anchoring the Dynamic Centre of your home. They make wonderful omphalos stones because they are very grounding and are not easily affected by other energy fields. They can establish a Dynamic Centre almost instantly in a home. Linghams are found only in the sacred Narmada river in India, where the swollen monsoon waters tumble them into their typical oval shape. They have a unique mineral composition which emits a powerful force field and there is a mystical quality that seems to emanate from them. To me they look like dragon's eggs just about to hatch. In India, linghams are worshipped in many temples, where they are anointed with oils and covered with brightly coloured flowers. In Tibet linghams rest under

---

Trance Walking to Find an Omphalos Stone

To trance walk, allow yourself to be relaxed with your mind unfocused. To enter this state, take three very deep breaths and imagine that you are breathing through the centre of your forehead, which is called the 'third eye' in eastern mystic traditions. This will help activate your intuition. Then imagine that you are putting out a psychic 'call' for a perfect omphalos stone. This creates an energetic cord between you and your stone. Then begin to walk. You will recognise your stone when you find it because there will be something about it that seems special. To someone else it might look ordinary, but to you it will be like no other stone in the area.

the dais of the lamas. Traditionally, the stone is positioned upright on a small stand called the yoni. The lingham symbolises the Yang, or male forces of the universe, while the yoni symbolises the Yin, or female influences. Together they represent the male and female aspects of God.

When used to designate the centre of your home. your lingham should be placed upright in some kind of circular container such as a small bowl. Linghams should be anointed with sandalwood oil on a regular basis to maintain their energy level. If you live in a multi-storey block of flats, lingham are particularly good for anchoring your home's centre to the earth.

Creating an altar

Creating an altar to anchor the Dynamic Centre is another powerful way both to ground and ignite energy in your home. When you place an altar in the Dynamic Centre, you are creating a focal point where spiritual energy can emanate into your home throughout the day. It is essential that you dedicate this altar to the heart of your home, its Dynamic Centre. You may have many altars in your home but this particular altar is designated as your home's centre-point. This altar should keep in step with your life. It should not be some static collection of objects which you set up and then abandon. Each day it can be refreshed with a candle, incense or flower.

Maintaining your home's centre

Once you have established a true sense of the centre in your home or workplace, it is essential to honour it so that it continues to radiate health and vibrant energy throughout your space. To do this, you will want to perform periodic cleansing. A light misting of the air with spring water will renew the energy of your home's centre. Fresh flowers enhance its energy. A small bowl of rice can be a traditional way of honouring the sacred centre of a home. When your home is centred, you will feel centred in your life. And when you come from your centre, anything is possible.

16

The Four Sacred Elements

MY CHEROKEE grandparents lived on a ranch in Oklahoma. On their land was a large hill called Blue Mound, so named because when you looked at it from a distance it appeared to be blue. It wasn't easy to walk up Blue Mound, but I loved to climb it, because when I got to the top I felt as though I could see the entire universe. It was the place where I sensed a perfect balance of the elements – Air, Water, Fire and Earth. From my vantage place, I'd feel the warmth of the sun on my face and watch the winds sweep across the plains below. I would lie on my back in the high grasses and, comforted by the feeling of the earth beneath me, watch the big fluffy clouds drift by. One day I saw a rainstorm in the distance and waited with anticipation as it crept closer and closer until, with one crackling thunderbolt, the sky seemed to open overhead, sending a deluge of water pounding down on me from the heavens. I laughed with joy. I had never felt so alive, so much a part of the world.

Human beings divide reality into separate components. We measure time in terms of decades, years, months, days, hours, minutes, seconds, and even nanoseconds. And we have divided the mysterious panorama of nature into separate parts that we label the elements. In truth, nature is a melding and blending of the elements – a vast cauldron of Air, Water, Fire and Earth. None can exist without the others. It is not just that they interact with each other, because in a profound sense each element has an imprint of the others within it. The tree that grows from the earth takes energy from the sun, water from the rain, and oxygen from the air: all are needed to sustain life.

However, it is often only through separating and defining the natural forces around us that discernment and wisdom can evolve. But when we do this, when we divide nature into four (or five) elements, we must remember that this is only a symbolic system which can never encompass reality. Wholeness resides in harmonic forces which exist outside the perception of our senses and which *are symbolised by the elements*. It is this realm, where balance and harmony reign supreme, that gives birth to miracles.

When I first learned about feng shui I was enthralled. Here was a system that validated what I sensed about living spaces, as well as what I had learned from my own Native American traditions. However, I continually stumbled over the five-element theory in Chinese feng shui. This system divided the forces of nature into the elements of Wood, Water, Fire, Earth, and Metal. I recognised the brilliance of the system and acknowledged that it worked very well in many instances. And yet, perhaps because of my Native America heritage, it didn't quite fit for me. I yearned to find a method that could feed my soul, one that would honour the *four* elements of my roots, my land and my culture.

My intimate connection with the four elements grew out of my experiences with the Native American Medicine Wheel. To the Native American, the elements are not only the physical elements of *real* air, water, fire and earth, they are also the four conditions of matter. Air refers to all gases; Water includes all fluids; Fire represents all radiant and electrical phenomena; and Earth symbolises all solids. I began to see that the elemental wisdom taught by the Native Americans, as well as by the ancient Greeks and Europeans, could have enormous value for balancing the energy in homes and workplaces. From an ancestral perspective, my connection to the four elements was rooted not only in my Native American heritage, but also in the traditions of my Scottish ancestors. This was the system which felt the most comfortable to me.

For a long time I searched for a way to synthesise the four elements of the West with the five elements of the East. Although I tried a number of different approaches, I never found a satisfactory way to correlate the two systems. Finally I realised that both systems had value, *but they were separate systems*. This was a revelation for me. As soon as I began applying the four elements of my ancestors to my feng shui consultations, magic happened. I had discovered a system whose roots went deep into the soil of my homeland.

In presenting it here I wish to show no disrespect for the Chinese system of five elements; indeed, I have enormous regard for that system. I work with the four elements because in doing so I honour my own heritage and culture, and because it feels best for me. I believe that gaining a historical perspective about the four elements, and using the unique qualities of each one, can enable you to create a very special energy in your home.

HISTORY OF THE FOUR ELEMENTS

Ancient traditions   The earliest religions were earth-based. The earth was believed to be a conscious being who made her bounty available to humans. She was the Earth Mother, a Great Goddess to be revered. In early cultures around the world, the elements of Air, Water, Fire and Earth were honoured and called upon to bring harmony and prosperity to the land. Life was considered to be in balance when these elements were in an equilibrium. Rituals honouring the four elements have continued into modern times in the cultures of Native Americans, and in Wiccan, paganistic and shamanistic religions.

Native Americans   The number four has always had deep significance for Native Americans. They honoured the four directions, the four winds, the four quarters of the universe, and the four elements. The symbolism of the four elements welded all separate pieces of reality into one cohesive whole. Each element was personified and homage was given to the Spirits of Air, Water, Fire and Earth. The four elements were thought to be the primal essence of all life on earth, and each one brought a gift that gave balance to the people. The Spirit of the Air gave the wind with its cooling breezes in the summer. The Spirit of the Water brought refreshing rains. The Spirit of the Fire gave warmth from the sun, and the Spirit of the Earth brought forth the hills, the mountains and all the creatures of the earth. The underlying energy of all the elements was the Creator, the source of all life.

Ancient India   In Ancient India the four elements were called Vayu (Air), Apas (Water), Tejas (Fire), and Privithi (Earth). A fifth component, Akasha (Ether) was the essence from which all life flowed, similar to the Native American belief that the centre-point of all the elements was the Creator.

Persia   Mithraism was a mystery school of Persian origin that declared that man had to rule the elements before he could truly reach spiritual attainment. Initiates underwent rigorous rites of Air, Water, Fire and Earth. Each elemental rite was said to test a particular aspect of the initiate's nature.

Egypt   The great Egyptian sage, Hermes Trismegistus; believed fervently in the power of the four elements, and that reflection on them could provide a deeper understanding and appreciation of life. He also believed in the *prima materia*, the essence of the universe, and that each human carried this essence inside of him.

Greek philosophy   In the fourth century BC, a Greek philosopher named Empedocles declared that life had four basic elements: Air, Water, Fire and Earth. Aristotle and Plato, two of the greatest philosophers of the classical world, embraced the idea. Aristotle talked too about 'ether', also called *prima materia* – the prime material of the universe – an echo of the Native American and ancient Indian belief in a Divine essence that sourced all the elements. The *prima materia* had no physical form, but within its essence was the potential of matter. Hippocrates, honoured as the father of medicine, declared that a patient's health depended upon a balance of the four bodily fluids or humours, which correspond to four elements. He also believed that no physician could practise effectively without an understanding of the elemental aspects of heavenly influences.

Medieval alchemists   Medieval alchemists built on the foundation laid by the Greeks to expand their own ideas about the four elements. Many people think alchemists were engaged solely in efforts to turn base metals into gold, but in a deeper sense their mission was to transform the baser aspects of humanity into more divine qualities. Gold was a perfect symbol for this quest because it didn't rust and thus represented divine immortality.

In addition to believing that the four elements were the base components of life on earth, the alchemists also felt that they were symbols of man's connection to the universe. Air represented the spirit, Earth corresponded to the body; Water symbolised creation; and Fire stood for transforming energy. In general, Earth and Water were related to the female principle, and Air and Fire represented the male principle. The early alchemists also believed that the elements were all supported by an energy that was called the 'Quintessence', which was an essence of spirit.

Other traditions and the four elements

In *The Masks of God: Primitive Mythology*, Joseph Campbell observed that many ancient cultures shared similar views about the four elements.

He noticed multiple commonalities between the beliefs of Mayan-Aztec cultures and those of Egypt and Mesopotamia. All of these ancient cultures revered the power of the four directions and the four elements.[1] In comparing the five-element system of China with the four-element systems of other cultures, Joseph Campbell said, 'The systems differ, yet they are derived from the same root.'[2]

The great Sufi poet Rumi wrote that the four elements were the foundation of life, and that they had a profound effect upon the human spirit. This renowned mystic also wrote about the energy underlying the four elements, which unifies them and is the source of all life.

Cells and the four elements

Not only do we need the four elements to live – the Air to breathe, the Water to drink, the Fire for warmth and the Earth for food – but each cell in our body is like a tiny Medicine Wheel – a macrocosm of the microcosm – which needs the four elements to survive. Every cell needs Water for hydration, Air for oxidation, Earth for nutrients, and Fire for the bio-electrical energy that surges through it.

Astrology and the four elements

Since earliest times human beings have looked to the stars and constellations for meaning. One of the oldest human artefacts ever found, dating from about 34,000 years ago, is a Cro-Magnon slab of bone that was apparently notched to mark the phases of the moon. From those early beginnings astrology grew around the world. One of the main tenets of astrology maintains that each sign of the zodiac corresponds to one of the four elements of nature. For example, Aries is the first sign of the zodiac and is a Fire sign. It is followed by Taurus, an Earth sign, then Gemini, an Air sign, which is followed in turn by Cancer, a Water sign. This cycle continues around the zodiac, with all twelve signs divided evenly between the four elements.

The Fire signs are thought to be vibrant, lively, adventuresome, impatient and ebullient. Earth signs are considered stable, dependable, very grounded and logical. Air signs are associated with communication, lofty ideals, reflection and ideas for the future. Water elements are said to be emotional, sensitive, intuitive, private and compassionate.[3]

Animals and the four elements

Human beings have always personalised the world around them. This basic tendency presumably led to the association of particular animals with the elements. The animals assigned to the elements vary from culture to culture, and even from tribe to tribe within a culture. However, the practice is universal and probably arose because it is easier to relate to the traits of animals than to disembodied principles. For example, it might seem difficult to communicate with the Spirit of the Air because it lacks tangible form. It is easier to communicate with the eagle, which is often associated with the Air element.

Although it is valuable to assign qualities to various elements, it is important also to keep in mind that all elements emerge out of the same energy, and in nature the elements are not separate from each other. In practising Medicine Wheel Feng Shui™ I do not assign an element to a specific direction, because in nature all four elements exist in every direction. You don't find air only in the east or south – air exists in all directions. All elements are interconnected and are a melding of energy patterns that create life.

Modern architecture and the four elements

Some present-day architects acquire creative inspiration from the four elements. Nader Khalili, a remarkable architect and author of several books, is noted for his passion for building ecologically sustainable, affordable homes. Khalili feels that it is essential to integrate the elements of Air, Water, Fire and Earth into our homes. He says that incorporating the four elements into his work has infused it with a spiritual dimension.

Tom Bender is an architect who is a leader in the ecological building movement and the winner of AIA (American Institute of Architects) and UIA (International Union of Architects) competitions for sustainable community solutions. Tom says that he draws on his understanding of the four elements to create his buildings, which are renowned for their sense of harmony with nature, as well as their aesthetic beauty.

FOUR ELEMENTS FOR HEALING

For many years I worked as a healer using a system I developed called Four Directions Healing. I also taught this system to other therapists. The therapy was based on the idea that the elements have an effect on the psyche. I found that when a client visualised each of the four elements, *each element evoked a particular emotional response, as well as different types of memories*. Sometimes the sessions were quite dramatic.

During my session with Robert I asked him to visualise images of the earth, such as mountains, boulders and valleys. While he was envisioning these scenes, I asked him how he felt. He reported feeling comfort and deep relaxation. When I asked him if any memories were emerging, he said that pleasant childhood memories were floating through his mind. I then asked him to visualise images of water – waterfalls, rivers, rainfall. This time he began to cry silently. When I asked what he was feeling, he told me that he had remembered a sad moment from his childhood that he had previously forgotten. Using resolution techniques we were able to process his sadness so that it could heal.

The remarkable thing about this elemental approach to therapy is the way that it reveals the emotional impact the elements have on us. Someone who feels completely calm and relaxed visualising one element might have a completely different response to another one. I believe that our memories, beliefs and emotions are tied in some mysterious and organic way to the elements of nature. By activating these elements within us, it seems that we also activate quadrants of our souls. A proverb from India states that everyone is a house with four rooms – physical, mental, emotional and spiritual rooms – but unless we go into every room every day we are not a complete person. I found that the elements were a powerful vehicle for entering these rooms.

When I trained therapists to use my Four Directions Healing system, I found that their skill in using these methods was directly proportional to their ability to shift their consciousness and become one with the elements. A powerful way to attune to the elements is to spend time in nature. For example, lying on the earth and imagining your body dissolving into it, until you feel the mountains and valleys inside your soul, can redefine the way you experience the world around you.

ELEMENTS AS ARCHETYPES

Each element can be thought of as an archetype associated with particular qualities. You will find that you are more closely associated with the qualities of one element than with those of any other. *Discovering the element with which you are most aligned can be very valuable so you can create a home that is in harmony with your personal element rather than at odds with it.*

Although you may find aspects of yourself in all of the elemental personality types described below, there will be one that most closely reflects your personal approach to life. Some people will find that there is a certain amount of crossover in their affiliation with elements. You may find that you are more of an air person in one part of your life, with water qualities predominating in another area. An example of this might be someone who operates in a highly organised, intellectual way at work (Air Clan person), but has a more emotional, intuitive style at home (Water Clan person).

1 Archetypal Air Clan person

Affirming qualities Air Clan people are known for their grace and diplomacy. They are often intellectual and drawn to the arts. They can be idealistic, with a humanitarian focus, and are usually extremely open-minded. They like to feel free and unbounded, and tend to be articulate, artistic, gracious and innovative. They can make good teachers. Air Clan people are good at forming bridges between divergent groups and bringing people closer together. The Air Clan individual always has a strategy for life. Where others are guided by the heart or their emotions, the Air Clan person is guided by logic and rational thinking. Air Clan people often have a master plan for their life and evaluate the events of their life in terms of this plan. They do not take risks easily and will spend a great deal of time assessing facts before making changes. They are organised and cautious.

It would be unusual for an Air Clan person to have a home filled with mementos of the past or sentimental objects. The homes of Air Clan people are usually uncluttered and contain objects that are well-designed and aesthetically pleasing.

Restrictive qualities Sometimes Air Clan people can be indecisive because they see all points of view. They tend to take an overly intellectual approach to a situation where a gut response might be more appropriate. Their concern for the many often obscures awareness of the needs of people closest to them.

Symbolism The Air element is Mental Power. It is freedom, movement, expansion, uplift and exhilaration.

2 Archetypal Water Clan person

Affirming qualities Water Clan people tend to experience the world through their emotions and feelings. They often find themselves in caretaking positions, and they make good protectors of the young or helpless. They are naturally empathic and sensitive to the feelings of others. They are always ready to lend a helping hand without drawing attention to themselves. They nurture hope and faith in others and usually are loyal friends. There is a quiet heroism in the Water Clan person. Relationships are important to Water Clan people. They yearn for what is real and honest in all their dealings with others. They also need to know that they are part of a family. The past is important to them because it provides a context for relationships.

Restrictive qualities   Under stress Water Clan people have a tendency either to keep their emotions dammed up inside or else flood everybody and everything with their feelings. Alternatively they can have the tendency to fixate on one thing to the detriment of all other areas of life. Water Clan individuals may have difficulty letting go.

Symbolism   The Water element is Emotional Power. It is fluidity, nurture, compassion and healing.

3 *Archetypal Fire Clan person*

Affirming qualities   Fire Clan people are fast-moving and intense. They tend to be visionaries who are always looking to the future; sometimes they are able to foretell the future. They make good leaders, as they often have the ability to inspire others. But they also have a need for privacy in order to restore their energy and replenish their souls. The Fire Clan person's need for retreat can arise out of an inability to set boundaries with others. However, this difficulty is inextricably linked with the very qualities which make Fire Clan people such strong visionaries.

Because they need time to be alone, Fire Clan people are very cautious about letting others into their private domain. They are much better at one-on-one interactions, but, conversely are excellent at inspiring large groups. They tend to skip small talk and get right to the heart of the matter. They have the ability to reach straight into a person's core to see the truth of what is most important.

Fire clan people are known for courage, optimism and pioneering spirit. They are good at initiating projects. Without constant stimulation, they stagnate. What might seem like excessive activity is linked to their life force. A fire that stops moving is dead.

Restrictive qualities   People of the Fire Clan can seem hyperactive, volatile and overpowering. They may have difficulty seeing a project through to completion and they are easily bored. Others may find them too intense, and they have a tendency to burn themselves out. Fire Clan people can also be very self-critical. They are their own worst judge. Sometimes they overcompensate for their difficulty in establishing personal boundaries by seeming cool and aloof.

Symbolism   The Fire element is Spirit Power. It is radiance, illumination and vitality.

4 Archetypal Earth Clan person

Affirming qualities   Earth Clan people are very aligned with the earth and will vigorously defend their young and the less fortunate. They take pride in their physical bodies and sometimes identify themselves primarily in this way. Security is important to them. Earth Clan individuals are seldom talkative unless the subject is one they feel impassioned about. They have an affinity for working with plants, wood and minerals, and therefore often excel in areas such as gardening, carpentry or stonemasonry.

There are two basic sub-groups within the Earth Clan. One type is stable, practical, earthy, grounded, solid and persevering – someone who would be considered a salt-of-the-earth-type individual. People who fall into this group are creative and original, especially when working with their hands. They can be slow and deliberate in their actions and discerning in their view of the world.

The second type of Earth Clan people are adventurers. These earthy souls are high-spirited and ready to take on any challenge. They thumb their nose at convention and are noncomformist in attitude. Unwilling to submit to authority, they often enjoy being the one in control. Adventurer Earth Clan individuals love to party and are passionate about life. They have good instincts and tend to respond on a gut level rather than out of careful deliberation.

Restrictive qualities   Sometimes Earth Clan people can become very attached to an idea. They may experience difficulty changing their mind, even when faced with overwhelming evidence that it would be in their best interest to do so. Sometimes rigid, narrow-minded and incredibly stubborn, they can be closed off from their feelings. In relationships, they may be afraid to make a long-term commitment, but they are extremely loyal once the commitment is made. They are often intolerant of people if they perceive them as clinging or needy, and they are drawn to physical vitality in others.

Symbolism: The Earth element is Physical Power. It is fertility, attainment, achievement, stability and abundance.

Bringing the elements into your home

Whenever you include the elements in your home, you will bring a richness of spirit that will nurture your soul. Use the information contained in Chapters 9 to 12 to identify the specific qualities of each element that you wish to activate, then use the information in Chapter 17 to combine the four elements to create the ideal elemental home for you.

17

The Elemental Home

As I OPENED the gate into Chellie's garden I knew I had entered into a magical realm. Delicate windflowers were swaying slightly in the warm summer breeze. Handmade birdhouses were nestled on poles amidst the flowers. A quaint statue of a cherub held a shallow birdbath in his chubby hands, and a fragrant honeysuckle cascaded down a garden wall.

The artistic touches throughout Chellie's home mirrored the whimsical charm of the garden. The curtains had panels of soft hand-dyed fabric. A Norwegian carving of an old fisherman seemed to wink at me from a nearby shelf. The fridge door was covered with the finger paintings of Chellie's two young boys. As we sat down to tea, I knew that I was in a quintessential Water Element home, a place where I could kick off my shoes and be myself.

Most people have a stronger affinity with one element than with the others. This alignment grows out of their basic personality type and approach to life. Homes, too, are usually more strongly aligned with one of the elements. One home will feel like a Water Element home, while another will be aligned with the Earth element. Although the majority of homes have characteristics associated with more than one element, their aura still falls within one of the four elemental groups. Learning the elemental alignment of your home will enable you to assess how well it is working for you. Including some aspects from all of the four elements will lend balance and integration to your home, while selecting one main element to work with will help you to create an environment that will nourish your soul.

The information in this chapter is designed to help you identify the elemental influences in your home. It is based on information I have gathered around the world and that I have used in my own practice, but it is intended only as a guide. There are always exceptions to any set of rules. Some of the ideas here may work better in one environment or culture than in another. If you find that this is true for you, please do not hesitate to use what works and ignore the pieces that don't fit your situation. There is no right interpretation and there is certainly truth in all of them. It is my hope that the following information will stimulate you to find the truth in your own home, so that you can make it a place of magic and beauty.

THE AIR HOME

When you walk into an Air home you will find an environment that is lofty, airy and expansive. The Air home is defined by clean sleek lines and classical style. Elegance and understated good taste are hallmarks of Air design. You might see a Ming vase tucked into an alcove, or a stunning ikebana flower arrangement. A sense of organisation and balance pervades this home. Each thing has its place and usually everything is in its place. Even when there is messiness, a sense of basic order is still apparent beneath the disarray. Minimalist designs, Zen-like simplicity and modern elegance are all favoured styles.

This environment does not appear to have occurred through chance or whimsy. Although Air rooms can be warm and inviting, they will none the less have a studied, rather than random, feel to them. This home, upon closer inspection, will reveal well-organised cupboards and shelves, with the contents arranged according to type, size, function or colour. The electrical, plumbing and air-conditioning systems will usually be well maintained. In an Air environment, the focus will be on the classic lines of the architecture and furnishings, rather than on decorative touches applied to them. You might also find:

Interior style Light, airy, spacious, elegant, formal, classic, lofty, simple, sleek lines, open, spacious. In this home you might find skylights, slate, track lighting, tall windows, open space beneath sofas and beds.

Accessories   Books, fine art, tall vases, narrow armoire, tall bookcases, electrical gadgets, food processors, excellent stereo equipment, metal, floor-to-ceiling curtains, black-and-white photographs, mobiles, wind chimes, tall lamps with light directed upwards, shoji screens.

Textures, patterns, fabrics   Sheers, solids, crisp cotton, damask and chintz, stripes.

Shapes   Rectangular.

Building features   Taller than wide, high ceilings, tall windows, columns.

Building style   Modern, minimalist, colonial, Scandinavian, industrial, art deco, high-tech design.

Metals   Aluminium, stainless steel, chrome.

Plants   Iris, spiky tall leaves, orchids, lilies, daffodils.

Aromas Lemon, lime, pine, eucalyptus, juniper.

Lighting   Halogen, bright, white, crisp, well-defined.

Animals (photos, drawings or figurines)   Birds in general, but particularly the eagle, hawk and falcon.

Music   Classical (Vivaldi, Mozart, Bach), flute, wind instruments, some types of jazz.

Garden   Formal or classical style. Spacious, sweeping lawns with well-defined borders and groomed hedges. Tall trees, such as eucalyptus, aspens and evergreens. Tall greenery, such as bamboo and other reeds. Formal statuary, columns, fountains, winged angels.

Surrounding landscape   Vast vistas, panoramic views, building situated on the top or side of a hill or mountain, open spaces, plains.

THE WATER HOME

The first thing you will feel when you walk into a typical Water home is warmth and comfort. It feels good to be there. This home is often filled with the traditional comforts of home: bread baking in the oven, handmade quilts on the beds, a dog curled in front of the hearth, a soft comfortable couch, flowered curtains blowing in the wind, roses blooming just outside the window.

You won't find trendy uncomfortable chairs here. Decorating decisions stem from a basic desire for what is real. Never mind if one of the table legs has chew marks on it – the puppy was young and didn't know any better. There is a sense of honesty and naturalness to the Water home. In place of the hands-off *objets d'art* favoured in an Air home, you will find hand-crafted things which seem to invite handling. The fibres are 100 per cent cotton, rather than polyester or silk, and the coffee mugs will probably be hand-painted pottery with a small chip here or there.

There is rarely a sense of pretence in a Water home. It is a home for living in, not for show. It promotes feelings of community and belonging no matter who lives in it. Objects are chosen for sentimental value. The drawing of a child, a handmade wreath, a special shell found on a holiday at the seaside, the less-than-beautiful lamp that was a present from a loved friend: all these will be cherished in the Water home.

Relationships are of utmost importance to the Water Clan person and the Water house reflects this. Clustered photos on the mantelpiece and piano, a fridge covered with children's drawings, poems and family photos: all are characteristic of this kind of home. The Water home is also the most romantic home. Floral prints, lace curtains, scented soaps and beeswax candles add to the generous feeling of emotional comfort here.

The feeling in a Water home is comfortable, flowing, feminine, nurturing and natural. Some Water homes will have the solid, honest simplicity found in Shaker designs; others may be filled, even cluttered, with mementoes. You may also find:

Interior style   Natural, simple and well-kept, with plain oak and pine furniture, or cosy, filled with sentimental objects, lots of cushions, lace, ruffles, French country-style, soft textures, charmingly mismatched furniture, rounded corners, draped fabrics, deep comfortable sofas.

Accessories   Fountains, aquariums, round ceramic vases decorated with flowers, bowls of water, roses, fresh flowers and ones made of silk, teddy bears and toys, trunks with mementoes, antiques, vintage throws and shawls, handmade objects worn with age, Blue Willow-pattern plates on the wall, heirlooms, trinkets, photos of friends and family, pictures or figurines of children and young animals, fairies, angels and unicorns, handmade quilts, plants, old baskets.

Textures, patterns, fabrics   Fabrics that drape and flow, French country designs, Pierre Deux or Laura Ashley fabrics, calicos, floral prints, ginghams, cottons, pastel chiffons, pastel stripes or checks, soft wool.

Shapes   Circles.

Building features Homy (whether simple or ornate), fretwork, Victorian ornamentation, bay windows, curved walkways, ivy, climbing roses or other flowering creepers, rounded corners, curved roof lines, lush vegetation close to house.

Building style Country cottage, Victorian or earlier period, crafts-man-style bungalow.

Metals Silver, pewter, hand-cut tin.

Plants Many flowers, especially tulips, roses, daisies, lavender, African violets, philodendron, prayer plants, ferns.

Aromas Florals, lavender, rose, jasmine, ylang ylang, neroli.

Lighting Soft, warm, muted, shaded, rounded Japanese rice paper lanterns, glowing, lit from within, many candles.

Animals (photos, drawings or figurines) Water animals, such as dolphins, whales, seals and fish and any type of young animal; also pandas, koalas, and polar bears.

Music Melodious and pastoral music, Chopin, Brahms, New Age music, nature sounds, country and western, lullabies.

Garden Enclosed cosy spaces with meandering pathways, comfortable benches and places to rest. Pools and fountains. Many flowers, especially ones reminiscent of English country gardens, such as roses, violets, lupins, and lavender. Pastel colours, sweet scents. Birdhouses, birdbaths. Hanging baskets. Statues of Kwan Yin or Venus. Secret places, hidden bowers.

Surrounding landscape Rolling hills and softly rounded land forms. Streams, slow-flowing rivers, ponds, pools, mists, rain. Trees with rounded tops, such as maples and willows. Full, leafy bushes.

THE FIRE HOME

Because of their intensity and high energy level, Fire Clan people often create homes as places of retreat. The predominant theme of most Fire homes is privacy. Because their nature makes them able to inspire others and often draws large numbers of people to them, Fire Clan people need a home that counterbalances these tendencies, a place where they can go to restore their energy and replenish their soul. The Fire home reflects a desire to tame the chaos and bring balance to life.

Fire Clan people are also highly intuitive and often have the ability to see into the future. These qualities give their homes a wonderful atmosphere of spirituality. It is common to find altars here, or clusters of objects placed in symmetrical arrangements that resemble altars. Focus is very important, and often furnishings are arranged around a focal point in the room. In addition, there is usually a focus point for the entire home.

The Fire home is filled with objects that are well made and of timeless appeal. These will be grouped together in daring combinations and arrangements that somehow work together beautifully. For example, you might find an eighteenth-century chair with cushions from Africa. A Fire home may have some of the same classic items found in an Air home, but here they will be casually grouped together rather than placed in a formal arrangement. A Fire home may have some areas that aren't meant to be touched or lived in; they are for display only.

The Fire home may have long curtains falling into bunched folds on the floor. Abundant swags, fat tassels and other decorations speaking of abundance and luxury are common here. Gorgeous fabrics fill the Fire home, adorning the windows and beds and furniture. Rooms may contain an abundance of cushions, tablecloths, draperies and graceful throws, and all are sumptuous and exquisite.

The Fire home may contain small intimate spaces hidden behind closed doors, making for an ambience very unlike the open expansive one of the Air home. A fire that is too big burns out of control, hence rooms in a Fire home will have a sense of containment and intimacy. Corners are filled with statues, plants, screens and draped fabrics, thus bringing the edges of the room closer to the centre. The focal point in every Fire room can be compared to a flame in a dark room – all eyes are drawn to it. In this home you'll find dimmers on light switches everywhere. This allows control of the amount of overhead light so as to maximise the effect of the focal point in the room. In the daytime the curtains are often thrown back so that the light of the sun can flood in.

Another type of Fire house could be described as the 'Unconfined-Fire home' or the 'Extroverted Fire home'. This home has hard edges and vibrant yet erratic colours. There is a sense of sharp, brilliant intensity here. Colours might seem to jump and clash with each other: intense reds combined with bright greens, jet black with sunflower yellow. There is something incredibly exciting and exhilarating about the energy found in this type of home. Here you might find a modern metal sculpture in the centre of the living room and a huge abstract painting leaning against the wall, its surface covered with wild splashes of orange and black.

Often there will be neither carpets nor curtains in this type of home. The sound of steps on the floor echoes throughout the entire home. The energy is highly charged and personal interactions are intense. The phone will ring, someone runs to gets it and then immediately dashes out of the door. People seldom walk here; they run. This type of home can be great for those who need to bring some excitement or exhilaration into their life. For example, it might work well for people who have so much water energy in their life they are drowning in their emotions.

The atmosphere in a Fire home is either private and sanctuary-like, calming, rich and eclectic, or it is erratic, bright, vibrant, sharp, brilliant. The categories below contain descriptions of both types of Fire homes. Because the two Fire styles are very distinct from each other, descriptions under the various headings have been divided with the numerals '1' for the Introverted Fire home and '2' for the Extroverted home. In a Fire home you may find:

Interior style
1 Private-sanctuary feeling, muted edges, hidden corners, calming, rich, eclectic. Here you might find drapes, fringes, canopy beds, elegant centrepieces, gilded Buddhas, chandeliers, candles, tapestries, thick wall-to-wall carpeting, oriental rugs, fireplaces.
2 Erratic, bright, vibrant, sharp, immediate, brilliant, intense features. Ringing phones, electronic equipment, an interior constantly being rearranged with things being added and removed. Revolving cycle of frequent messes and clean-ups as distinct from the constant state of clutter in the Water home. Exhilarating, erratic, sometimes dizzying combinations of colour, texture, smells and sound. Few or no photos of family or ancestors.

Accessories
1 Candles, leaded crystals in the window to bring rainbow and fire energy into the home, jewel-like glass, beautiful frames, intimate table settings, tasseled cushions, pairs of objects, rich fabrics, ornate objects grouped with hand-crafted ones.
2 Sharp angles, pyramids. Clocks, especially with second hand movement. Electrical equipment, television, stereo appliances, track lighting. Items grouped in threes, large bold paintings, modern sculpture.

Textures, patterns, fabrics
1 Rich fabrics such as velvets and jacquards. Brocade, silk, textured wools, rich solids, intricate designs, stripes, hand-woven fabrics in beautiful colours.
2 Zigzags, herringbone, checks, electric and very vibrant colours, rough textures, plastics and vinyls, black leather.

Shapes   Triangle, pyramid.

Building features

1 Confined symmetry, traditional architecture. Brick, stone or wood construction, or a combination of these.

2 Sharp corners and edges, erratic angles, very large windows, innovative roof lines, unusual layout of rooms.

Building style

1 Tudor, Baroque, châteaux, eclectic mix of the old and the new.

2 Modern, highly dramatic.

Metals

1 Gold, wrought iron, copper.

2 Stainless steel, aluminum.

Plants

1 Ferns, ivy, begonias, chrysanthemums.

2 Indoor trees, plants with spiky leaves, spider plants, fast growers.

Aromas

1 & 2   Cedar, sage, piñon.

Lighting

1 Muted or dimmed lights, candles, many lamps with warm bulbs.

2 Bright, vibrant lights, coloured light bulbs.

Animals (photos, drawings or figurines)

1 & 2   Phoenix, thunderbird, reptiles, lizards, snakes.

Music

1 Nature sounds, Beethoven, soft jazz, New Age music, ethnic music.

2 Loud, dynamic, vibrant music.

Garden

1 Softly monochromatic colours with ivy-covered fences, or there may be a somewhat wild and overgrown mix of flowers, shrubs and herbs growing together in a beautiful lush way. Unusual mix of colours and textures create a startlingly beautiful effect. Small private areas surrounded by latticed fencing or hedges. Intimate benches, garden swings, areas for relaxation and contemplation of the garden. Beautiful garden gates of wood or iron leading into small enclosed areas.

2 Modernistic layout of stones, topiary trees, dramatic plantings of unusual plants. Multi-level terraces. Cacti, sand and sharp-leaved succulents.

Surrounding landscape

1 & 2   Sharp mountain peaks, desert, cliffs, dramatic landscape.

THE EARTH HOME

The first impression on entering an Earth home is the eclectically organic atmosphere. This home often contains rich textures, treasures from many lands, big earthen pots, anything made of wood, wrought iron, beautiful baskets, and a wonderful array of scents, from sandalwood and frankincense to a whiff of ratatouille wafting from the kitchen. It's also a home that says: 'Forget the rules – this is what I like.'

There are two kinds of Earth home. The first style is natural and organic and honours a return to the earth. In this home you might find natural fabrics, unbleached muslin and linen, natural sisal, unglazed pottery, handmade baskets, lots of plants, oversized cushions on the floor, a Native American drum hanging on the wall, primitive art from Africa or South America, and an Indian blanket thrown over the bed.

The second type of Earth home is the most sensual home of all the elemental homes. It is richly luxurious, a complete feast for the eyes, ears, nose and fingers. It invites the senses to heighten. In this home you might find velvets, velour, satin, sumptuous textures. It is a passionate environment, juicy with diversity. Here you might find a gold brocade sofa plump with an eclectic mix of cushions covered in antique fabrics, animal prints, paisley designs and needlepoint. On the walls there may be paintings ranging from classical to modern, all in elaborate gilded frames. An ornate altar with an African statue could be standing next to an old Spanish carving of St Francis among an abundance of candles and incense. In an Earth home you may find:

Interior style Earthy, warm, eclectic, grounded, abundant, fertile, solid, secure, unchanging, rich and sensual. In this home you might find large, squat overstuffed sofas and chairs. Mediterranean style, western style, Mexican style, medieval-gothic style. Heavy rustic wooden furniture. Tile or wood floors. Big oversized wooden cabinets, an iron potbellied stove, brick interior walls. Earth environments don't change as much over time as others. Once set up, they tend to remain the same over time.

Accessories Lots of plants, bunches of dried herbs, pots hanging in the kitchen, wooden salad bowls, wood carvings, cast-iron kettle on the range. Earthen pottery, macramé, animal-print fabrics. Wrought-iron candle holders and elaborate fire screens. Tassels, jugs, rocks, stones. Flowers hung upside down to dry, potpourri, short squat vases, Mexican/Spanish earthenware dishes. Terracotta tiles and dishes, primitive art, brightly coloured teapots, folk art from exotic lands, baskets and pots with lids, trunks.

Textures, patterns, fabrics   Natural fabrics, linens, sisal, unbelted muslin, canvas, ethnic designs, batiks, rich velvets, velour, satin, silks and brocades.

Shapes   Square.

Building features   Square, squat, close to the earth, with box-like features. This is a house that seems to have grown out of the earth. It will often share features with the natural environment surrounding it. For instance, a log home in the northwest pine forests of America is a perfect example of an Earth home.

Building style   Wooden houses, Southwest American style, log cabin, western-ranch style, Mediterranean, Spanish hacienda, castle. Adobe, brick, stone, wood or plaster construction.

Metal   Iron, gold, brass, copper.

Plants   Window-box gardens with herbs, lettuce, chives. Dahlias, geraniums, zinnias. Garlic and onions. Garden vegetables, especially root vegetables.

Aromas   Sandalwood, frankincense, myrrh, cedar, bergamot, tea-tree oil, eucalyptus, rosemary, thyme, oregano.

Lighting   Warm, rich lighting. Candlelight. Muted and glowing lamps.

Animals   (photos, drawings or figurines)   Photos, drawings or statues of elephants, turtles, tortoises, hippopotamus, rhinoceros, bears.

Music   Wagner, classic rock, heavy metal, blues, jazz, folk and country, any music with a steady beat or a lot of bass.

Garden   Earth home gardens are rarely predictable. Here you are likely to find a small statue of a frog or an elf among the bushes, a whirligig in the flowers, or an iron sculpture made of old machine parts. The Earth garden will delight your senses with its wonderful array of sights and smells. Just as the Earth home needs to reflect the land forms around it, so too the Earth garden needs to honour the native plants of the area. Although it is fine to include plants not native to the region, the overall feel of the garden should be consistent with the local climate and culture.

Surrounding landscape   Low rolling hills, plateaux, cliffs and forested areas. Earth homes look and feel best when they appear to blend in with the landscape around them. For example, a New England clapboard home would appear very unnatural and ill at ease in the red plateaux

of Arizona in the United States. An Earth home has a primal connection to its locality, so it should appear almost to have grown out of the land.

ELEMENTAL COLOURS

In elemental homes, you will find many colour schemes. For instance, one Earth home might be filled with tones of brown, terracotta and beige, while another has avocado green, pumpkin and cream. Both are good examples of Earth home colour schemes and yet they would appear very different from each other. Any home usually contains a range of colours, which may not seem to be associated with one element. However, there are two important concepts to consider when working with colour in the elemental home. The first and most important is the *activating colour* for a particular element, and the second is the *range of colours* usually associated with an element.

The activating colour for an element is a powerful tool that can be used to balance immediately the energy in a home where there is elemental disharmony. In order to know when and how to use this tool, you must first know the range of colours commonly associated with the elements.

For example, if a home is decorated in neutrals colours such as beige, yellow and tan (which are Air home colours) and the residents are complaining that they are having trouble taking action on the projects in their lives, there may be too much Air element in the home. They are thinking too much about a project rather than taking action. It might be valuable to activate the Fire element. Since red is Fire's activating colour, creating a focal point for the living room with an arrangement of red candles or a large bouquet of red tulips can help bring more decisiveness into the home. It doesn't need to be a lot of red; even a small amount of colour will work. Doing this will change the energy of the room and can also help the people there to feel more active and decisive. The conscious mind might resist this idea and think that there is no logical reason why this should work. None the less, the subconscious mind is powerfully affected by even the smallest of symbolic changes and colour is a remarkable way to impact the subconscious mind.

Activating Colour for the Elements	
Air	Yellow (mental clarity)
Water	Blue (emotional balance)
Fire	Red (activating force)
Earth	Green (grounding energy)

> ### *Range of Colours Associated with the Elements*
>
> **Air**   Neutral colours: white, beige, pale yellow, cream, tan, grey, black
> **Water**   Pastel shades of all colours and white
> **Fire**   1: Monochromatic schemes of rich shades of any colour
>   2: Vibrant, bright, clear colours
> **Earth**   Rich earth colours: burnt umber, rust, copper, orange, gold,
>   brown, terracotta, cream, aubergine, and all shades of green

It is important to note that an elemental home may not always be decorated in colours usually associated with an element. A Water home might be decorated with vibrant florals rather than pastel ones. It would still have the energy characteristics of a Water home, but the vibrant colours would also add balance from the Fire element to the primary Water feeling of the space.

Diagnosing and treating elemental colour imbalances in the home is not simple, because most homes have many colours in them. This is an area where your intuition will be a great help to you. Learning to work with colour is highly rewarding, because colour often produces instant, highly dramatic results in a home.

ELEMENTAL ENVIRONMENTS

Your environment will either support you or diminish your energy, and adjusting the elemental influences in your home can turn a draining environment into one where you will flourish. All people have aspects of each of the elements within them and so do homes. However, usually one element will predominate and will define the primary alignment of the person or home. Knowing your elemental alignment, and that of your home, can be helpful in creating the home you want. Here are some of the ways that environments and people match up.

An Air person

in an Air home may feel organised, punctual, centred and focused, but may sometimes have difficulty with decisions.

in a Fire home may feel disjointed, ill-tempered, uncentred and exhausted because air is consumed by fire.

in a Water home may feel too many emotions. Air people typically are not sentimental and can find this emotional environment overwhelming.

in an Earth home may feel too grounded and a bit claustrophobic when surrounded by all the belongings in an Earth home. The spirit of an Air person needs to feel free to soar. This can be impeded by an Earth environment. Also, the Earth home is completely grounded in the concepts of here and now, and this can be difficult for the Air person who likes to see the big picture.

A Water person

in an Air home may feel that life is too impersonal, and that he or she is not very connected to others.

in a Fire home may feel caught up in angry emotions, because fire mixed with water results in steam.

in a Water home may feel comforted and nurtured. However, they can also be continually experiencing an ocean of emotions.

in an Earth home may feel comfortable, if a bit sluggish at times. The water person may have a tendency to gain weight in this environment.

A Fire person

in an Air home may feel unprotected and sometimes a bit out of control, because air fuels fire.

in a Fire home may feel sublimely happy and focused, or exhausted because they are burning the candle at both ends.

in a Water home may feel their natural enthusiasm for life is continually dampened. This is a bad combination.

in an Earth home may feel stagnant and held back from moving forward in life, because earth puts out fire.

An Earth person

in an Air home may feel completely without creature comforts and never truly at home.

in a Fire home may feel happy and have a good time, because the Earth person's sociability when combined with the erratic energy of second type of Fire home will result in great parties. However, an Earth person may feel lonely in the Introverted Fire home.

in a Water home may feel agitated and have difficulties getting projects off the ground.

in an Earth home may feel grounded, steady, abundant and safe, but an Earth person's body may become stagnant and his or her thinking can become narrow-minded.

ELEMENTAL DECORATING

Knowledge of the elements can be a very helpful tool in decorating your home. A home doesn't only reflect your taste, it can help you to define your priorities and shape your future. Generally it's best to live in a home that basically matches your elemental character. However, there are some emotional and psychic drawbacks if it matches you too perfectly. The most beneficial environments will mostly reflect your elemental type but will also bring in aspects from the other elements to create balance. Even if your home is not the best match for your needs, you can greatly improve it by adjusting its elemental balance. Symbolic representations of the elements will activate their forces within your home and will make it a much more healthful environment for everyone living there.

Judy, nurse who had recently been laid off her job, called me shortly after her mother died. She was a Water Clan person and her house clearly reflected this in many ways. Her sofa was slipcovered in a blue floral design. Ruffled curtains framed her windows and a photograph of kittens hung on the wall. She also had a colour print of a waterfall prominently displayed in the living room. All of this water energy might be overwhelming for someone who was going through a period of deep grief.

After we talked together, I suggested that she add some red accents to her home to activate the energy of Fire (to help dry up some of the Water energy). I encouraged her to remove the decorative cloth tapestry covering her unused fireplace and to start having a cosy fire there every night. I also recommended that she leave her curtains open wide during the day to bring in the energy of sunlight. Judy added some red cord cushions to her sofa and invested in a rose-red duvet cover for her bed. Although, understandably, she still felt sad, she said the red colour was helping her deep depression to subside, leaving her free to move on in her life.

Adding elemental aspects

It is not necessary to redecorate your entire home to create a sense of elemental balance. Even adding small aspects of an element to one room will powerfully shift the energy throughout your space and will improve the health and energy of everyone living there. The case of Robert, a divorcee in his mid-forties, is an excellent example of how this can work. Following a difficult break-up, he had been single for several years and was having trouble developing any long-term love interests. He told me that the women he dated complained he was cold and aloof. When I visited his modern apartment, I found a quintessential Air home. The walls were lined with floor-to-ceiling book shelves, and the books on them were categorised by subject and alphabetised by title. As we went around his home he pointed out its beautiful architectural details. The elegant white cover on his bed was tightly tucked in all around the edges. The upholstered pillow covers were perfectly lined up and without a wrinkle. A typical Air Clan person, Robert worked for the accounting division of a prestigious law firm.

I felt that it was important for Robert to activate the elements of Fire and Water and Earth in his home to increase feelings of warmth and connection. I asked him if he had any photos of his family. He said that he had a number of photo albums that he kept in a cupboard. To energise the Water element, I suggested that he buy some beautiful frames for some of these and display them on his mantel in the living room and on a table next to his bed. I explained that the Water element is characterised by feelings of closeness in relationships, and that by celebrating these qualities with his photos he would be activating these qualities in his life. I also recommended that he enhance the Water qualities of his bedroom by adding an array of pastel silk pillows to his bed.

To activate the passionate qualities of Fire, I suggested placing a group of crimson candles in his living room. I asked him to light them every day while focusing on his intention to kindle love in his life. I also suggested that he drape a red wool shawl across his cream-coloured sofa. I recommended, too, that he invest in some plants to activate the Earth element and create a less sterile feeling in his home.

These were a few of the changes I suggested Robert make in his home to balance its elemental energy. He agreed to try all of them. The next month he called to report that he was having some great dates and he had felt relaxed and comfortable. He felt confident he would eventually find the kind of relationship he was looking for.

The following are suggestions for changes you can make to activate the energy of the elements in your home. These are not comprehensive. The ideas here are intended to get you started.

To Activate More Air Element

Hang mobiles, play flute music, add yellow accessories, open the windows every day and invite the Spirit of the Air into your life. Organise your cupboards, create an orderly system for your books, CDs or other collections of items you own. Add bowls of lemons and limes.

To Activate More Water Element

Add aquariums or bowls of water, hang pictures or photographs of water, purchase a home fountain. Display photos of friends and family, add stuffed animals, figurines or pictures of young animals. Buy flowers, add floral prints and cool colours – blues, lavenders, turquoise – or pastels of any colour.

To Activate More Fire Element

Burn candles, make a fire in the fireplace, add red and bright colours, metal sculptures with sharp edges. Open your curtains to let sunshine in, hang cut crystals in windows to bring rainbow fire energy, hang a chandelier.

To Activate More Earth Element

Add earthenware, ceramic pots, wrought iron, and anything made of wood. Add objects in earth colours. Display rocks, stones, and baskets on the floor. Purchase plants or silk plants.

Using the Elements to Balance an Environment

- Do you need more movement or vitality?
  Activate: Fire element
  Decrease: Earth element
- Do you need more stability?
  Activate: Earth element
  Decrease: Fire element
- Do you need more clarity?
  Activate: Air element
  Decrease: Water element
- Do you need more nurturing?
  Activate: Water element
  Decrease: Air element
- Are you constantly feeling immersed in your emotions?
  Activate: Air element
  Decrease: Water element
- Do you often feel ungrounded, as though you are floating?
  Activate: Earth element
  Decrease: Air element
- Do you feel sluggish and have trouble initiating projects?
  Activate: Fire element
  Decrease: Earth element

Elemental Energy of Outdoor Environments

When deciding how to balance the elements in your home, be sure to consider the influence of the elements outdoors. For example, I live in Seattle, which is situated close to the sea and is famous for its grey rainy days. In addition, our house is located next to a lake in the city. As a result we have a surfeit of Water energy here. To create the most balanced environment, we decided on a home balanced between the Fire and Earth elements and we avoid any elements that would increase the energy of Water. The rich reds and coppery rust colours on the walls, heavy earthenware pots, marble statues, plants, and platters of stones on the floor throughout our home bring a feeling of warmth and grounding here.

The following are descriptions of outdoor environments that are primarily aligned with one element. The local natural environment will have an effect on the energy of your home. I have included some of the features and vegetation that are likely to be found there. Of course, many areas will have combinations of more than one kind of elemental energy.

Air environment Breezy, windy areas, mountain tops, elevated areas or open plains. Cottonwood trees, aspens, eucalyptus, tall timber, bamboo.

Water environment Areas with streams, lakes, rivers, or by the sea. Rain, fog, mists. Bogs, marshes, intensely green grass and other vegetation.

Fire environment Deserts, heaths, rugged or jagged rock formations. Hot and dry. Cactus, piñon trees, sage, scrub brushes.

Earth environment Rolling hills, cliffs, rocky canyons, forests, woods. Rocks and boulders, many trees.

18

Medicine Wheel Energy Map

YOU STAND at the centre of a multitude of cosmic forces flowing around you and through you. The strengthening rhythms of the earth lie beneath your feet. The energising radiance of the sun shines down upon you. The waters of this blue planet refresh you. The powerful winds from the four directions swirl around you, opening up your mind to new possibilities. You are the centre-point of the wheel in which the four directions join. You are the connecting link between earth and heaven.

When you understand the principles of the four elements and directions, when you know at a deep level that you stand in the centre of these powerful forces, then you can create a home balanced by the transformative energy of the Medicine Wheel. This is what I call Medicine Wheel Feng Shui©. In this chapter I want to show you how to use what you have learned to create magic in your home or workplace. Using your intuition to guide you, you can apply your knowledge of the forces of nature to heal and transform the energy of your space. Using an example of a home in Seattle, I will show you how to bring all of the techniques together to create an environment that is dynamic and whole.

An overlay grid system for your home

The diagrams on page 243 show the layout of a two-storey home that belongs to Suzanne and David, who live there with their teenage son Josh. The Medicine Wheel overlay can be superimposed over both upper floors. This house happens to be aligned on a nearly perfect north/south axis, but many homes will not be laid out according to this configuration. This is not important. You will simply align the overlay according to the directions as they enter your home.

It is important to get to know a family before making any feng shui recommendations. Suzanne, David and Josh are a successful, happy family who told me they were satisfied with their lives, but did wish that they could spend more time together. All three of them are very active and, as a result, life often takes them in different directions. Even when they were all at home, they were usually in different parts of the house, involved in separate activities. Consequently, they often ate at different times and had different sleep schedules. (I wasn't surprised by all their activity, because within the home I found many symbols of Fire energy, which is the element of constant movement and change. I sensed the need for more Earth energy in the home to help stabilise all the fluctuating Fire energy.)

Discovering what you (or clients) want to accomplish out of a feng shui consultation is essential, because this lets you know how to focus your intention. It determines your actions and lets you know if you have been successful once you have finished. This family's goal of spending more time in one another's company provided the focus for our work together. We wanted to create an environment that would be more grounded and less erratic. Here are just a few of the suggestions I made using the Medicine Wheel overlay.

East There were two sets of stairs in the eastern quadrant of this home. One set led upstairs, and the other led to the basement (not pictured). Stairs can be a metaphor for travel or change, as they are transitions between spaces. Stairs in the east (the sector of new beginnings, ideas or projects) can indicate career changes, new areas of interest, or travel. On one of the stair landings, there was an urn containing beautiful glass eggs, which also are symbolic of new beginnings. (I often find that people will unwittingly put objects in their home that reflect a subconscious awareness of the relationship between the object and the directional area of the home where it is placed.)

I asked Suzanne and David if there had been many changes in their life or if they had travelled much since living in this home. They laughed and reported that in the seven years they had lived there they had visited seventeen countries between them. Both of them had gone through

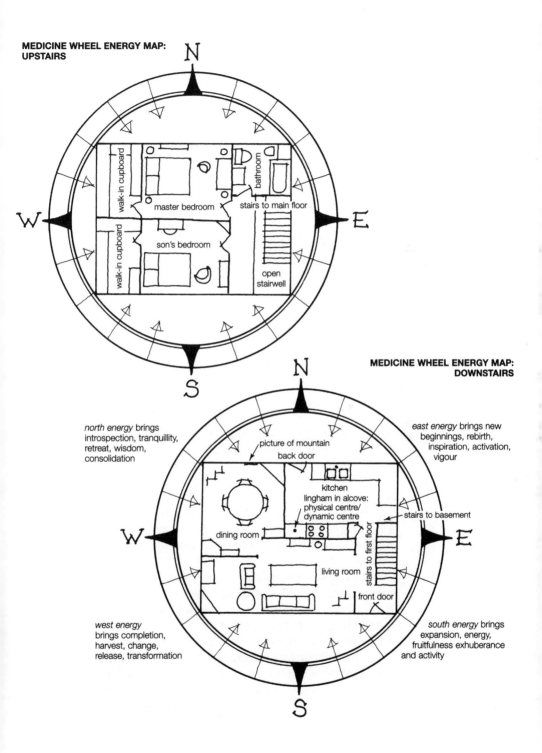

MEDICINE WHEEL ENERGY MAP: UPSTAIRS

N

walk-in cupboard

master bedroom

bathroom

stairs to main floor

walk-in cupboard

son's bedroom

open stairwell

W

E

S

MEDICINE WHEEL ENERGY MAP: DOWNSTAIRS

N

north energy brings introspection, tranquillity, retreat, wisdom, consolidation

east energy brings new beginnings, rebirth, inspiration, activation, vigour

picture of mountain

back door

kitchen

lingham in alcove: physical centre/ dynamic centre

stairs to basement

dining room

stairs to first floor

living room

front door

W

E

west energy brings completion, harvest, change, release, transformation

south energy brings expansion, energy, fruitfulness exhuberance and activity

S

career changes, and their son had also had a major change of focus in his life. He had recently decided to study psychology instead of botany following his graduation from high school.

The well-maintained entrance to this home faced south and was in the eastern part of the house, indicating that the energy coming into it carried the vitality of new beginnings from the east and the fruitfulness of the south. Since the entrance to a home sets a template for the energy throughout, it was little wonder that the lives of this home's inhabitants had been prosperous and continually full of changes.

Because they already enjoyed many benefits of eastern energy in their home, I made only one recommendation for this quadrant. There was a large plant at the top of the stairs on the eastern side of the home. I suggested that they fertilise it in the springtime, as a metaphor for keeping their many activities fertile and alive. I also suggested placing large stones around the base of the plant to bring in the Earth element, as this would symbolise stability for their many projects.

South The living room was located in the southern part of the home. Energy from the south brings vitality and expansion, and this is the area associated with growth and the beginning of harvest. To honour the abundance in their lives, I suggested they place symbols of fruitfulness in the living room, such as a bowl of fruit or a painting of flowers. The south also represents the expansive expression of self. As this was the room where the family spent the most time, I suggested that they mutually create an altar on the mantel with personal objects clustered close together to symbolise a deepening of family ties. (An altar created in this way would also help balance the expansive energy of the south and help consolidate the family energy.) In addition, I recommended they place something that represented the Earth element on the altar, such as pebbles, to bring a groundedness to their family (and help balance the Fire energy in the home). The altar would act as a continual affirmation of their commitment to spend more time together.

West The western quadrant of the home contained part of the dining room on the main floor. Although this room was beautifully decorated, the family almost never ate there. Meals were usually casually consumed in the living room. Since west is the direction associated with completion, I asked the family if they ever experienced trouble finishing projects. They all looked a bit sheepish and explained that incomplete projects were a recurring theme in their lives. I asked them to list some unfinished projects that they wanted to conclude. We then rolled this list up, made a small shrine in the dining room and dedicated it to 'completions'.

I also suggested they paint the dining room's white walls an earthy tone and place a basket of stones on the floor; this, I explained would activate the element of Earth, which is helpful for completing projects. (Just as the Fire element helps you *initiate* your projects, the Water element helps you *nurture* them, the Air element helps you *analyse* different aspects of your project, and the Earth element helps you to *complete* them.) When I checked with them later, they told me that they were using the dining room together much more often, and that it had taken very little effort to finish up the projects they had listed for completion.

North   The kitchen (and part of the dining room) lay in the northern quadrant of the home, I felt that the consolidating energy of the north could be used to bring the family together. There was nowhere to sit down in the kitchen, so people usually just leaned against the counters. I recommended they add some wooden stools in the kitchen to activate the Earth element and provide places to sit that would enhance family unity. We also discussed painting the all-white kitchen a beautiful shade of green, which also would activate Earth energy here. The new colour scheme was stunning and the wooden stools turned the room into a natural gathering place. All three members of the family talked of how cosy the kitchen now felt and how they were drawn to the room throughout the day for a cup of tea, or a snack, and to chat.

It was natural that changes in the kitchen would have a powerful effect on the family, because we had determined that the physical centre of the home was located here. By making changes so that it became a gathering place for the family, it now also functioned as a Dynamic Centre. To honour this, a lingham was lovingly placed in an alcove which happened to be located in the exact centre of the home. This stone grounded the energy here and radiated it throughout the home.

I also encouraged them to place a photograph of a mountain, which represents stability and cohesion of Earth energy, in the northern part of the dining room with the intention of bringing these qualities more into their family life.

This family was doing well before their consultation, but after making these changes they said they felt closer than ever. Utilising the power of east, south, west and north and the sacred centre, and the energy of Air, Fire, Water and Earth, they were able to create a true place of centre, a home in which to share their love.

19

The Journey Home

IT'S WINTER. I'm sitting by a blazing fire. I love the crackling sound it makes and the wonderful smell of pine that fills my home. It's dark outside and the windows are fogging over, but I can hear the gentle tap of rain against them. It feels so good to curl up by the fire on such a blustery day, cupping my hands around a steaming mug of tea.

This afternoon I took a walk by the lake. The air was cold and grey. A chilling mist soaked through my clothes, wetting my hair, my skin. The branches of the trees were bare and dead leaves formed dark patchwork on the ground. Sometimes I think I can hear the voices of the trees as they whisper among themselves, but today they were silent. Some days I'm sure that I feel the pulse of the earth beneath my feet, but today she seemed to be in deep slumber.

Everything appeared so lifeless and forlorn until a small chickadee hopped on a branch in front of me. Her little head bobbed to one side and then the other as she viewed me through shiny black eyes. When I moved closer to get a better look at her, I noticed tiny green shoots emerging from the tips of the branches where she perched. I was amazed to find these promises of spring on such a cold and dreary day. My keys fell and, when I reached among the leaves to retrieve them, I found iris shoots pushing out of the dark earth. Even in the darkest time of winter, signs of renewal and burgeoning life were everywhere.

It was already dark when I reached home, but before going in I looked up. The clouds had parted to reveal winter stars, twinkling and bright. I imagined my forebears looking to the heavens on a clear winter night, seeing the vast expanse of stars and feeling a sense of comfort as they realised that their place in the great tapestry of life was secure.

And now, as I sit before the fire, it is as if I can hear the echo of my ancestors in my soul. Their voices remind me that my home isn't only the four walls of my house and all that they contain. My home is the earth, the clouds, an eagle's nest perched high in a cedar tree. It is the mountain stream that rushes down to the great sea. My home is within the Air, the Water, the Fire and the Earth. I am reminded that I am always home wherever I am.

In this book we have explored many ways to create a sanctuary for your soul. We have considered homes in the light of ancient sacred traditions and scientific perspectives, as well as their psychological associations. There are many points of view, and yet one thread connects them all: a voice calling us to remember what is truly important in our lives, our ultimate purpose on earth, and how we can best accomplish this. Beneath the mist of confusion lies the truth that we are all unique human beings. Each of us is important and, collectively, all are essential to the continuing evolution of our planet. There is a purpose for every one of us, and the spaces that we occupy can assist us on journeys of the soul.

At the end of the day, let us remember that it's not the quality of your house but the integrity of your heart that creates a home for the soul. Your home can magnify your hopes and dreams. It can be a place where your spirit thrives. But in order for this to happen, you must first have the courage to be honest and genuine, to share your love fully and deeply with those who are closest to you. You must reach into the depths of your being and ask what is most important to you, for it is out of the answer to this question that you will truly create a home for your soul.

It is my hope that every space you occupy in your life will nurture your spirit and help you to feel at home wherever you are.

Notes

Chapter 1:
Creating a Home for the Soul

1 As quoted in Lawlor, Anthony, *The Temple in the House: Finding the Sacred in Everyday Architecture*, New York: G. P. Putnam's Sons, 1994, p. 145.
2 Ibid.

Chapter 3:
Finding the Hidden Messages in Your Home

1 Lawlor, Anthony, *Home for the Soul*, New York: Clarkson Potter/ Publishers, 1997, pp. 163–4.
2 Liberman, Jacob, *Light: Medicine of the Future*, Santa Fe, New Mexico: Bear & Company, Publishing, 1991, p. 9.
3 Ibid., p. 41.

Chapter 5:
Using Your Intuition to Heal Your Home

1 Cytowic, Richard E., *The Man Who Tasted Shapes*, New York: Warner Books, 1993, pp. 3–6.
2 Ibid., pp. 144–152.
3 Ibid., p. 166.

Chapter 7:
Awakening Natural Forces in Your Home

1 Time-Life Books, *Earth Energies*, Alexandria, VA: Time-Life Books, 1991, p. 120.

2 Ibid.
3 Ibid., pp. 124–26.
4 Collinge, William, *Subtle Energy: Awakening to the Unseen Forces in Our Lives*, New York: Warner Books, 1998, pp. 102–3.
5 Ibid., p. 102.
6 Ibid., pp. 103–4.
7 Benyus, Janine M., *Biomimicry: Innovation Inspired by Nature*, New York: William Morrow and Company Inc., 1997, pp. 6–7.

Chapter 8:
Shapes and Patterns of the Universe

1 Note the similarity between her description of this shape and the geometrically 'ruffled' edge shapes of the labyrinth of Chartres Cathedral. The scooped moon-shapes along the edge are said to be an important and significant feature.
2 Lawlor, Robert, *Sacred Geometry*, London: Thames and Hudson, 1982, p. 58.
3 Briggs, John, Fractals: *The Patterns of Chaos*, New York: Touchstone, 1992, p. 16.
4 Ibid., p. 37.

Chapter 9:
The Spirit of Air

1 Reported in 'Unified We Share the Air', *Woman Spirit*, Issue 13, April 1997, p. 25.

2 Schwenk, Theodor. *Sensitive Chaos*, Stuttgart, Germany: Rudolph Steiner Press, 1985. p. 119.

3 For more information about this, please see my book *Sacred Space*.

4 Time-Life Books, *Earth Energies*, Alexandria, Virginia: Time-Life Books, 1991, pp. 110–12.

5 Ibid., pp. 110–11.

6 Ibid., pp. 131–32.

7 Campbell, Don, *The Mozart Effect*, New York: Avon Books, 1997, p. 82.

8 *Earth Energies*, pp. 132–33.

9 Ibid., p. 133.

10 Collinge, William, *Subtle Energy: Awakening to the Unseen Forces in Our Lives*, New York: Warner Books, 1998, p. 234.

11 Tompkins, Peter, and Bird, Christopher, *The Secret Life of Plants*, New York: Harper & Row, Publishers, 1973, p.148.

12 Ibid., pp. 14–15.

13 Reported in 'Classical or Baroque Music for Studying', *Woman Spirit*, Issue 13, April 1997, p. 13.

14 Campbell, Don, *The Mozart Effect*, New York: Avon Books, 1997, p. 14.

15 Cornell, Judith, *Mandala: Luminous Symbols for Healing*, Wheaton, Illinois: Quest Books, 1994, p. xvii.

16 Campbell, pp. 194–5.

17 Ibid., p. 194.

18 Ibid., pp. 36–7.

Chapter 10:
The Vitality of Water

1 Hitching, Francis, *Earth Magic*, New York: Pocket Books, 1976, pp. 214–15.

2 For a visual demonstration of how to create a home fountain, please see my video, *Instinctive Feng Shui for Creating Sacred Space*. Information about how to order this is included at the end of this book in the Resources section.

3 Collinge, William, *Subtle Energy: Awakening to the Unseen Forces in Our Lives*, New York: Warner Books, 1998, pp. 73–4.

4 Hitching, pp. 184–5.

5 Day, Christopher, *Places of the Soul: Architecture and Environmental Design as a Healing Art*, London: Aquarian/Thorsons, 1990, p. 39.

6 Moore, Alanna, 'Are You Under Geopathic Stress? Research from the New Field of Geobiology', *Australian Wellbeing*, No. 15, 1986, p. 97.

7 Tompkins, Peter and Bird, Christopher, *The Secret Life of Plants*, New York: Harper & Row, Publishers, 1973, p. 307.

8 Ibid., pp. 307–11.

9 Ibid. (See Resource section for information on how to obtain flower remedies.)

10 Devereux, Paul, Steele, John, and Kubrin, David, *EarthMind: Communicating with the Living World of Gaia*, Rochester, Vermont: Destiny Books, 1989, p. 176.

Chapter 11:
The Power of Fire

1 Alexander, Christopher, et al, *A Pattern Language: Towns, Buildings, Construction*, New York: Oxford University Press, 1977, p. 514.

2 Time-Life Books, *Time and Space*, Alexandria, Virginia: Time-Life Books, 1990, p. 79.

3 As quoted in: Alexander, Jane, *Spirit of the Home*, London: Thorsons, 1998, p. 16.

4 Pagram, Beverly, *Home and Heart: Simple, Beautiful Ways to Create Spirit, Harmony & Warmth in Every Room*, Daybreak, Rodale Press, Inc., 1998, p. 22.

5 For more information about this, see my book *Altars*, (London: Rider, 1999).

6 Editors, Time-Life Books, *The Mind and Beyond*, Alexandria, Virginia: Time-Life Books, 1991, p. 52.

7 Tarkan, Laurie, *Electromagnetic Fields: What You Need to Know to Protect Your Health*, New York: Bantam Books, 1994, pp. 14–15.

8 For fairly inexpensive sources for gauss meters, see the Resources section at the end of this book.

Chapter 12:
The Wisdom of the Earth

1 Eliade, Mircea, *Myths, Dreams and Mysteries,* translated by Philip Mairet, New York: Harper & Row, 1960.
2 Neihardt, John G., *Black Elk Speaks,* New York: Pocket Books, 1972, pp. 29, 31.
3 Collinge, William, *Subtle Energy: Awakening to the Unseen Forces in Our Lives,* New York: Warner Books, 1998, p. 75.
4 Ibid., p. 74.
5 Moore, Alanna, 'Are You Under Geopathic Stress? Research from the New Field of Geobiology', *Australian Wellbeing,* No. 15, 1986, pp. 94–5.
6 Collinge, pp. 74–7.
7 Ibid., pp. 77–8.
8 Article in *The Washington Post,* 12/12/97.
9 See Resources section at the end of this book for additional reading about magnets and magnet products.

Chapter 13:
Introduction to Medicine Wheel Feng Shui

1 Neihardt, John G., *Black Elk Speaks,* New York: Pocket Books, 1972, p. 44.

Chapter 14:
The Cardinal Directions

1 Bleakley, Alan, *Fruits of the Moon Tree: The Medicine Wheel and Transpersonal Psychology,* Bath, England: Gateway Books, 1988, p. 9.
2 Neihardt, John G., *Black Elk Speaks,* New York: Pocket Books, 1972, p. 2.

Chapter 15:
Finding the Centre of Your Home

1 Anderson, Richard Feather, *Yoga Journal,* Oct. 1986, p. 29.
2 Time-Life Books, *Earth Energies,* Alexandria, Virginia: Time-Life Books, 1991, pp. 33–4, 52.
3 Pennick, Nigel, *The Ancient Science of Geomancy: Living in Harmony with the Earth,* Sebastopol, California: CRCS Publications, 1979, pp. 44–5.

Chapter 16:
The Four Sacred Elements

1 Campbell, Joseph, *The Masks of God: Primitive Mythology,* New York: Viking Press, 1959, p. 212.
2 Ibid., p. 452.
3 Time-Life Books, *Cosmic Connections,* Alexandria, Virginia: Time-Life Books, 1990, p. 122.

Resources

Intuition

In United States: Non-profit educational and scientific organisations. Catalogue with information, books and full range of dowsing supplies, including aurameters, L-rods and pendulums: The American Society of Dowsers, PO Box 24, Danville, VT 05828-0024, USA; tel: (802) 684-3417; fax: (802) 684-2565; Email: ASD@dowsers.org.

In England: British Society of Dowsers, General Secretary, Sycamore Barn, Tamley Lane, Hastingleigh, Ashford, Kent TN25 5HW, England; tel: 44-1233-750253; Email: bsd@dowsers.demon.co.uk; Website: www.dowsers.demon.co.uk.

In Australia: Dowsers Society of NSW, Mrs E. Miksevicius, 126 Fiddens Wharf Road, Killara, NSW 2071, Australia.

Dowsing video: *Discover Dowsing: Learn to Bridge Logic with Intuition,* filmed by Bradley Boatman Productions, Santa Barbara, CA 93130, USA.

Patterns

Labyrinth catalogue and newsletter: Grace Cathedral Veriditas, 1100 California St., San Francisco, CA 94108, USA; tel: 1-415-749-6356 (m–f 9–5 PST); fax: 1-415-749-6357; Website: www.gracecathedral.org/veriditas.

Video about fractals: scientific explanation of the Mandelbrot set and fractals, narrated by Arthur C. Clarke. Beautiful images of computer-produced fractals. *Fractals: The Colors of Infinity,* Filmed for the Humanities and Sciences, PO Box 2053, Princeton, NJ 08543, USA; tel: in USA toll-free: 1-800-257-5126; or: 1-609-275-1400.

Air

Meter for measuring sound levels; available in both analog and digital models: Tandy Corporation, 700 One Tandy Center, Fort Worth, Texas 76109, USA; tel: (817) 390-3300; tel. order line: 1-800-843-7422; Website: www.radioshack.com.

Colour & Aroma Therapy Products

Complete line of colour and aroma harmonic products (excellent):

In Australia: Aura Light, 'Unicornis', Obi Obi Road, Mapleton, MS 956, QLD. 4560, Australia.

In England: Aura Light, Rainbow Farm, Buckland, Bampton, Oxfordshire OX18 2AA, England.

Another line of colour therapy products: Aura-Soma Products, Dev Aura, Tetford, Lincs. LN9 6QL, England.

Sources for essential oils: Tisserand Aromatherapy Products, Brighton BN3 ZRS, England. Also available from most major health food stores.
In Essence, 3 Abbott Street, Fairfield, Victoria 3078, Australia. I have used these products for years, and continue to admire them.

Lifetree Aromatix, 3949 Longbridge Ave, Sherman Oaks, CA 91423, USA. Information packet & order form can be obtained for $2.50.

Video about geometric shapes created by the vibration of sounds. Remarkable images: Cymatic Soundscapes, MACROmedia, PO Box 279, Epping, NH 03042, USA.

Excellent recordings of nature sounds and other healing music: Symbiosis, PO Box 2000, Richmond, Surrey. TW9 3IH, England.

Water

For books on qualities of flowers, please see the following titles in the Bibliography section: *The Bach Flower Remedies* by Edward Bach, MD and F. J. Wheeler MD; *Flower Essence Repertory* by Patricia Kaminski and Richard Katz.

Sources for flower essences: Bach Flower Remedies, The Dr Edward Bach Healing Centre, Mount Vernon, Sotwell, Wallingford, Oxon, England. Also available from most major health food stores.
Alaskan Flower Essence Project, PO Box 1369, Homer, AK 99603-1369, US; tel: toll-free in the USA & Canada: 1-800-545-9309; tel: (907) 235-2188; fax: (907) 235-2777; Email: Info@alaskanessences.com; Website: www.alaskanessences.com.
Australian Bush Flower Essences, Essential Energies, 54 Clifton Street, Richmond, Melbourne 3121. Australia.
Perlandra Flower Essences, PO Box 3603, Warrenton, VA 20188, USA; tel: toll-free in the USA & Canada: 1-800-960-8806; tel: (540) 937-2153; fax: (540) 937-3360; Website: http://perelandra-ltd.com.

For a list of dowser organisations, please see information listed under Intuition resources

Denise Linn's video on creating Sacred Space; contains demonstration on how to build a home fountain: *Instinctive Feng Shui for Creating Sacred Space*. Available worldwide from: QED Recording Services, Lancaster Road, New Barnet, Herts. EN4 8AS, England; Website: http://www.qed-productions.com; Email: enquiry@qed-productions.com.

Available in the USA from: Denise Linn Seminars, PO Box 75657, Seattle, WA 98125-0657, USA.

Living water videos: *Sacred Living Geometry: The Enlightened Theories of Viktor Schauberger* (2 tapes). Presented by Callum Coats, Laura Lee Press, PO Box 3010, Bellevue, WA 98009, USA. Call for a free catalogue (in the USA toll-free): 1-800-243-1438.
Nature Was My Teacher: The Vision of Viktor Schauberger, Borderland Sciences, PO Box 220, Bayside, CA 95524, USA.

Fire

Catalogue with great selection of home planetariums and fluorescent stars: Edmunds Scientifics, 101 E. Gloucester Pike, Barrington, NJ 08007, USA; tel: 1-800-728-6999; Website: www.edusci.com.

For books about colour, please see the following titles in the bibliography: *The Symbolism of Color* by Faber Birren; *Discover the Magic of Colour* by Lilian Verner Bonds.

Source for computer shields, home and business shielding: Field Management Services, 123 North Laurel Ave., Los Angeles, CA 90048, USA; tel: (323) 937-1562; fax: (323) 934-2101; Email: FMS@FMS-Corp.com; Website: http://www.FMS.Corp.com.

Earth

Source for Healthy Home supplies: International Institute of Bau-Biologies, Helmut Ziehe, Box 387, Clearwater, FL 33757, USA; tel: (813) 461-4371.

Sources for magnetic health products: *In the United States:* Nikken Technology, Independent Distributors: Dave and Kathy Herbert, 2805 Doaks Ferry Rd NW, Salem, OR 97304, USA; tel (503) 375-0501. Numerous magnetic products, including sleeping pads.
In England: Nikken Technology. Gina Lazenby, PO Box 2133, London W1A 1RL, England.
In Canada: Dr Dean Bonlie, MagnetiCO Sleep Pad, Inc., #109, 5421 - 11 Street NE, Calgary, Alberta T2E 6M4, Canada; tel: 1-800-265-1119; tel: (403) 730-0883; fax: (403) 730 0885; Website: www.magneticosleep.com.

Bibliography

Alexander, Christopher, and Ishikawa, Sara, et al, *A Pattern Language: Towns, Building, Construction*. New York: Oxford University Press, 1977.

Alexander, Jane, *Spirit of the Home*. London: Thorsons, 1998.

Andrews, Ted, *Crystal Balls and Crystal Bowls*. St Paul, Minnesota: Llewellyn Publications, 1994.

Bach, Edward, MD, and Wheeler, F. J., MD, *The Bach Flower Remedies*. New Canaan, Connecticut: Keats Publishing, Inc., 1979.

Barrie, Thomas, *Spiritual Path, Sacred Path: Myth, Ritual and Meaning in Architecture*. Boston and London: Shambala, 1996.

Bender, Tom, *The Heart of Place*. Nehalem, Oregon: Bender Press, 1993.

Birren, Faber, *The Symbolism of Color*. Secaucus, New Jersey: Citadel Press, 1988.

Bleakley, Alan, *Fruits of the Moon Tree: The Medicine Wheel and Transpersonal Psychology*. Bath, England: Gateway Books, 1984.

Bonds, Lillian Verner, *Discover the Magic of Colour*. London: Optima. A Division of Little, Brown and Company (UK) Limited, 1993.

Bower, John, *The Healthy Home*. New York; Carol Publishing, 1991.

Briggs, John, *Fractals: The Patterns of Chaos*. New York: Touchstone, 1992.

Campbell, Joseph, *Hero with a Thousand Faces*. Princeton: Princeton University Press, 2nd edition, 1968.

Campbell, Joseph, *The Mask of God: Primitive Mythology*. New York: Viking Press, 1959.

Cornell, Judith, Ph.D., *Mandala: Luminous Symbols for Healing*. Wheaton, Illinois: Quest Books, 1994.

Cytowic, Richard E., MD, *The Man Who Tasted Shapes*. New York: Warner Books, 1993.

Day, Christopher, *Places of the Soul: Architecture and Environmental Design as a Healing Art*. London: Aquarian Press, 1990.

Devereux, Paul, *Shamanism and the Mystery Lines: Ley Lines, Spirit Paths, Shapeshifting and Out of Body Experiences*. St Paul, Minnesota: Llewellyn Publications, 1994.

Devereux, Paul, Steel, John, and Kubrin, David, *Earth Mind: Communicating with the Living World of Gaia*. Rochester, Vermont: Destiny, 1989.

Eliade, Mircea, *The Sacred and the Profane: the Nature of Religion*. New York: Harcourt, Brace, Jovanovich, 1959.

Fischer-Rizzi, Susanne, *Complete Aromatherapy Handbook: Essential Oils for Radiant Health*. New York: Sterling Publishing Co., Inc., 1990.

Freke, Timothy, and Wa'na'Ne'Che' (Renault, Dennis), *Native American Spirituality*. London: Thorsons, 1996.

Hitching, Francis, *Earth Magic*. New York: Simon & Schuster, 1976.

BIBLIOGRAPHY

Inkeles, Gordon, and Schenke, Iris, *Ergonomic Living: How to Create a User-Friendly Home and Office*. New York: Fireside, 1994.

Jansen, Eva Rudy, Singing Bowls: *A Practical Handbook of Instruction and Use*. Holland: Binkey Kok Publications, 1990.

Jung, Carl, *Memories, Dreams, Reflections*. London: Fontana Library, 1969.

Kaminski, Patricia, and Katz, Richard, *Flower Essence Repertory*. Nevada City, California: Society Press, 1994.

Lawlor, Anthony, *Temple in the House*. New York: Jeremy P. Tarcher, Putnam Books, 1994.

Lee, Vinny, *Quiet Places*. Pleasantville, New York: Reader's Digest, 1998.

Lennon, Robin, *Home Design from the Inside Out*. New York: Arkana, Penguin, 1997.

Marcus, Claire Cooper, *House as Mirror of Self*. Berkeley: Conari Press, 1995.

Molyneaux, Brian Leigh, *The Sacred Earth: Spirits of the Landscape, Ancient Alignments and Sacred Sites, Creation and Fertility*. Boston: Little Brown and Company, 1995.

Neihardt, John, *Black Elk Speaks*. University of Nebraska Press, 1961. (Originally published in 1932 by William Morrow & Company.)

Pagram, Beverley, *Home and Heart: Simple Beautiful Ways to Create Spirit, Harmony and Warmth in Every Room*. Daybreak, Rodale Press, 1998.

Pennick, Nigel, *The Ancient Science of Geomancy: Living in Harmony with the Earth*. London: Thames and Hudson Ltd., 1979.

Rossbach, Sarah, and Prof. Lin Yun, *Living Color*. New York: Kodansha International, 1994.

Schwenk, Theodor, *Sensitive Chaos*. Stuttgart, Germany: Rudolph Steiner Press, 1965.

Swan, James A., *The Power of Place: Sacred Ground in Natural and Human Environments*. Wheaton, Illinois: Quest Books, 1991.

Swan, James, and Swan, Roberta, *Dialogues with the Living Earth*. Wheaton, Illinois: Quest Books, 1996.

Tame, David, *The Secret Power of Music: The Transformation of Self and Society through Musical Energy*. Rochester, Vermont: Destiny Books, 1984.

Tarkan, Laurie, *Electromagnetic Fields: What You Need to Know to Protect Your Health*. New York: Bantam, 1994.

Tompkins, Peter, and Bird, Christopher, *The Secret Life of Plants*. New York: Harper and Row, Publishers, 1973.

Feng shui certification course:

Denise Linn offers professional certification training programmes in Interior Alignment™ and Instinctive Feng Shui™. To receive information about this course and her other courses around the world, contact: Denise Linn Seminars, PO Box 75657, Seattle, WA 98125-0657, USA.

Audio and video tapes:

Denise Linn has a series of audio tapes on a variety of topics, as well as a video, *Instinctive Feng Shui for Creating Sacred Space*, which provides effective step-by-step techniques to balance the energy in your home and workplace. For information on ordering these tapes, contact: QED Recording Services Ltd., Lancaster Road, New Barnet, Herts. EN4 8AS, UK; tel: +44 (0) 181-441-7722; fax: +44 (0) 181-441-0777; http://www.qed-productions.com; Email: enquiry@qed-productions.com.

Index

INDEX